THE CREATION OF A CRUSADER

AMERICAN ABOLITIONISM AND ANTISLAVERY
JOHN DAVID SMITH, SERIES EDITOR

*The Imperfect Revolution: Anthony Burns and the Landscape
of Race in Antebellum America*
GORDON S. BARKER

A Self-Evident Lie: Southern Slavery and the Threat to American Freedom
JEREMY J. TEWELL

Denmark Vesey's Revolt: The Slave Plot That Lit a Fuse to Fort Sumter
JOHN LOFTON   NEW INTRODUCTION BY PETER C. HOFFER

*To Plead Our Own Cause: African Americans in Massachusetts
and the Making of the Antislavery Movement*
CHRISTOPHER CAMERON

*African Canadians in Union Blue: Volunteering for the Cause
in the Civil War*
RICHARD M. REID

*One Nation Divided by Slavery: Remembering the American Revolution
While Marching toward the Civil War*
MICHAEL F. CONLIN

*Her Voice Will Be on the Side of Right: Gender and Power in Women's
Antebellum Antislavery Fiction*
HOLLY M. KENT

*The Creation of a Crusader: Senator Thomas Morris and the Birth
of the Antislavery Movement*
DAVID C. CRAGO

The Creation of a Crusader

*Senator Thomas Morris and the Birth
of the Antislavery Movement*

DAVID C. CRAGO

THE KENT STATE UNIVERSITY PRESS
Kent, Ohio

© 2023 by The Kent State University Press, Kent, Ohio 44242
All rights reserved
ISBN 978-1-60635-463-6
Published in the United States of America

No part of this book may be used or reproduced, in any manner whatsoever, without written permission from the Publisher, except in the case of short quotations in critical reviews or articles.

Cataloging information for this title is available at the Library of Congress.

27 26 25 24 23   5 4 3 2 1

Contents

Acknowledgments vii

Introduction 1

1 Avoiding Anything Like Agitation 8

2 They Are Attempting to Overwhelm Us 22

3 Keeper of the Jeffersonian Conscience 38

4 The Absolute Creed of the Abolitionists 51

5 I Ask No Forgiveness 66

6 The Beacon Fires of Liberty 83

7 A Rotten Branch to Be Lopped Off 95

8 A Torrent of Eloquence and Argument 109

9 Independent Opinions and Ultra Doctrines 123

10 The Power to Abolish Slavery in Every State 143

Conclusion 161

Notes 168

Index 233

Acknowledgments

This book has been many years in the making. I have set it aside and returned to it so many times over the years that any effort to acknowledge those who have contributed to it is certain to fall victim to my memory. I recognize that I will unintentionally fail to recall many whom I should acknowledge. Of these, I ask forgiveness.

In many respects this book is the product of a lifetime's fascination with the subject. I first encountered Thomas Morris as a passing reference in a text assigned in Robert Durden's undergraduate history seminar at Duke University. Morris's Ohio background, and the seeming incongruity of a southern Ohio Jacksonian senator becoming a leading abolitionist, intrigued me. The following year, Sydney Nathans graciously agreed to supervise an independent study that allowed me to write my honors thesis on Senator Morris. Both Dr. Durden and Dr. Nathans were remarkable scholars, but more importantly for this book, they were also extraordinary teachers who instilled in their students a lifelong curiosity and desire to understand.

The course of my career took me away from Jacksonian senators, but in 2019 I was able to return full-time to the faculty of the College of Law at Ohio Northern University and consideration of Morris's role in political antislavery. I am grateful to Dean Charles Rose for providing both the opportunity and resources to allow me to focus on this long-delayed study. The professional staff of the Taggart Law Library (Nancy Armstrong,

Dustin Johnston-Green, and Kaylan Ellis), in particular, were extraordinarily helpful. Their enthusiasm for the project and their ingenuity and persistence in locating frequently obscure materials was a marvel. Without their ability to provide these resources in Ada, I would not have been able to meet my teaching obligations and complete this book.

My faculty colleagues, Steve Veltri and Bruce Frohnen, generously and willingly took time out of their own teaching and research schedule to read earlier drafts of the manuscript. They provided not only thoughtful and insightful comments but also welcome encouragement. Without both this project would not have been completed. John David Smith, the editor of the Kent State University Press's American Abolitionism and Antislavery series, and the anonymous outside reviewer suggested avenues of approach and additional sources for further investigation, which enhanced my portrait of Morris.

Tasha Miller and Julie Krupp tirelessly and professionally prepared the numerous drafts and revisions required to complete the project. Their contribution cannot be overstated. Over the past three years, Allison Young, Katherine Naugle, and Madison Putnam have diligently and skillfully assisted with the project. Without their combined efforts the work could not have been completed. I am grateful to Jennifer Moore for recommending them to me.

Finally, and most importantly, my wife Camille Hanby Crago, who has endured more discussions of nineteenth-century antebellum politics and constitutional theory than any one person should ever have to do. Her persistence in encouraging me to complete this project and her support throughout was essential. I could not have done it without her.

If in spite of the contributions and best efforts of these and others I have unintentionally overlooked, errors remain, they are mine.

This the only known likeness of Thomas Morris in existence. It was done nearly eighty years after his death as part of the Grant Centennial sponsored by the Ohio Historical Association (*Ohio Archaeological and Historical Quarterly* 31 [1922]: 351–52).

It is rather remarkable that there is in existence no portrait of Senator Morris. His reputation in his day extended beyond the borders of his state. His espousal of the anti-slavery cause made him the candidate of the Liberty Party for Vice-President of the United States in 1844. A long search, however, for a portrait some years ago led to the conclusion that none is in existence. An effort was made to find a painting, daguerreotype or print to complete a list of portraits of United States senators but none was found.

On the occasion of the Grant Centenary the writer met in Bethel Doctor W. E. Thompson, who in his eighty-seventh year is still actively engaged in the practice of medicine. He is perhaps the only man living who has a distinct recollection of the personal appearance of Senator Morris. His description was so detailed and apparently accurate that he was requested to assist in the reproduction of a likeness of Morris. To this he kindly assented.

A competent person was then sought to make a sketch corresponding to the picture preserved in the memory of Doctor Thompson. Such an artist was found in Richard M. Brand of the Columbus *Evening Dispatch*. He made a number of sketches which were submitted to Doctor Thompson who suggested modifications until one was produced that met his approval. From this drawing the portrait was made which appears elsewhere in this issue of the QUARTERLY. It is a faithful reproduction of the features of Senator Morris as Doctor Thompson graphically recalls them. For this service the Society is under obligations to Doctor Thompson and Mr. Brand who have spent considerable time in making the presentation of such a portrait possible.

The quest for a portrait of Senator Morris made while he was living, has not ceased. It is possible that one may yet be found.

More than one hundred years later, no other likeness has been found.

Introduction

In February 1860, Abraham Lincoln journeyed from Illinois to New York to launch his effort to secure the Republican nomination for president. At Cooper Union, Lincoln told his audience that "neither the word 'slave' nor 'slavery' is to be found in the Constitution." Instead, "wherever in that instrument the slave is alluded to, he is called a 'person.'" As a result, "we deny that a right to property in slaves has any existence in the Constitution."[1] In making this declaration, Lincoln was echoing another self-educated frontier lawyer. More than two decades earlier, Ohio Senator Thomas Morris confronted John C. Calhoun's claim that the Constitution protected the right to slave property. Dismissing Calhoun's argument, Morris told the Senate "the word slave or slavery is not to be found in the Constitution . . . The slave is treated as a person, not a thing." As a result, "I deny that the right . . . of the master to his slave property, is founded on or arises from" the Constitution.[2] The constitutional underpinnings of the political campaign to abolish slavery, which culminated in Lincoln's election, were announced on the floor of the Senate that day in 1836.

For more than 150 years Morris has "generally left historians baffled."[3] At the time Morris challenged Calhoun's constitutional arguments, he had been in the Senate less than three years but had held elective office for nearly thirty. In 1836 Morris was "the leading hard money Jacksonian Senator," who consistently voted to support the president's economic policy and views of state sovereignty.[4] Throughout his political career he had opposed corporations, monopolies, and banks as bastions of inequality and privilege but prior to his confrontation with Calhoun, he had publicly addressed slavery only once. In the aftermath of Nat Turner's rebellion, Morris had chaired an Ohio General Assembly joint committee that concluded free Blacks should be colonized outside the United States and recommended congressional appropriations to support the colonization effort.[5] He shared Jackson's distrust of Henry Clay's Bank of the United States and John Calhoun's disunionist nullification theories, but neither support for Jackson and colonization, nor opposition to Clay and Calhoun, augured support for abolition.

Not only Morris's deeply held Jacksonian beliefs but his personal background has contributed to scholars' bewilderment at Morris's abolitionism. In many respects, Morris was the antithesis of the typical abolitionist. At a time when most members of antislavery societies were motivated by evangelical Protestantism to attack the sin of slavery,[6] Morris was neither "a religious man" nor a member of a church.[7] He lacked formal education, had owned and operated a tavern, had been imprisoned for debt, and had been charged with a felony early in life. He spent his entire adult life in southern Ohio counties bordering the Ohio River and slaveholding Kentucky, far from the abolition hotbed of Ohio's Western Reserve. Yet during the 1830s "he was the only senator of either party to openly denounce the gag rule and defend the abolitionists."[8]

That Morris should be cast in this role has not only puzzled historians, it surprised his contemporaries. He had been an ardent Jeffersonian, states' rights democrat committed to legislative primacy and opposed to any sort of governmentally conferred privilege. For the first two years of his term in the United States Senate, he had been the loyal but largely silent supporter of Jackson. His opposition as an Ohio legislator to the Bank of the United States and nullification had earned him the notice of the national party leadership,[9] but had not translated into electoral success outside his home county. Although he represented Clermont County in the Ohio General Assembly almost continuously from 1807 to 1832, he had lost a bid to be elected to Congress in the fall of 1832. His election to the United States Senate in December 1832 resulted more from his long service in the general assembly than statewide popularity.

Morris was first elected to public office in 1806, but his antislavery career did not begin until January 7, 1836, when he presented two petitions from citizens of Ohio seeking the abolition of slavery in the District of Columbia. The presentation of similar petitions in the House of Representatives three weeks earlier had resulted in an uproar. Although Morris could hardly have been unaware of the turmoil in the House, two days earlier his Whig colleague in the Senate had offered antislavery petitions, which were quietly received and referred to committee. Morris had intentionally delayed presenting petitions until he had seen the Senate's reaction to those petitions. When Calhoun erupted from the desk next to his, Morris was stunned. He had not expected to create controversy, but the events of that January day propelled Morris into the center of the abolition crusade and the emergence of political and constitutional antislavery.

Morris's position, first as a United States senator and then as a political "martyr" for his antislavery stance, gave his views a prominence and authority as abolitionists took their first steps into electoral politics. "Antislavery politics, or free soilism, grew out of abolition. . . . Political abolitionists established the precedent of third-party politics, . . . developed arguments on the unconstitutionality of slavery, the unrepublican character of the Slave Power, and a free labor critique of slavery."[10] Morris played a prominent, frequently creative role in each of these developments. His ideas became central to the political discourse of the era and were embedded in the antislavery understanding of the Constitution. The genesis of the constitutional provisions accommodating slavery is beyond the scope of this study, but "did antislavery advocates distort the Constitution in order to legitimize their case, as proslavery and certain radical abolitionist critics charged? Or did the Constitution, with all of its concessions to slavery, also provide the means to hasten slavery's demise?"[11] In other words, regardless of the subjective intent of any individual framer or ratifier, was the Constitution as written a proslavery charter? Because Morris was in the vanguard of the development of the antislavery interpretation of the Constitution, crafting a credible answer to these questions requires an understanding of the origin, content, and evolution of his thought.

Morris did not come to the Senate with an antislavery agenda or constitutional theory. For him (as for others who followed), "the growth of an antislavery ideology . . . depended in large measure on the growth of proslavery thought."[12] Calhoun's aggressive response to the abolitionists' mail campaign in the summer of 1835 and petitions directed at abolishing slavery in the District of Columbia caused Morris to perceive new threats to personal liberty and to rethink his understanding of slavery's relationship to the Constitution. Conditioned by his Jacksonian outlook to fear expansion of governmental power or grant of privilege, Morris saw Calhoun's demands to suppress abolitionist mailings and to limit the reception of abolitionist petitions, as well as his assertion of a federal constitutional property right in slaves, as seeking special protection for slave owners. When Morris expressed this understanding in Jacksonian rhetoric, the Slave Power was born.

Not only the concept of the Slave Power, but virtually all of what became antislavery constitutionalism found early public expression, if not its origin, in Morris's speeches and writings: the Constitution as an antislavery document;[13] the nature of slavery as a "local" institution requiring positive law for its creation;[14] the understanding of slaves as "persons" within the meaning of the Constitution;[15] the lack of power on the part of Congress to establish slavery in the District of Columbia or the territories;[16] the imperative of equal and exact justice regardless of race;[17] and the unconstitutionality of the Fugitive Slave Law[18] all emerged in Morris's responses to the demands of the Slave Power for constitutional protection. All were given national exposure, first through the publication of the debates in the Senate and then through the distribution of his speeches and letters by the antislavery press. All became integral parts of the antislavery constitution and were critical to the development of the Liberty Party whose "politics until 1845 derived from constitutional thought."[19] All came to be accepted as fundamental by the Free-Soilers and Republicans.[20]

Political and constitutional antislavery, then, were built on Morris's ideas. The Slave Power, the lack of congressional power to enact slavery anywhere, the absence of constitutional recognition of property in man, and the imperative of equal and exact justice for all animated antislavery political thought throughout the years leading to the election of 1860. Most of the elements of the antislavery constitution that supported what James Oakes has characterized as "the Antislavery Project" of the 1850s were articulated by Morris from his Senate seat next to Calhoun in the 1830s.[21] Morris's definition of the political reality of the Slave Power ultimately came to shape the national debate over slavery in the years leading to the Civil War.[22] His warnings about the consequences for the free states of Calhoun's constitutional construction appeared prescient in the aftermath of *Dred Scott*. Nevertheless, Morris remains "one of the forgotten men of the early antislavery movement."[23]

Without the benefit of a comprehensive study of the evolution of Morris's thought historians have generally missed his contribution entirely or misunderstood his views. While he is acknowledged as having introduced the concept of the Slave Power into the antebellum political lexicon,[24] Morris's role in the origination and articulation of the elements of antislavery constitutionalism is most often overlooked.[25] He is portrayed, at best, as a role player consigned to the margins of the political antislavery movement. Historians have simply failed to recognize Morris's importance in the development of political and constitutional antislavery thought.[26]

In many respects, the lack of any collection of his personal papers or letters has limited scholarly assessment of Morris's career. Although Morris kept a diary and corresponded privately with his family (at least during his term in the United States Senate),[27] none of those items appears to have survived. Moreover, Morris rarely corresponded privately with others in the antislavery or Liberty Party organization. While Morris's views and actions were discussed in correspondence between other antislavery activists, letters to or from him are strikingly absent from collections of his colleagues' papers.[28] As a result, Morris's views and impact must be pieced together from the comments of his contemporaries, his Senate speeches, his published letters, and newspaper accounts of his activities.[29] The difficulty of this task is compounded by the effort (particularly after Salmon Chase joined the Liberty Party) of his more moderate Ohio colleagues in the political antislavery effort to diminish the impact of Morris's increasingly radical constitutional views by refusing to print his letters, speeches, and resolutions.[30] These efforts, which angered Morris, were only marginally effective at limiting his influence on his contemporaries but have hampered historians' attempts at assessing Morris's impact.

Not only is there no collection of Morris's papers, but unlike many of his contemporaries Morris did not publish his arguments in fugitive slave cases (Salmon Chase), nor did he systematically develop his theories in books (William Goodell), or pamphlets (Theodore Weld). Although Chase, Goodell, and Weld adopted many of Morris's ideas, Morris did not attempt to collect, organize, and publish his views.[31] The difficulty of uncovering how Morris understood slavery's relationship to the Constitution caused many early scholars, if they discussed Morris at all, to assume that his antislavery views remained constant over his career. As a result, they attributed to Morris whatever view—ranging from support for colonization to

6 THE CREATION OF A CRUSADER

immediate emancipation—he may have held when they found him. Depending on the commentator, then, Morris has been described as a "rabid abolitionist" or a "conservative antislavery man."[32]

These characterizations of Morris's views may also have contributed to subsequent historians' lack of interest in Morris. If he could be easily pigeonholed, there would be little point in pursuing the development of his thought. Morris's constitutional understanding, however, was conceived not in the stillness of the library but in the rough-and-tumble world of political contests in the antebellum era. As a result, his theories were far from static. They evolved in response to his perception of the Slave Power threat. The necessity of defeating that power caused Morris to adopt increasingly creative and radical constitutional doctrines. He had entered the Senate as a supporter of colonization, but by the time of his death, Morris had concluded that not only was slavery unconstitutional in the District of Columbia and the territories, the Constitution empowered Congress to emancipate slaves regardless of where they were held.

The brevity of Morris's prominence in political antislavery has also contributed to scholars' lack of attention. Writing at the end of the nineteenth century, Theodore Smith concluded that the absence of scholarly recognition of Morris's significance to the antislavery effort was the result of Morris's preference. According to Smith, "Morris's modesty was so great as to lead him in the period from 1841–44 to prefer to exercise his talents in the comparatively humble sphere of local canvassing." His absence from national conventions or meetings "allowed men more eloquent, but of far less political ability, to overshadow him."[33] Morris's anger at the effort of the editor of the *Philanthropist* to exclude his views and labors from its columns,[34] however, belies any notion of modesty on Morris's part. His present obscurity cannot be said to result from humility.

But there is a grain of truth in Smith's recognition of Morris's absence from the nation's stage. Antislavery, in the 1830s, "was a young people's movement. Most of its leaders . . . were in their twenties."[35] However, Morris was sixty years old when he first challenged Calhoun in the Senate and sixty-five when first nominated by the Liberty Party as its vice presidential candidate. Although Liberty Party organizations outside Ohio consistently sought Morris's attendance at their conventions, he was often physically unable to attend. Over the final three years of his life Morris struggled with "ill health and family afflictions"[36] that prevented him from attending meetings at venues outside Ohio and made him particularly susceptible

INTRODUCTION

to Bailey's effort to minimize awareness of Morris's views. His death one month after the 1844 election ended his antislavery career. When historians have surveyed the actors present at the creation of the Republican Party, the election of Lincoln, or the adoption of the 1866 Civil Rights Act, Morris is nowhere to be found. Many of his Liberty Party colleagues, however, were. Historians have chosen to focus on the stories of those who witnessed the ultimate success of political antislavery. Nevertheless, that Morris's ideas were integral to that success is undeniable.

In many respects Morris's journey from an opponent of slavery in the abstract, to a champion of Northern rights in opposition to the Slave Power, to an advocate of constitutional restrictions on the expansion of slavery, to a proponent of the necessity of congressional power to abolish slavery and to provide equal justice for all was a path many would follow in the years leading up to and including the Civil War. Morris's progress on that journey was marked by the mileposts of his increasingly radical constitutional thought. More than a decade after Morris's death, Salmon Chase correctly assessed Morris's role: "He was far beyond the time he lived in. ... Few anti-slavery men ... with all the light thrown on the subject, saw this matter as clearly as he did."[37] *The Creation of a Crusader* is the story of how Morris came to see the Slave Power and the Constitution clearly and to convey that vision to the political movement for emancipation.

CHAPTER I

Avoiding Anything Like Agitation

The morning snow had turned to a cold rain by the time the junior senator from Ohio sought recognition from the chair.[1] He had several petitions from Ohio citizens—requests from the rapidly growing antislavery societies seeking the elimination of slavery in the District of Columbia—to offer. Although similar petitions, and Southern objections to them, had convulsed the House of Representatives for days, his Whig colleague from Ohio, Thomas Ewing, had offered several similar petitions two days earlier in the Senate without any objection.[2] Thomas Morris expected a similar response to his motion. From the desk next to his, however, John C. Calhoun leaped to his feet in opposition.[3] As Morris listened to Calhoun's objections, he must have found Calhoun's understanding of the Constitution puzzling. He may have found the fact that he was the one confronting the South Carolina senator surprising.

Morris had emigrated to Ohio from Virginia as a nineteen-year-old and settled in Columbia just east of Cincinnati. Lacking any formal education, he had gone to work as a clerk in a store owned by John Smith. A few years later, he moved his family further east to Clermont County and opened a tavern. The business struggled and Morris began reading Blackstone as a path to greater success. In 1804 he was admitted to the bar as the first resident attorney in Clermont County.[4]

Two years later he was elected to the Ohio House of Representatives and immediately burst onto the political stage in Ohio. He was designated the lead prosecutor in impeachment proceedings brought against two members of the Ohio Supreme Court for declaring provisions of Ohio law related to the jurisdiction of justice of the peace courts unconstitutional. Although he was a thirty-two-year-old lawyer with little trial experience, he was given the task of managing the impeachment prosecution. In undertaking this task, Morris aligned himself with Thomas Worthington and the popular sovereignty wing of the Ohio Jeffersonians.[5] Drawing heavily on the charges adopted by congressional Jeffersonians a few years earlier against United States Supreme Court Justice Samuel Chase, Morris attacked the Ohio judges for their usurpation of power.[6] Since at the time the Ohio legislature elected the Supreme Court justices, Morris argued that the justices could not defy the "will" of the general assembly. The impeachment effort ultimately failed to obtain the two-thirds majority needed to convict in the Ohio Senate, but Morris had embarked on a career focused on protecting the people from the power of elites.

Throughout his long career in the Ohio legislature, Morris worked to limit the power of judges, protect debtors, and tax corporations.[7] Wary of economic or social elites, he tended to personalize political differences. Indeed, he gained recognition when Ohio elections "were between personalities rather than between parties or factions."[8] Morris cut his political teeth in this rough-and-tumble world of shifting alliances, personal feuds, and rancor. Although early state politics had divided along national party lines, by "1815 Ohio elections became more unstructured, unpredictable, and even anarchic . . . Electioneering and self-promotion spread slander and personal rancor increased . . . The pattern of chaotic, largely personal elections at the local and county levels would be overwhelmed only slowly."[9]

With the breakup of Democratic-Republicans in the aftermath of the 1824 presidential election, Morris joined the ranks of the Democracy. When the Jacksonians gained control of the Ohio legislature in 1832, they selected Morris, now their senior statesman, as the first Democratic senator from Ohio. His election resulted largely from his length of service in the general assembly. Three candidates, Benjamin Tappan, John Milton Goodenow, and Morris, sought the Senate seat. On the first ballot Tappan and Morris each received thirty votes with Goodenow garnering the remaining seven. Goodenow, a bitter enemy of Tappan ("his hatred of Tappan had taken possession of his whole soul"), then withdrew and threw his support to Morris.[10]

The new senator had never represented any area other than Clermont County, nor was he overwhelmingly popular in other areas of the state.[11] Morris had twice unsuccessfully sought election to Congress as a representative. The second time was in the fall of 1832 prior to his election to the Senate. Although he was consistently popular in Clermont County, he could never generate enough votes outside its boundaries to win. His seniority, however, had made him the party leader in the general assembly.[12] "Morris was the very embodiment of a Jeffersonian Democrat."[13] Ohio Democrats were certain they had elected a committed Jeffersonian who could be relied on to support President Jackson in Washington.

Morris took his seat in the Senate in the midst of a political firestorm. Over the summer, President Jackson had ordered the removal of the government's deposits from the Bank of the United States. When William Duane, the secretary of the Treasury, refused, Jackson dismissed him and appointed Roger Taney. The new secretary, although not confirmed by the Senate, began removing the deposits on October 1. The Bank responded to this action by dramatically reducing the availability of credit and triggering a financial panic.

The "Panic Session" of Congress provided an opportunity for Jackson's opponents to strike. Because the House of Representatives was controlled by Jackson's supporters, "all of a sudden the quiet, sedate, drab, patrician, and uninteresting Senate of the United States became the arena for one of the greatest political cock fights in American history."[14] For the next three months, the Senate did little but debate Henry Clay's motion to censure Jackson. Morris had gone to Washington deeply suspicious of the Bank of the United States and the Southern advocates of nullification. The censure debate persuaded Morris that Calhoun (the nullifier) and Clay (the Bank) had joined forces. Although he said little, he never waivered from his support for Jackson.

Jackson thought that the Bank of the United States was "aristocratic and oppressive."[15] In 1832 Morris had forced a strong anti-Bank resolution through the state Democratic convention. A correspondent from the national administration told Morris that his actions had "place[d] Ohio in the front rank of the Democracy of the country, and redeem[ed] her character from the imputation of being governed by a monied monopoly."[16] On the move by South Carolina to nullify an act of Congress, Morris, while still in the Ohio legislature, took an equally strong position. Although John McClean, a justice of the United States Supreme Court, told him "there is a danger of too much action," Morris chose to ignore his advice.[17] "The first object of the American people," the senator-elect said, "should be to cherish the most ardent attachment to the Constitution." He believed "the doctrine that a state has the power to nullify a law of General Government [was] revolutionary in its character." He supported the use of force, if necessary, to bring South Carolina into line.[18]

The maneuvers in the Twenty-Third Congress to obtain the recharter of the Bank confirmed his suspicions. He feared "the dangerous power of the Bank" and thought no "curse [had ever] fallen on this Republic equal to the Bank."[19] Upon his arrival in the Senate, Morris had been given a seat between Calhoun and Willie P. Mangum, a senator from North Carolina, and so found himself "in the midst of the Nullifiers." As the session progressed, he saw a growing cooperation between the "nullifiers" and the Bank party. George McDuffie, South Carolina's other senator and "the great intellectual champion of Nullification," had made "Biddle his idol and Jackson his Devil," and from what Morris could see, McDuffie spoke the "language of the Southern majority."[20]

In recognizing the developing affinity between the South and the Bank of the United States, Morris was certainly not unique. The French traveler Michael Chevalier commented at length positively on Southern support for the Bank.[21] Morris's perception of the relationship, however, differed from the view of Chevalier. Even in Morris's private letters to his son, the Jacksonian rhetoric of monsters pervaded. Supporters of the Bank and the advocates of nullification represented two organized groups that sought to attack the Constitution.[22] Morris's understanding of the Bank struggle only deepened his initial distrust and suspicions of Calhoun and the Southern nullifiers.

During the Twenty-Third Congress, Morris behaved in exactly the expected manner; he rarely pressed himself on the Senate. When he did speak, he generally confined himself to issues of particular importance to Ohio.[23] On major issues he preferred to let Thomas Benton, Silas Wright, or some other prominent Jacksonian engage Clay and Daniel Webster. Throughout this session of Congress, Morris "set in [his] place . . . endeavoring to learn what sort of stuff the Senate [was] made of."[24] Ohio Democrats appeared content with Morris's actions. The *Western Hemisphere* reported that "Morris [would] be cheered, and applauded, and sustained for his course during the session."[25] A group of central Ohio Democrats sponsored a public dinner at the State House in Morris's honor and complimented him for having "manfully resisted the grasp of a power [the money power] which put itself above the people."[26]

Nevertheless, in the fall of 1835, prior to Morris's return to Washington, several Ohio Democrats sought to interest him in accepting an appointment to the Ohio Supreme Court. The plan was for Morris to resign from the Senate to accept a seat on the court. The Democrat-controlled general assembly would then elect Benjamin Tappan to replace Morris in the Senate. Initially the proponents believed they could obtain Morris's agreement to the plan. Morris had briefly served on the Ohio Supreme Court in the aftermath of the impeachment effort two decades earlier and had been greatly disappointed when the general assembly failed to reelect him to the bench.[27] Moreover, his interest in and attention to Senate business had flagged significantly and he had become frustrated at being in the minority. During his first session in the Senate (December 1833 to March 1834), Morris never missed a roll-call vote. Over the next twelve months, however, he missed over 30 percent of roll calls—a voting record poor enough to place him in the bottom 20 percent of all senators.[28] By December (perhaps motivated by animus against some of the plan's proponents) he had changed his mind about resigning and returned to Washington.[29]

When the new Congress met in December 1835, the Democrats had gained control of the Senate. With two years of experience and his party now in the majority, Morris assumed a more active role in the Senate. He proposed legislation to limit the sale of public land to actual settlers in an attempt to stop the inflationary speculation in land. On the question of admitting Michigan to the Union, he forcefully defended Ohio's claim to disputed areas along the border between the two states. He also came to the aid of the national party leadership and spoke against Clay's proposal for the distribution of the proceeds from public land sales and in support of Jackson's nominations to the Supreme Court. When his Whig colleague from Ohio ignored the general assembly's instructions to vote in favor of expunging the Senate's censure of Jackson, Morris delivered a partisan-charged reprimand.[30] Ohio's Jacksonians could not have hoped for more.

During the summer of 1835, however, a new issue had intruded into the political debate. Tariffs and banks no longer occupied center stage: "organized antislavery was unquestionably the paramount issue of the day."[31] The issue was immediately injected into the nascent presidential campaign.[32] Throughout the nation "crowds gathered to hear mayors and alderman, bankers and lawyers, ministers and priests denounce abolitionists as amalgamationists, dopes, fanatics, foreign agents, and incendiaries."[33] Southern Ohio experienced this uproar over antislavery tracts during the summer as well.[34]

The American Anti-Slavery Society had adopted a plan to blanket the country with antislavery literature. The pamphlets, targeted at religious and community leaders across the nation, were designed to "rebuke the . . . proslavery loyalists" and change public opinion to make resistance to abolition fruitless. Southerners were not amenable to the plan.[35] In July 1835 the postmaster in Charleston, South Carolina, discovered antislavery pamphlets and tracts in mail addressed to South Carolina citizens. Claiming that these materials, although addressed to white Carolinians, were in reality "a call for black revolution," the postmaster locked up these tracts until the Postmaster General Amos Kendall could tell him how to proceed.[36] Kendall responded to the Charleston postmaster's urgent request for instructions by telling him "You must . . . decide for yourself what is best."[37] Kendall then sought Jackson's guidance. President Jackson agreed with the Charleston postmaster when he described the mailing of antislavery pamphlets as a "wicked plan of exciting the Negroes to insurrection and to massacre."[38]

The residents of Charleston, however, needed no instruction from the president. Within twenty-four hours of the pamphlets' arrival, a mob, led by Robert Hayne, had taken the pamphlets from the post office and burned them. This action touched off a series of similar mob attacks directed at antislavery literature and advocates across the country.[39] During the summer of 1835, the country "was in a state of hysteria." In the South, slaveholders saw the pamphlets "as nothing short of a terrorist attack . . . that justified almost any countermeasure including . . . restrictions on civil liberties."[40] To at least one observer, it appeared that "the abolitionists, a few thousand crazy-headed blockheads, have actually frightened fifteen million people out of their senses."[41] As John Quincy Adams confided to his diary, "there is a great fermentation upon this subject of slavery at this time in all parts of the Union."[42]

In the midst of the uproar over the abolitionist activity, the presidential campaign began. For apparently entirely "personal reasons," Jackson had selected Martin Van Buren, the vice president, as his designated successor. The Democrats, meeting in Baltimore, had unanimously concurred in the selection on May 22, 1835.[43] Nevertheless, the president's opponents, both within and without his party, were not about to let Van Buren's succession occur without a struggle. His "biggest problem was not the small group of abolitionists in his midst at home, but the important and vocal group of Calhounites and Southern Whigs who realized they could use the abolitionists against" him.[44] A vigorous response to the incendiary publications controversy could provide a vehicle for Van Buren to reemphasize his loyalty to the South.[45] Jackson moved quickly to take advantage of this opportunity.

The president asked his postmaster, Amos Kendall, to review the circumstances surrounding the "incendiary publications" and report to Congress on proposed solutions. Near the end of his annual message to Congress, Jackson referred to the events of the prior months:

> In connection with these provisions in relation to the Post-Office Department, I must also invite your attention to the painful excitement produced in the South by attempts to circulate through the mails inflammatory appeals addressed to the passions of the slaves, in prints and in various sorts of publications, calculated to stimulate them to insurrection and to produce all the horrors of servile war. There is doubtless no respectable portion of our countrymen who can be so far misled as to feel any other sentiment than that of indignant regret at conduct so destructive of the harmony and peace of the country, and so repugnant to the principles of our national compact and to the dictates of humanity and religion.[46]

Jackson concluded by calling "the special attention of Congress to the subject" and suggesting "the propriety of passing such a law as will prohibit, under severe penalties, the circulation in the Southern States, through the mail, of incendiary publications intended to instigate the slaves to insurrection."[47] Not since the controversy surrounding Missouri's admission to the Union had the issue of slavery been so clearly presented to Congress.[48] For Calhoun, the events of the summer and the president's proposal provided just the opportunity he sought to resurrect his political fortunes.[49]

Slavery had long been a matter of public discussion in Ohio. The American Colonization Society had been active in the state for many years and widely supported by prominent politicians. According to one Society agent in Ohio, "among the members we number the Governor, Auditor and Treasurer of the State, Speaker of the Senate, a considerable number of Senators and Representatives."[50] In 1824, in the aftermath of the Missouri Crisis, the Ohio General Assembly had adopted resolutions describing slavery as a sin requiring a national solution and calling for a federal program of emancipation and colonization.[51] Following Nat Turner's rebellion in Virginia, the general assembly again turned its attention to emancipation and colonization supported by the federal government. The governor believed that the events in Virginia would cause free Blacks to migrate out of the slave states to Ohio.

Although since its admission to the union Ohio had been "constructing the harshest black code in the free states,"[52] the governor asked the general assembly to consider adopting more stringent laws to prevent Blacks from relocating to the state. In the Ohio House a committee was appointed to develop a response. The committee concluded that Blacks were "forever excluded . . . from all hopes of equality" and they "would always be unequal." The best policy would be to strengthen the Black laws.[53]

If Blacks were not allowed to emigrate to Ohio, some method of diverting them from Ohio's borders would be necessary. Morris was appointed to a select committee to examine again the possibilities of colonization as a solution to slavery. He drafted the report adopted by the Ohio legislature. In his report Morris did not dissent from the views taken by the House Committee. Instead, he gave an exposition of his views of slavery. He felt that although slavery was "a moral evil" and "undoubtedly our greatest national sin," the general assembly had no "right to interfere between the slave and his owner."[54] In articulating this position, Morris was confirming his acceptance of the "federal consensus," regarding slavery in the states. The text of the Constitution, while containing no explicit prohibition on congressional action against slavery in the states, was also silent on any federal power to act on it in the states. Absent an explicit grant of power to emancipate slaves held in the states, the consensus was that "only the states could abolish or regulate slavery within their jurisdictions."[55] "No other constitutional precept so profoundly shaped the contours of antislavery politics in the years between the founding of the nation and the Civil War."[56]

Morris thought it obvious that "the States in the adoption of the federal compact, recognized slavery among the existing order of things." To support that statement, he cited the constitutional provisions on the slave trade and the return of fugitive slaves. Nevertheless, he did not believe that anyone "who reflects seriously on the subject" could think that slavery "can be perpetual." Instead, "the time is not far in advance when it must terminate." Influenced by the Nat Turner revolt of the previous summer, Morris feared that slavery would by "the terrible scourge of insurrection" result in a war of "extermination" and acknowledged that he was "not insensible to the horror and heart-rending scenes that must ensure from servile war waged

16 THE CREATION OF A CRUSADER

by the colored population of our country." For this reason, he thought it necessary to free "our country of its colored population . . . [which] seems to be required as the only means of preventing the shedding of human blood."[57]

Following this lengthy preamble of arguments in favor of colonization, Morris concluded with his recommendations:

> It is, therefore, seriously recommended to this people, as well as to the government of the United States, whether it is not worthy of the attention of Congress, as well as the different state legislatures, to extend their care and fostering hand to the benevolent efforts of the Colonization Society, by affording pecuniary supplies and the means of transportation to all free persons of color who are willing to emigrate to Liberia. This would not only be an act of naked justice to this long oppressed race of men, but seem to be required as the only means of preventing the shedding of human blood, and as a necessary measure for the security of ourselves and our posterity.[58]

In 1832 Morris shared the almost universal opinion in the North that slavery was wrong. He did not, however, believe that the North could do anything about slavery as it existed in the Southern states. Dealing with the already free Blacks concerned him more than abolishing slavery.

In recommending public support for colonization, Morris was in line with other Ohio leaders. Tom Corwin, then a Whig congressman from Ohio, concurred, noting "that the removal from amongst us, of this class, if not necessary to internal tranquility as a nation, is at least indispensable to the perfection of our social and political systems." For Corwin, "the evils resulting from the free black people" in areas where slavery existed were obvious. He noted that Ohio looked "with most intense interest to the operations of this Society, chiefly for the reason that . . . they yet hope to rid themselves of this anomalous population, whose existence amongst them, they justly considered the only evil to which their condition, as members of the confederacy, subjects them."[59]

Governor Robert Lucas, a Jacksonian, had been elected president of the Ohio branch of the colonization society in 1834. In that year, however, agents of the newly formed American Anti-Slavery Society began to work in Ohio,[60] and by April 1835 the Ohio Anti-Slavery Society was formed at a meeting in Zanesville attended by over one hundred delegates from twenty-five counties.[61] These organizational activities, occurring concurrently with the incendiary publications uproar, precipitated a strong backlash in Ohio. Agents of the American Anti-Slavery Society were assaulted by mobs and large antiabolition rallies were held across the state.[62]

The incendiary publications controversy and resulting violence thrust the abolitionist demands and civil liberty issues to the forefront of political debate. Although in the view of some antislavery leaders, the Southern response had done more "than could have been done by the arguments of a thousand agents to convince the sober and disinterested of slavery's crime,"[63] the South's success at preventing the circulation of the pamphlets made the prospect of achieving the goal of changing slaveholders' opinion doubtful. The cost of the project, coupled with the financial distress of its primary backers,[64] made continuation of the campaign problematic. By the time Congress convened in December 1835, the abolitionists had moved on to a different strategy.

Petitions directed at the institution of slavery had been sent to Congress for years.[65] In the second session of the first Congress, petitions from Pennsylvania Quakers and the Pennsylvania Abolition Society had asked Congress to use all its powers to abolish slavery. Despite the Constitutional Convention's deliberate exclusion of "slavery" from the text, Southern representatives in Congress consistently claimed the federal government had no authority over slavery anywhere. Anticipating much of the debate four decades later, Southern members claimed that because Congress had no power over slavery, the petitions should be rejected as unconstitutional.[66] Nevertheless, antislavery advocates continued to petition Congress. The Pennsylvania Abolition Society in conjunction with the American Convention of Abolition Societies, had pressed the issue in 1829. The petition had been referred to the Committee on the District of Columbia, which recommended against taking any action. The Committee's recommendation was accepted by the House. When John Quincy Adams returned to the House of Representatives in 1831, one of his first acts was to submit fifteen petitions seeking the abolition of slavery in the District of Columbia.[67] The Bank, the tariff, and nullification, however, dominated Congress during Jackson's first term. After 1829, antislavery petitions were quietly referred to committee, never to be acted upon.

When the American Anti-Slavery Society's efforts to blanket the South with antislavery pamphlets triggered President Jackson's recommendation to censor the mail and, in any event, proved unsuccessful at converting slaveholders,[68] the society turned to petitioning Congress. The tone of these petitions, however, changed dramatically from those of earlier years. The prior petitioning efforts had been couched in deferential terms and delivered with discretion, seeking gradual change. No longer would abolitionists follow a course of moderation. Suddenly "massive petitions" demanding the immediate abolition of slavery in the District of Columbia began to arrive in Congress.[69]

Although the Ohio Anti-Slavery Society had been actively involved in soliciting such petitions for nearly a year,[70] during the prior session of Congress none had been sent to Morris. By the start of the first session of the Twenty-Fourth Congress, however, he had received a large number of these petitions. On January 7, 1836, he presented "several petitions from the citizens of Ohio . . . praying for the abolition of slavery in the District of Columbia."[71] Two days earlier, Morris's Whig colleague from Ohio, Thomas Ewing, had also presented similar antislavery petitions. These petitions were received and tabled without debate.[72] The effort to introduce antislavery petitions two weeks earlier in the House, however, had touched off a firestorm. South Carolina congressman, James Hammond, after earlier voting to receive and table antislavery petitions, moved to refuse to receive any more such petitions. Whether the motion for a "gag rule" was an "impromptu" idea of Hammond's or not, it created an inflammatory issue for the members of the House.[73]

Antislavery petitions created a dilemma for the administration. While Northern opinion regarding sending unsolicited antislavery tracts to slaveholders raised memories of Nat Turner, refusing to accept petitions to Congress struck directly at rights protected by the First Amendment. Although the Jacksonian leadership was quite comfortable with censorship of the mails, refusing to receive petitions was another thing entirely. Moreover, the effort appeared to be another Calhounite scheme to embarrass Van Buren. The challenge was to find a response that "would placate southern feelings without alienating" the North.[74] Following the Baltimore nominating convention in 1835, the *Washington Globe* had claimed "the whole democracy of the North . . . are opposed, upon constitutional principles, as well as upon views of sound policy, to any attempt of the abolitionists" to achieve their goals.[75] In considering the House action on antislavery petitions, however, the *Washington Globe* "declared the right of petition was an 'unlimited natural right,'" rejected the argument that Congress could refuse petitions of any kind, and contended that the national legis-

AVOIDING ANYTHING LIKE AGITATION

lature had the same authority in the District as any state legislature over the question of slavery.[76]

Calhoun, however, had no intention of letting the opportunity pass him by; for him, the advent of the antislavery incendiary publications and petition campaigns was an opportunity to rally the South and perhaps derail Van Buren's election.[77] When Morris moved that the petitions he presented be referred to the Committee on the District of Columbia, Calhoun immediately objected and asked that a vote first be taken on their reception by the Senate. He contended that the petitions "deeply, basely and maliciously slandered" his constituents.[78] Moreover, Congress lacked the power to address slavery anywhere. As Calhoun read the Fifth Amendment: "no man shall be deprived of his liberty or property without due process of law." Because "slaves of this District were property," they could not be freed under Congress's legislative power over the District or anywhere. He asserted that the antislavery petitions were "sundering the bonds" of the union and that they were more dangerous than the incendiary publications.[79]

Morris, surprised by Calhoun's attack, followed the apparently accepted Jacksonian position announced by the *Washington Globe*. He first reaffirmed his commitment to the federal consensus by denying "in the most explicit terms the power of Congress to interpose in any manner whatsoever with question of Slavery in any of the States." The petitioners did not request any such action, "nor would he, in any instance, give countenance or support" to any effort directed at abolition in the states, but he rejected Calhoun's claim that Congress lacked power to legislate in regard to slavery in the District. Rather, Morris believed that Congress possessed "primary, complete and exclusive legislation" over the District, and "that a contrary opinion, which he had heard lately expressed, was entirely new to him."[80]

Perhaps more importantly in his view, even if Calhoun was correct that Congress lacked the power to abolish slavery in the District of Columbia, the First Amendment still required that the Senate accept petitions: "If the right of petitioning Congress was deemed of so much importance as to be declared by the Constitution a right which Congress should not abridge, with what propriety then shall one branch of Congress undertake to declare the petitions shall not be received on the grounds that the objection is not in the power of Congress to grant, or that the words used by the petitions are such as ought not to be heard."[81] To Morris, if Congress "could prescribe the matter and the form in which petitions should be presented, ... there was at once an end to the right of petitioning." The petitioners, therefore, had a right to present themselves to the Senate, "placing their feet on the Constitution of their country." He believed that they should "be heard in their petitions," but that then the senators "could dispose of those petitions as in their wisdom they may think proper."[82]

Although Morris could hardly have been unaware of the developments in the House, the lack of a similar gag-rule effort in response to Ewing's presentation of petitions persuaded Morris that no such effort would be made in the Senate. He told the Senate that he had "refrained from presenting [the petitions] until he had an opportunity to see what was done with others of like tenor."[83] The debate on Morris's petitions finally halted when James Buchanan, then a senator from Pennsylvania, announced that he also had petitions seeking abolition in the District to present and moved that further debate be postponed.

A few days later,[84] after Buchanan had presented this apparently more subdued petition from some Pennsylvania Quakers also calling for abolition in the District, Morris sought leave to withdraw his petitions. Noting that Calhoun's "objections did not apply to the petition" presented by Buchanan, Morris hoped that the question of the right to petition might be resolved "unembarrassed by the language in which the petition was drawn." He told his colleagues that "it was his sincere desire to avoid anything like agitation or excitement" in the Senate. He only argued for the right "of the people peaceable to assemble and petition for the redress of grievance."[85] Whatever may have been his motivation, by withdrawing his petitions Morris could hardly be said to have "met the proposal of a gag rule triumphantly."[86] The Senate debate over reception of the petitions continued off and on for nearly two months. Although Morris said he intended to make his views known before the vote on the petitions, he never followed through.

In hindsight, Morris's claim to wish to avoid "excitement" appears disingenuous, but there are several reasons to believe the statement sincere. His delay in presenting the petitions coupled with his almost invisible performance during his first two years in the Senate make him an unlikely candidate for an antislavery agitator. Although he subsequently claimed to have believed Congress should do something about slavery in the District ever since he arrived in the Senate, he had never raised the issue prior to presenting the petitions in January 1836. This reluctance to engage in debate had been characteristic of Morris's tenure in the Senate up to that point. Three weeks after the votes on the petitions, Morris told the Senate that "it was true that he had been a silent member of that body, almost entirely; so that his friends here and elsewhere had, in good degree censured him." He said he had "refrained from speaking while there was [*sic*] so many gentlemen willing to speak." Indeed, "not wishing to push himself into notice by public speaking, he felt entirely satisfied to give his colleagues every opportunity to do so."[87] Whatever may have been his reasons, prior to the vote on reception of the petitions, Morris did not speak on the issue again, nor did he attempt to resubmit the petitions he had withdrawn.

Morris's motivation in this initial petition controversy in the Senate resulted not from any strong abolitionist sentiment but from his commitment to the right of petition. In this belief he found most of the Northern senators in agreement. On the motion of Buchanan to receive the Quakers' petitions, Morris voted with the majority in favor of acceptance.[88] This action, however, certainly did not make him an abolitionist since a majority of the senators from the slaveholding states also voted to receive the petitions. Two days later, Morris again voted with the majority in favor of a Buchanan motion. But this time the motion rejected the prayer of the petitioners.[89]

CHAPTER 2

They Are Attempting to Overwhelm Us

The Jacksonians' "Address to the People of the United States," issued following their Baltimore presidential nominating convention in May 1835, told the nation: "No man, nor set of men, can interfere, or even wish to interfere, with the reserved rights of the States, embracing their domestic institutions and social relations, and call himself a Democratic Republican, or a friend of the Union."[1] This position was consistent not only with the federal consensus, but with Morris's statements contained in his Colonization Report for the general assembly three years earlier. During the debate over the Senate's reception of the abolitionists' petitions, Morris had not renounced this statement nor deviated from its understanding. If the senator had any serious desire in the early spring of 1836 to break with the Jacksonians over abolition, the remainder of the Senate session provided him with multiple opportunities to make the break.

In early March, as the debate on abolition petitions was winding down in the Senate, Martin Van Buren again decided to make his views on slavery public. His goal was to shore up his Southern support for his presidential campaign by reassuring the South of his commitment to protect slavery. On March 11, as the Senate voted to deny the request of Buchanan's petitions, the *Washington Globe* published a letter to Junius Amis from Van Buren that confirmed the orthodox Jacksonian position on slavery for the presidential campaign. This statement had three points:

1. Congress has no right or power to interfere with slavery in the states.
2. Even if Congress had the power, it would be inappropriate to interfere with slavery in the District of Columbia and any action directed toward abolition in the District (without the consent of Maryland and Virginia) could lead to the destruction of the union.
3. Further efforts of abolitionists against slavery would increase "public odium" toward them.

Van Buren committed that he would "go in to the presidential chair the inflexible and uncompromising opponent" of any action against slavery in Washington, DC. In Van Buren's view, the blame for the current excitement lay entirely with the abolitionist agitators.[2]

Morris had spent most of his first two years in the Senate sitting "still in [his] place . . . endeavoring to learn of what sort of stuff the Senate is made."[3] In the final months of the session, following action on the antislavery petitions, his reticence to speak ended. Arkansas's application for admission to the union as a slave state presented Morris with the opportunity to take exception to Van Buren's position. The antislavery press had taken a clear stand against it, and petitions circulated opposing it.[4] The abolitionist view of the issue was stated starkly by the Ohio Anti-Slavery Society:

> If slavery be a crime, the act of admission involves us as a nation in its guilt. This act we consider moral sanction on the part of the whole United States to the system of slavery . . . It may be said that the right of Arkansas to be received as a slave state, was secured by the Missouri Compromise bill of 1822; But the compromise no more justifies our conduct in this instance, than one sin can justify any immoral act, as its own legitimate product.[5]

In the House, the Jacksonians were forced to resort to all-night sessions and parliamentary maneuvering to defeat efforts led by John Quincy Adams to block the admission because of the slavery provisions in the Arkansas Constitution.[6]

Morris, however, had no difficulty voting in favor of Arkansas's statehood. One of his fellow senators (Swift of Vermont) refused to vote for admission because the term "perpetual slavery" appeared in the proposed state constitution.[7] After Swift's statement regarding Arkansas's recognition of slavery, Morris made several remarks that some early historians, reading back from a later perspective, mistakenly interpreted to reflect the abolitionist position.[8] Far from being an expression of an abolitionist sentiment, his speech rejected the antislavery justification for opposing Arkansas's application for admission in the union.

Morris began by saying that he believed "slavery to be wrong in principle and mischievous in practice," and therefore he wanted to be clear about the basis of his vote. He objected to the recognition of slavery in the Arkansas constitution as a "fundamental principle in her government." He acknowledged that "the wrong, in a moral sense, with which [he] viewed slavery" would justify a vote against the admissions of Arkansas if he "believed he had the power to do so." Morris believed that "the Constitution under which [he] acted clearly required" that he vote to admit Arkansas. Since the Ordinance of 1787 did not apply to Arkansas nor did the Missouri Compromise ban slavery in Arkansas, and it had not entered into any agreement with the United States that slavery should not be admitted into the state, Morris concluded:

> [Arkansas had] the right to choose this lot . . . though I regret that they have made this choice, yet believing that this Government has no right to interfere with the question of slavery in any of the states, or prescribe what shall or shall not be considered property in the different states, or by what tenure property of any kind shall be holden, I cannot, as a member of this body, refuse my vote to admit this state into the Union because her constitution recognized the existence of slavery.[9]

Morris's view was the antithesis of the abolitionist position. He denied that the extension of slavery was an issue in the admission of Arkansas. Although "in a moral sense" he believed "slavery to be wrong in principle," he viewed slavery as a state issue and rejected any idea that Congress had the power to proscribe a state's domestic institutions.[10] In short, although Congress could have prohibited slavery in the Arkansas Territory, because it had not done so, the federal consensus applied to Arkansas's application for statehood.

His argument was entirely consistent with the general Northern view on the morality of slavery and the Jacksonian position on congressional power over slavery in the states. Although "the vast majority of Democrats agreed that slavery was 'an evil in the abstract,' few were greatly exercised over the moral issues involved. Slavery was . . . best dealt with by those in the locality where it existed."[11] His vote to admit Arkansas was contrary to the abolitionist stance and completely in line with the general Democratic view of slavery and the national party's efforts to aid Van Buren's election.

Texas's move for independence also threatened to become an issue in the presidential campaign and provided another opportunity for Morris to break from the Jacksonian line. Southerners had long looked at Texas as a natural area of expansion, but many Northerners (not just abolitionists) were uncomfortable with the prospect of increasing Southern power.[12] The abolitionists recognized the role of slavery in Texas's move for independence, and opposed any recognition of Texas as an independent country. Morris, however, initially supported the Texas revolution and quickly sought Senate support for the revolutionaries. On April 26 Morris presented resolutions from a meeting in Cincinnati "suggesting the expediency of acknowledging the independence of that country" and asked that the resolutions be referred to the Committee on Foreign Relations. In offering the resolutions, Morris endorsed the request and noted that "he accorded fully with the feelings expressed in the proceedings." Although Senator Walker from Mississippi supported Morris's request, cooler heads believed that referring the question on recognition to a committee was premature. Morris agreed to have his motion tabled.[13]

A month later, Senator Walker attempted to present similar resolutions from a meeting in Louisiana urging recognition of Texas's independence. When the chair ruled the form of the resolutions improper, Walker sought to bring up Morris's tabled resolutions. Morris now thought the "recognition of Texas involved a question which did not meet the eye and which was beyond mere recognition of her independence." As a result, he believed "the observance of prudence was necessary" and that Walker's motion was "premature and hasty." When he was accused of "being under the influence of the Executive," Morris denied that Jackson had caused him to back off from his earlier support for recognition of Texas's independence. Nevertheless, he did not oppose the resolution's reference to committee. The Senate then agreed to refer all such memorials to the Committee on Foreign Relations.[14]

The Senate's action on antislavery petitions, the admission of Arkansas, and the recognition of Texas's independence did not conclude its slavery-related agenda. The censorship of the mails remained. This was the issue that had caused Jackson to bring slavery back to Congress. The president had recommended the passage of a federal statute that would prevent the mailing of "incendiary publications" into the South. To many, this proposal raised serious freedom-of-speech concerns. In addressing the Ohio General Assembly in December 1835, Ohio Governor Lucas articulated "the conservative point of view with which a larger portion of the State undoubtedly agreed."[15] Although critical of abolitionists, the Jacksonian governor understood slavery and the right to freedom of speech in terms with which Morris would agree:

> The community, of late, appears to have been thrown into commotion on the subject of slavery in the southern states, and as citizens of a common country, we cannot view that commotion with indifference. *We have not one word to say in favor of the principle of slavery.* We view it abstractedly, as both moral and political evil; but it was interwoven in our political system at its first organization, and its existence has been continued in many of the states as a part of their local policy. With this policy we have no right to interfere. Each state has the constitutional right to regulate its own internal affairs; and it was with extreme regret we witnessed the recent excitement in the slaveholding states, produced by the misguided zeal of individuals residing in the free states. The conduct of these individuals we sincerely deprecate; and the public sentiment of the people of Ohio has stamped their conduct with the seal of disapprobation; and will doubtless continue their exertions to allay all excitement with regard to this delicate question, as far as the moral force and controlling influence of public opinion can extend; but we are firmly of the opinion that no legislative acts can be passed on this subject, as suggested by some of the southern states, without an entire disregard to the Constitution of the state of Ohio. The constitution declares "that the printing press shall be open and free to every citizen who wishes to examine the proceedings of any branch of government, or the conduct of any public officer; and no law shall ever restrain the right thereof." Every citizen has an indisputable right to speak, write or print upon any subject as he thinks proper, being liable for the abuse of that liberty.[16]

Calhoun believed that Jackson's proposal to have the federal government involved in preventing the mailing of antislavery materials could be interpreted to empower Congress to abolish slavery. To Calhoun, the creation of a Northern antislavery majority was to be feared more than the impact of the antislavery pamphlets on the South. Despite these fears, he recognized in the president's proposal "an opportunity to unite the South by magnifying the importance of the abolitionists."[17] He sought (and obtained) the creation of a special committee (which he chaired) comprised of mostly Southern senators to consider and report on the proposed legislation.[18] By the time this issue reached the floor of the Senate, however, the administration was firmly opposed to the bill reported by Calhoun's committee.[19] According to one leading Jacksonian, Calhoun's report on the subject of incendiary publications was "inflammatory" and full of "insidiousness" and was not agreed to by a majority of the special committee.[20]

Not only did Calhoun deny that slavery was evil, he asserted that the antislavery publications tended "to excite to insurrection and servile war." He also claimed that allowing the publications to be mailed in the South would "end in completely alienating the two great sections of the union."[21] Calhoun's report continued that the existence of the union imposed a duty "on the States within whose limits the danger originates to arrest its further progress."[22] He then returned to the petition issue, claiming that "the general government has no right or authority over the subject of slavery," so that Congress's receipt of the petitions was "obnoxious and dangerous." Failure, then, to adopt the reported bill (which would require local postmasters to comply with state laws regulating the content of the mail) "would be virtually to co-operate with the abolitionists." The result would again justify nullification.[23]

After withdrawing his petitions, Morris did not speak again on the petition issue before the Senate had voted to accept the petitions and to reject their request. Nearly a month after the decision to deny the request of the antislavery petitions, the presentation of resolutions from the legislature of Maine on incendiary publications provided Morris with the opportunity to explain his views on antislavery petitions, as well as to attempt a little revisionist history on the Senate floor. In presenting the Maine resolution, Senator Ruggles noted that they passed "through both Houses of the legislature of Maine without one word of exciting debate." He thought the behavior was "worthy of imitation in this body" when abolition petitions were presented.[24] Calhoun, noting that he assumed Senator Ruggles was referring to him, replied that as long as the petitions referred to Southerners as "pirates, murderers and villains he would take the liberty to treat such denunciations with the scorn they deserve." Senator Brown from North Carolina attempted to calm the debate by saying he "had not heard those terms in the petitions and that prudence would suggest not using those terms."[25]

Calhoun responded by asking for the petitions that Morris had withdrawn. Morris apparently still had the petitions in his desk on the Senate floor and handed them to Calhoun, but noted that he did "not consent for them to be used." After acknowledging Morris's request, Calhoun nevertheless proceeded to read portions of the petitions that he found offensive. Among the phrases that troubled Calhoun were the claims that slaveholders "traffic in human flesh," that "dealing in slaves . . . had solemnly been declared piracy by the laws of . . . all Christian nations," and that "slavery was sinful . . . because it corrupted public morals." Calhoun concluded by threatening "interposition" should the Congress fail to act favorably on his proposed bill.[26]

Calhoun's unauthorized use of the petitions and attack on the petitioners triggered a response from Morris. He saw nothing wrong with the language of the petitions. Although he had withdrawn the petitions "at the solicitation of his friends," Morris "then and now thought [the petitions] were perfectly unexceptionable." Instead, he accused Calhoun of engaging in the conduct he objected to in the petitions. Morris said the petitioners "had been termed miserable fanatics, vile incendiaries and charged with an intention to dissolve the Union." Morris then went beyond the contents of the petitions to address the substance of the petitioners' requests. He acknowledged that "when he first took his seat . . . as a Senator," he had told a colleague from Georgia that "he believed that Congress had a right to legislate in the subject of slavery in the District of Columbia," and "that sound policy required that something should be done with regard to it." His position had changed: "He was now convinced from information since acquired that it was not expedient for Congress to touch the subject." Finally, Morris said the *Congressional Globe* report of him voting to reject the prayer of the petitions was incorrect. He could not, "consistently with his views, vote to reject a petition without giving the subject of it a fair examination."[27] Whether the *Congressional Globe* or Morris's subsequent revision was correct regarding his vote on receiving the antislavery petitions, he did not believe Congress should act on slavery in the District.

The debate on the bill, combined with Calhoun's threat of interposition unless the bill passed and his attack on Morris' constituents, prompted Morris to act.[28] A few days after the exchange with Calhoun on the language of the petitions, and the day after Calhoun's nullification threat, Morris addressed the incendiary publications bill directly. In his first major speech after more than two years in the Senate, he challenged the constitutionality of Calhoun's bill and attacked Calhoun and the South directly.[29] Morris said that he would "tremble for the liberties" of his country were Congress to adopt the principle that the mails could be opened without a warrant. Indeed, "the very suggestion, coming from the quarter it does [that is, Calhoun], is sufficient to give alarm." To Morris, the proposed bill was simply one more effort to declare that citizens of the free states "have no right to talk—to preach or to pray on the subject of slavery" with the result that "liberty of thought, of speech, and of the press shall be . . . if not prohibited, rendered to a great degree useless. All of this is required . . . out of respect for the laws of one or more of the slaveholding states." Morris "denied the whole argument."[30] While his comments so far had addressed only the incendiary publications bill, after listening to Calhoun and considering his arguments for three months, Morris was ready to contradict the South Carolinian's constitutional theory and his constant claim that the South was under attack by abolitionists.

The word *slave* did not appear anywhere in the Constitution. Most historians, however, have long recognized that the Constitution contained several "clauses . . . that directly or indirectly accommodated" slavery.[31] These include the three-fifths clause (article I, section 2) for apportioning representation and the corresponding limit on direct taxes (article I, section 2 and 9); the prohibition on abolishing the international slave trade before 1808 (article I, section 9) and what became known as the Fugitive Slave Clause (article IV, section 2). This combination of avoidance of the word *slavery* with a series of clauses accommodating its existence has led some recent commentators to conclude that "the founders' Constitution simultaneously evades, legalizes and calibrates slavery."[32] Others go further and argue that the "Constitution rested on a compromise that was understood from the start to be amoral or even immoral: namely the preservation and perpetuation of slavery."[33] In other words, they claim that these provisions created a "carefully constituted document that preserved and protected slavery." To these commentators, the absence of the word *slave* was because "the founders did not want to explicitly acknowledge their hypocrisy. They sought instead to shroud it."[34]

Other historians, while acknowledging that the framers recognized that "slavery would have to be tolerated and even shielded as a creation of individual states," argue that they were also determined that "nowhere in the Constitution would it be deemed legitimate."[35] Instead, "the framers did not merely refuse to allow the word slavery into the document, they went out of their way to refer to slaves as 'persons held to service' ... a deliberate choice that reflected the influence of antislavery jurisprudence at the time."[36] In other words, "the convention was intent not on deviously avoiding the word 'slavery', but on excluding from the Constitution the very idea that there could be property in man."[37] Both sides of the current debate on slavery's role in the Constitution believe the founders intended what they wrote, but disagree entirely on what the framers intended by the language they chose.[38]

No provision of the Constitution, however, contained an express prohibition on congressional action to abolish slavery.[39] Other provisions did give Congress the express power to legislate in at least two specific areas where slavery could be implicated: the District of Columbia (article I, section 8) and the territories and admission of states (article IV, section 3, clauses 1 and 2). The abolitionist petitions inundating Congress in 1836 were targeted at these two areas of express congressional power.[40] The federal consensus did not address either of these powers, nor did either clause contain any reference to slavery. The issue Morris confronted in considering Calhoun's argument, like the debate between historians today, was whether the provisions accommodating slavery's existence, coupled with the Fifth Amendment, created a constitutional guarantee of slavery.

Calhoun claimed that slaves were property, and that the Fifth Amendment precluded Congress taking property without due process. As a result, the Constitution guaranteed slavery and prohibited abolition in the District. In Calhoun's mind, because the petitions sought abolition in the District, they were seeking action beyond Congress's constitutional power and, therefore, did not have to be received.[41] For the Fifth Amendment's prohibition of taking property to apply to bar congressional power to abolish slavery in the District, however, Calhoun needed to demonstrate that slaves were considered property under the Constitution. To establish this point, he turned to the Fugitive Slave Clause, an argument that had been used extensively by Southerners during the Missouri Crisis and would later be adopted by Chief Justice Taney as the predicate for his opinion in *Dred Scott*.[42] Although some contemporary historians agree that the "provision insured the legal sanctity of slaves as property,[43] as Don Fehrenbacher noted, "the wording scarcely invites such an interpretation." As adopted, the clause "drew no distinction between free and non-free persons" and "carried no connotation of property." The provision made no mention of the federal government but "was designed as limitation on state authority" to prevent the adoption of personal liberty laws."[44]

When Morris had arrived in the Senate, he felt himself "surrounded by these great men" (Benton, Clay, Webster, and Calhoun). Nevertheless, he told his son, "I trust I shall be able to think and act for myself."[45] Morris had taken three months "thinking for himself" to work out his response to Calhoun's property-based claim that the Constitution guaranteed slavery. There is no evidence that prior to his arrival in the Senate, he had given slavery's status under the Constitution any thought beyond what he had expressed in his colonization report four years earlier: slavery was evil; the Constitution recognized it as existing but anticipated its end in the not-too-distant future; and the federal consensus meant Congress could not act on slavery in the states. His expression of surprise at the notion that Congress lacked power to abolish slavery in the District, while perhaps uninformed, appears genuine. Although during the Missouri Crisis "northerners cited various clauses to justify a more general claim that the Constitution itself was an antislavery document,"[46] Morris never referenced that earlier debate. He did not appear familiar with the contents of the argument. He had simply not come to Washington with any developed antislavery constitutional theory. He had, however, come to Washington with an opinion of Calhoun. Jackson's friends described Calhoun as "the most wicked and despicable of American Statesman." Morris could not have agreed more.[47] Nothing Calhoun had done in the Senate since Morris's arrival had changed Morris's view.[48]

Although he was deeply suspicious of anything Calhoun proposed, in examining Calhoun's claims, Morris set out not to discover an antislavery constitution but to determine the merits of Calhoun's pro-slavery constitutional understanding. Morris applied the "plain meaning rule" of interpretation common to lawyers in the early nineteenth century. As Chief Justice Marshall had explained several years earlier, "although the spirit of an instrument, especially a constitution, is to be respected not less than its letter, yet the spirit is to be collected chiefly from its words." Deviation from this standard of interpretation was appropriate only if "the absurdity and injustice of applying the provision to the case, would be so monstrous that all mankind would, without hesitation, unite in rejecting the application."[49] In other words, under the established rules of constitutional interpretation, the words used by the framers were the key to the meaning of the text. The merits of Calhoun's claims, then, had to be measured against the words the framers used.

A few weeks earlier, Morris had concluded that the Constitution required that he vote to admit Arkansas (the antithesis of the abolitionist position), but in considering Calhoun's theory, what Morris found was a Constitution that distinguished persons from property. The constitutional text simply did not support a reading that guaranteed slavery or limited congressional power to abolish slavery in the District. Two weeks earlier, Morris acknowledged "that he had been a silent member" of the Senate for most of his term. Although he had "heard many arguments which he thought both weak and fallacious," he had let other senators respond. Calhoun's constitutional arguments, however, were apparently so "fallacious" that Morris could no longer refrain from responding.[50]

When Morris had presented his petitions in January, he had believed that Congress's "exclusive" power to legislate for the District justified the petitioners.[51] Calhoun's defense of slavery as property protected by the Fifth Amendment required a different response. Phrasing the issue in terms with which modern historians would be comfortable, Morris began by noting that the Senate was repeatedly being asked to "acknowledge that slavery is guaranteed by the Constitution." Morris thought that this was "the important point in the whole controversy."

> I deny that the right of property is guaranteed by the Constitution of the United States, or that the right of the master to his slave as property, is founded on, or arises from, that instrument. Property in slaves, as well as other things, is a mere creature of law, and in this country is entirely the creature of the State laws. The words *slave* or *slavery*, is not to be found in the Constitution of the United States; and by a bare perusal of that instrument, without a knowledge of the past, no one would suppose that slavery existed in any form in this Republic.[52]

This understanding that property in slaves was entirely a creature of state laws would become "the constitutional basis for the politics that in time led to slavery's destruction."[53]

More specifically, neither the Fugitive Slave Clause nor the three-fifths clause supported Calhoun's claim to a constitutional guarantee of slave property:

The slave is treated as a person, not a thing; and as a person, not as property, is represented in Congress. Hence provision is made in the Constitution of the United States, that no person who is held to service or labor in one State, under the laws thereof, escaping into another, shall, in consequence of any law or regulation therein, be discharged from service or labor, but shall be delivered up on the claim of the party to whom such service or labor is due. This provision of the existence of a person held to service or labor, under the laws of a State, and in its application could well be understood to mean a white as a colored person, and one held to labor for a term of years, as well as a slave for life.[54]

Under the Constitution as written, slaves were persons; they could not be property.

Because the text of the Constitution did not anywhere recognize the possibility that persons could be property, Morris concluded that Calhoun was in effect attempting "to rewrite the Constitution," and his Fifth Amendment protection of property analysis collapsed.[55] Whatever may have been the status of slaves under state law, for purposes of the Constitution, they were persons. Thus, the Fifth Amendment did not limit congressional power to abolish slavery in the District, nor make the goals sought by the antislavery petitions unconstitutional.

Morris had concluded, however, that the implication of Calhoun's constitutional exegesis went far beyond the power of Congress in the District. He feared that should the notion that the Constitution guaranteed slavery be accepted, it would "produce that most mischievous consequences" to the nonslaveholding states.

If it be true, and can be maintained, the honorable Senator from South Carolina or any other gentleman, may bring his hundreds or thousands of slaves into the State of Ohio, cause them to labor there as long as shall suit his convenience, and withdraw them at pleasure, and no law or regulation of my State, no, not even the [Ohio] constitutional prohibition against slavery, could reach his case, or afford us any security against this innovation, for the law of Congress made in pursuance thereof, shall be, or is, the supreme law of the land.[56]

Finally, the conclusion for Morris was obvious:

34   THE CREATION OF A CRUSADER

> It seems to me that the free States have a thousand times more just cause for fear and alarm, while gentlemen so strongly assert their constitutional right to their slaves, that they will attempt to introduce slavery into the free States, than the slaveholding States have that we shall attempt to interfere in any manner with the question of slavery as settled by the laws of their own States. They are attempting to overwhelm us by the power of this Government, while we deny the right of Congress or the Legislature of any State to interfere with the internal regulations or police of another State.[57]

Not only was the Constitution not pro-slavery, slaveholders were attempting to use the Constitution illegitimately to justify asserting federal power against the free states.

Morris had also grown tired of Southern threats of dissolution. He thought this "a vain and idle threat calculated to effect no good." Nevertheless, he

> should always be disposed to believe, that persons who make such threats, desire what they threaten, and that their continuance in the family or firm, instead of being a benefit is always an injury to the remaining members. Dissolve the Union! Who has the right to do this? No State or individual has either the moral or constitutional right to dissolve or accede from the Union for any cause.[58]

In Calhoun's demands for the protection of slavery, Morris heard the echoes of nullification. In his claim for special privilege, Morris saw the shadow of the money power.

This speech marked a "watershed" not only in Morris's career but in political antislavery.[59] As James Oakes has recognized, "once slavery's defenders shifted the terms of the debate to the fundamental property right . . . it was no longer a question of whether Congress . . . should abolish slavery in the District. . . . now opponents of slavery had to address the question of whether Congress could do so."[60] Morris provided the answer. The seeds of both the Slave Power thesis and antislavery constitutionalism were sown in the Senate that day in April 1836. The *Congressional Globe* published the full text of the speech, guaranteeing nationwide readership, including Southern Jacksonian slaveholders. In Ohio, the new abolitionist paper, the *Philanthropist,* also printed the entire speech, assuring abolitionist familiarity (particularly the leadership of the American Anti-

Slavery Society) with Morris and his constitutional response to Calhoun's theories.[61] Over the next two decades, Morris's constitutional interpretation would form the core of antislavery constitutional thought.[62]

Concern for the power the South possessed by virtue of the three-fifths clause and Southern domination of the presidency and administrative offices had been expressed almost since the adoption of the Constitution.[63] Jefferson's narrow electoral defeat of John Adams and the embargo and the War of 1812 had raised the ire of New England Federalists to the extra votes given to slaveholders. The Missouri Crisis had created strong sectional resentment toward the increased Southern electoral strength resulting from the admission of new slave states. Observers in the North had frequently compared the number of federal officials from each section and commented on the preponderance of Southerners. Subsequently, abolitionists would tabulate the number of Southern office holders as evidence of the prevalence of the Slave Power.[64]

Although Morris would make use of these calculations later in his career, neither the number of Southern office holders nor the three-fifths clause was the issue. Instead of complaining about the three-fifths clause, Morris used the Constitution's consistent reference to "persons" to counter Calhoun's claim of constitutional protection for slavery. In the two weeks prior to his speech on incendiary publications, Morris had voted to admit Arkansas as a slave state and to confirm two Jackson appointments to the Supreme Court, including Roger Taney. Indeed, Morris voted to confirm every Supreme Court appointment made by Jackson or Van Buren during his term in the Senate.[65] The issue, to Morris's mind, was not the constitutional sources for Southern power, but rather the persistent demand for special privileges made by the slaveholding elite for the protection of the physical basis of their source of power—slavery. Like the money power, slaveholders were using their status to attack the rights and opportunities of non–slave owners. The immorality of slavery offended him, but the arrogant elitism of slave owners (personified by Calhoun) angered him.[66]

Calhoun's demand for the censorship of the mails crystallized suspicions Morris had harbored since the nullification crisis. During the debate on the recharter of the Bank, he had come to view the "money power" and the South as groups that could become linked. Now the South was asking for the same type of special treatment that the Bank had sought. The reasoning that denied Congress the right to interfere in the states' institutions also led to the denial of Congress's right to grant special protection to those institutions. Just as he had earlier feared control of the government by an unconstitutional monied monopoly, Morris now feared the growth of Southern power by unconstitutional demands. He would struggle against the slaveholders "attempting to overwhelm us by the power of the Government" for the rest of his political career.

As an early historian of the Liberty Party noted, "up to this time Morris had been a Jeffersonian Democrat, a rather rugged speaker, a clear thinker, and a reliable party man. He had shown no signs whatsoever of being in advance of his constituents on the Slavery question, nor did he in the Senate say anything on the topic during the first half of his term."[67] Not until Calhoun's demands made the threat to civil liberty from the slaveholding power real for him did he speak or act in support of abolitionists' right to free speech. As much as the senator's son may have wished Morris to have been motivated by a hatred of slavery instilled by his mother,[68] it was the demands of Slave Power, not the slave, that first prompted Morris to act.

The struggle over incendiary publications had solidified Morris's distrust of the South but had not changed his understanding of slavery. Morris was neither a "rabid abolitionist" by 1836 (as some historians have claimed),[69] nor did his actions support the contention that his position in 1836 was the result of his "moral vision of the political world."[70] Rather, he justified his ultimate vote against the petitioners' request for abolition in the District of Columbia on the grounds of "expediency."[71] His votes on the right of petition, Calhoun's bill to censor the mail, recognition of Texas independence, and the admission of Arkansas were all consistent with the Jacksonian party line in the spring of 1836.[72] Morris was simply not a moral crusader bent on destroying slavery. The leading Jacksonians (Blair, Kendal, Taney, Burton, Van Buren) all believed that "the rise of democratic government . . . had generated such fears and anxiety from its opposition . . . that a counterattack had been launched. . . . first the Bank, then nullification, most."[73] Morris agreed. He split from the party leadership only in ascribing blame for the unrest and controversy. Leading Jacksonians thought the abolitionists "in league with the Pro-Bank Whigs" and the nullifiers to harm the Democrat Party.[74] Morris saw the Bank supporters and nullifiers combining with slaveholders to attack the civil rights of the people (including the abolitionist). Van Buren blamed the abolitionists; Morris blamed Calhoun and the South.

In the winter of 1836, Morris differed from other Jacksonians "only in his tendency to apply Democratic principles to the slavery issue."[75] He saw Calhoun's demands as a continuation of the Bank and nullification struggle. To most Jacksonians, however, the abolitionists were a part of Calhoun's efforts to defeat Van Buren or to dismember the union.[76] They saw the abolitionists as "the rich, the elite, the privileged." Their agitation was part of a "concentrated plot" involving Northern elites, Southern nullifiers, and the abolitionists to break up the union.[77] Morris, however, saw only the conspiracy between the South and the nullifiers and the Bank's supporters. Events in Ohio on his return in the summer of 1836 would reinforce his view.

CHAPTER 3

Keeper of the Jeffersonian Conscience

The violent response to abolitionist efforts to mail antislavery publications to slave state residents and the antislavery petition campaign of 1835–36 thrust slavery into politics to a degree not seen since the Missouri statehood controversy. Abolitionists found few friends there. The antislavery organization was still small and largely unpopular even in the free states. Consequently, most politicians declined to support the efforts of the abolitionists. Morris emerged as one of the few national office holders willing to defend the actions of the abolitionists. In 1836, however, Morris was ideologically not an abolitionist but rather one of the "the keepers of the Jeffersonian conscience."[1] The incendiary publications debate and antislavery petition campaign had dramatically changed the political context within which he operated. The demands of the South (and Calhoun in particular) for special treatment of slavery had pushed Morris to defend the civil liberties of abolitionists and deny the validity of Calhoun's proslavery interpretation of the Constitution. His initial backing of antislavery efforts resulted not so much from his dislike of slavery as from his distrust of the aggressive slaveholding power's demands for its protection.

Much of the maneuvering in Congress in the spring of 1836 had been related to the presidential campaign. Indeed, "for the first time in American history, slavery lit up a presidential race."[2] In addition to the debates surrounding antislavery petitions and incendiary publications, monetary and fiscal policy played a prominent role in the campaign. In particular the Distribution Bill sent surplus funds in the Treasury to the states to be deposited into local banks, and limited those depository banks from issuing notes in small denominations. Debate on the bill had exposed a division within the Jacksonian ranks.[3] Conservatives supported the bill and the prospect of an increased money supply to support economic growth. Radicals, distrustful of banks and paper money, opposed the program. Morris, along with several leading Jacksonians, had spoken and voted against this plan. Despite his reservations, Jackson finally acquiesced to the Distribution Bill in the spring of 1836.[4] Jackson, however, had merely relented; he had not surrendered. On July 11, a week after Congress had adjourned, the president issued the *Specie Circular,* which required that all purchases of federal lands be paid for in specie. As the fall campaign began, Van Buren made clear his support for Jackson's hard-money policy.[5] Morris was in complete accord.

The fall of 1836 found Ohio awash in party politics. Not only were all statewide and legislative offices on the ballot, but the presidential contest focused everyone's attention. Van Buren tried to make the election a plebiscite on Jackson's policies of "limited government, hard money, fiscal responsibility and strong . . . foreign policy."[6] Morris remained a "firm believer in the principles which govern the Democrats" and thought Jackson had "done more for the liberty of his country than most men"[7] and supported Van Buren enthusiastically. When Jackson's "hard money" policy became central to the campaign, however, the party split between "Conservatives," who favored bank notes and paper currency, and those who supported the *Specie Circular.* Ohio did not escape this division. The state Democratic party split, with the left wing following the lead of New York's hard-money Locofocos.[8] As "the leading hard money Senator," Morris was firmly in the Ohio Locofoco camp.[9]

While Morris was confronting Calhoun in the Senate, the nascent abolitionist cause in southern Ohio received an added impetus when James G. Birney, a former slaveholder converted to abolition by Theodore Weld, was driven from Kentucky as a result of the furor over the incendiary publications and settled in Cincinnati in early 1836 while Morris was in Washington. Unable to publish his antislavery paper, the *Philanthropist,* in Cincinnati, Birney began publication in the town of New Richmond soon after his arrival. Despite the obvious danger,[10] Birney decided to move his paper into Cincinnati in April. The bitter opposition of the residents, however, had not abated. In mid-July, as Morris was returning to

Ohio from the Senate, a mob broke into the press room and "the press and materials found in it were defaced and destroyed." Several days later on July 23, a meeting of concerned citizens was held "to decide whether they would permit the publication or distribution of abolition papers." The meeting appointed a committee to request that Birney cease publication. The committee met with Birney on July 28. The next day Birney defiantly refused to comply with the committee's demands. On July 30 a mob of four thousand to five thousand destroyed Birney's office, threw the press into the Ohio River, and sought to tar and feather Birney.[11] Undaunted, Birney refused to cease publication.

In the midst of this mob violence directed at the *Philanthropist*, Morris found a rapidly growing abolitionist movement when he returned to his home in Clermont County in July 1836. In the spring John Rankin had covered the county with his abolition tracts and formed an antislavery society at New Richmond. By the time of the first state antislavery convention at the end of April, the Clermont County organization had grown to sixty members. After giving his writings time to circulate, Rankin returned to the county in August for another lecture tour. Although he did not meet Morris during his visit, Rankin found that antislavery sentiment had increased remarkably. Within three days Rankin formed additional societies in three different towns within the county.[12]

The members of the local county antislavery societies included several friends and members of Morris's family. John Jollife, the Clermont County prosecuting attorney and a protégé of Morris, joined the organization at Batavia, the county seat. Additionally, S. J. Morris, the postmaster at Bethel and one of Thomas Morris's sons, joined and became treasurer of his local society. By this time, Dr. Issac Beck, Morris's nephew, was already involved with Rankin in assisting fugitive slaves' escape.[13] Calhoun's description of antislavery society's members as fanatics, vile incendiaries, and disunionists struck directly at Morris's friends and family.

More importantly (at least politically), Alexander Campbell had been elected a vice president of the state antislavery society and designated the manager for the society in Clermont County. Campbell had been involved in Ohio politics with Morris for nearly thirty years. Campbell had served several terms in the general assembly with Morris, been the speaker of the Ohio House and a member of the "prosecution" team for the judicial impeachment attempt led by Morris, and served four years as a US senator from Ohio. Although Campbell had joined the Whig party, he and

Morris had remained friends and his public leadership in the Ohio Anti-Slavery organization provided Morris with political reassurance.[14]

At least as important (if not more so) for Morris was who was opposed to the abolitionist organization and publication of Birney's *Philanthropist*. In general (and Cincinnati in particular), "anti-abolitionism was stoked chiefly by prosperous conservatives of both major political parties."[15] The leadership of the "anti-abolitionists" was comprised of "gentlemen of the highest classes and respected professions in the city."[16] Two men in particular stand out. Among the leaders of the Cincinnati effort to silence Birney was Jacob Burnett. He and Morris had been on opposite sides for thirty years. Burnett was vice chair of the January 1836 meeting that warned Birney not to publish his paper in Cincinnati. Nevertheless, in April Birney moved the paper from New Richmond to Cincinnati. Things remained relatively calm until July 12, when a mob destroyed the press that printed the *Philanthropist*. When Birney persisted in publishing his paper, the citizens of Cincinnati appointed Burnett to lead a committee to ask Birney to cease. Burnett told Birney that "nineteen twentieths of the people of Cincinnati opposed" the paper and "160 men were ready to destroy it." When Birney refused, Burnett reported the results to the other city newspapers. That night a mob (which may have included Burnett) threw the press into the Ohio River.[17]

Morris and Burnett had been enemies since before Ohio was granted statehood. In 1801 Burnett had represented the plaintiff in an action on a debt Morris had contracted the prior year. The judgment was for eighty-eight dollars, which Morris was unable to pay. When the property Morris had available for levy (one horse and one cow) were insufficient to pay the judgment, Burnett obtained a writ to have Morris imprisoned for debt.[18] Their paths crossed again a few years later during the effort to impeach the Ohio Supreme Court justices. While Morris led the impeachment effort, Burnett defended the justices in their Senate trial. An early Federalist, Burnett served in the general assembly, was elected to the United States Senate and the Ohio Supreme Court, and served as a director of the Cincinnati branch of the Bank of the United States. By 1836 he was a wealthy senior attorney and prominent Whig in Cincinnati.[19] He was the aristocratic antithesis of everything Morris stood for politically.

Thomas Hamer was an enemy of more recent vintage. He had moved to Bethel in 1820 to serve as the local schoolteacher. He soon became acquainted with Morris, who "took all but parental charge" of Hamer. After reading law in Morris's office for a few months, Hamer was admitted to the bar on Morris's motion. Hamer moved to Georgetown to set up his law practice and followed Morris into politics.[20] For several years the two collaborated politically and professionally. While Morris served in the Ohio Senate, Hamer became speaker of the Ohio House. In 1824 Morris transferred a newspaper he published in Georgetown, Ohio, to Hamer. They occasionally served as cocounsel in criminal cases, including the case of *State v. Hess* involving the defendant's use of counterfeit United States bank notes. Their client was ultimately convicted through the use of lay witness testimony regarding the authenticity of the signature of Nicolas Biddle on the notes. Morris argued against the testimony's admissibility, but in affirming the conviction, the Ohio Supreme Court approved, for the first time, the use of handwriting experts to establish forgery.[21]

In 1832 both men ran for Congress from the same district. Morris had the endorsement of the state Jacksonian party (the Whig press described him as "the big gun of the Administration party"), but Hamer decided to challenge him and ran as an independent.[22] Morris carried Clermont County overwhelmingly; Hamer won the rest of the district and was elected. Only 153 votes separated the two.[23] The campaign was bitter; Morris felt betrayed by his protégé. Neither man forgave the other. By the time Morris had entered the Senate, the relationship had deteriorated to the point that "even the friends of [Hamer] became unacceptable to Morris," and he worked assiduously to discredit Hamer with Van Buren. For his part, Hamer described Morris as "universally odious" and claimed the hard-money views Morris shared with the Locofoco wing of the Democratic party were "raked up from the rubbish heap of a past generation."[24] While Morris was defending the abolitionists' right to petition, Hamer served on the House committee that developed the "gag rule" and opposed any discussion of slavery.

When Morris arrived in Ohio, the papers were filled with reports of the mob's attacks on the *Philanthropist* and discussions of the rights of the abolitionists to free speech.[25] To Morris, the leadership of Bank supporters in the violent effort to suppress publication of the *Philanthropist* was tangible evidence of the Bank's alliance with Southern slaveholders and confirmation of the threat slaveholders' demands posed to civil liberty. Perhaps equally important, Birney couched his refusal to cease publication in terms of a response to Southern aggression: "the demand is virtually the demand of slavery ideas who, having broken down all the safe guards of liberty in their own states" demand that Ohio follow suit. In Birney's mind, either "the slavery of the south or the liberty of the north must cease to exist."[26] A point of view strikingly similar to Morris's understanding of the threat posed by Calhoun's demands for slavery's protection.

By the fall of 1836, then, Morris could hardly escape the implications of the antislavery argument. His friends and family members' conversion, coupled with the organization's activities in his home county, must have made an impression on him. These were the people Calhoun was seeking to silence. In addition, the mob's assault on Birney demonstrated the lengths slavery's supporters would go to protect the institution, and heightened Morris's concern about Southern demands for the silencing of abolitionists. Finally, on a raw, damp day in September Birney and Morris met for the first time. Birney was attempting to organize additional antislavery societies in Brown and Clermont counties and had lectured to a small group in Bethel (the weather hindered attendance).

Following the lecture, Birney met Morris. Birney said he had followed the senator's course in Washington with great care and had generally viewed his actions favorably. During the conversation Birney became convinced that Morris shared a basic affinity with his views. Noting that there had been some speculation that Morris agreed with several abolitionist positions, Birney reported to Elizer Wright that he was "inclined to believe . . . that the general estimation of him in this respect [was] well founded."[27] Although Birney did not elaborate on the abolitionist positions with which Morris agreed, they almost certainly discussed the abolition petition campaign and the attacks on the *Philanthropist* and the possibility that abolition strength in the District would result in the defeat of Hamer (who had supported the gag rule in the House) in the fall election.[28]

They also likely discussed the early history of Ohio under the Northwest Ordinance. The Ordinance, which prohibited slavery north of the Ohio River, was adopted by the Confederation Congress while the constitutional convention met in Philadelphia. It was ratified by the first Congress and significantly influenced Morris's thinking about Congress's power over slavery in the territories. Within a few weeks of his first meeting with Morris, Birney published a series of articles on the topic. Included in the articles was an "anecdote" related to Birney by "one of [Jackson's] warm political friends living in the state" of a Black man voting for delegates to the Ohio constitutional convention of 1802. The description of the source of the story and Morris's own subsequent report of Blacks voting for convention delegates make him the most likely source for the story.[29]

Historians have often overstated the importance of this meeting. Theodore C. Smith claimed that "Birney's logic opened Morris' eyes" and attributed the Ohioan's position on petitions and incendiary publications to his relationship with the former slaveholder.[30] Not only can this claim simply not be accurate chronologically (Morris did not meet Birney until after he had adopted these positions in the Senate),[31] Birney did not claim to have changed Morris's mind on any issue. Moreover, for Birney "slavery was a sin of which men must repent"; for him, "the movement was religious, not political." Birney feared that politicizing the movement "might lead to compromise of principle in the interest of expediency"—precisely the basis for Morris's opposition to abolition in the District of Columbia.[32] Morris, a lifelong politician who had never joined a church, had voted to admit Arkansas as a slave state, and had concluded that abolishing slavery in the District was "inexpedient," continued to maintain these positions long after his meeting with Birney.

Rather, the conversation with Birney (particularly the likely discussion of the summer's riots) confirmed Morris's conviction that the elitist forces that supported nullification and the Bank of the United States were now allied to attack Northern freedom. Birney's belief that "the antagonistic principles of liberty and slavery [had] been roused into action and one or the other must be victorious" would have resonated with Morris.[33] The primary result of that dreary September afternoon was not a change in Morris's views but a confirmation of the tangible threat to liberty posed by Southern slaveholder power.

Birney and Morris met at least once more prior to Morris's return to Washington.[34] In November the local societies in Morris's home county met in Batavia to organize the Clermont County Anti-Slavery Society. Although he declined to join the Society, he made "several valuable suggestions" to it. Echoing Morris's remarks in the Senate during the debate on incendiary publications, the Society resolved "that the recent encroachments by the South on the indisputable rights of the North,—encroachments that are instigated by the spirit of slavery, are fearful omens of the utter prostration of our liberties." Morris spoke at length in support of the resolutions.[35] John Rankin, who along with Birney, helped conduct the meeting, commended the speech and hinted at Morris's basic philosophical motivation: "Senator Morris gave us an impressive address. It is hoped that Providence intends to make this man an instrument of good

KEEPER OF THE JEFFERSONIAN CONSCIENCE

in the Senate of the United States during the present contest for liberty. He is a republican in principle as well as in name."[36]

Birney's ambiguous (almost tepid) description of the extent of the congruence of Morris's views with abolitionism, coupled with Rankin attributing Morris's position to "republican" (political) principles make it unlikely that either man yet thought of Morris as an abolitionist.[37] Indeed, perhaps because of Morris's position on the admission of Arkansas, the Ohio State Anti-Slavery Society's petition opposing the annexation of Texas was sent to Thomas Ewing (not Morris) for presentation to the Senate during its next session. Although hopeful of his ultimate acceptance of their views, the leadership of the abolitionist movement in Ohio remained uncertain of Morris's commitment to antislavery beyond his support of abolitionists' rights of petition and free speech. John Rankin, a minister who emphasized the sin of slavery, instinctively perceived the basis of Morris's support—republican (that is, Jeffersonian) civil liberty principles.

When Morris took his seat for the short session of 1836–37, he found the Senate focused less on antislavery petitions and more on the *Specie Circular,* the sales of public lands, the recognition of Texas, and the censure of President Jackson three years earlier. On all of these issues, Morris proved to be a consistent supporter of the administration. Early in the session, his lame-duck Whig colleague from Ohio, Thomas Ewing, introduced a resolution to rescind the *Specie Circular.* Collaborating with several members of Jackson's party, the resolution was turned into a bill and adopted by the Senate on a 41–5 vote. Along with Thomas Benton and Silas Wright, Morris was among the few Democrats who did not desert the president.[38]

The effort to expunge the Senate's censure of President Jackson embroiled Morris in a strange series of events. Early in the session the Democrats had caucused at a Washington, DC, restaurant and committed to a plan of action on the expungement resolution. Anticipating the opposition's tactics, the Democrats agreed to refuse to adjourn once debate began and arranged for meals to be brought in to sustain an all-night session. In these efforts, Morris was a silent but reliable vote in favor of the expunging resolution.[39] The debate had attracted a large crowd so that the galleries were packed by the time the vote was taken. Many (whom Benton later described as "subaltern wretches") became overly hostile to the point that some senators decided to arm themselves, and Senator Benton's wife refused to leave his side out of fear for what might transpire. Several

46   THE CREATION OF A CRUSADER

of the most unruly observers were gathered directly above Benton. Once the vote was completed, the senator pointed out who he felt was the leader and asked the sergeant-at-arms to bring him to the bar of the Senate.[40]

Up to this point, Morris had remained silent. Senator Benton's demand that the individual creating the disturbance be detained by the sergeant-at-arms and brought to the bar of the Senate, however, precipitated a sharp exchange with Morris. When the individual had been brought before the senator, Benton then attempted to have him discharged, but the chair declined. Morris, however, found "the whole proceedings as very extraordinary." He believed that if the individual had done something "worthy of an arrest," he should be able to consult an attorney and prepare a defense. When the Senate voted on a motion to discharge the individual, Morris did not vote, but his involvement with the matter did not end.[41]

The next morning William Lloyd, the individual who had provoked Benton's ire, delivered a "memorial" to Morris and asked that he present it to the Senate. Apparently, Morris did not receive the memorial until after the Senate had moved on in its session past the time allotted for presentation of petitions. He returned it to Mr. Lloyd, who then chose to publish it along with unflattering comments about Morris's conduct in the matter. Two days later Morris requested, and was granted, time to respond to the newspaper report.[42] Morris reviewed the circumstances surrounding his inability to present the petition, acknowledged meeting Mr. Lloyd some days before the events, and noted that Mr. Lloyd was from Ohio. Morris was convinced that "publication was intended to go to the State in which [he] lived" and did not believe Lloyd "should have the power to misrepresent his course in the Senate."[43]

Recognition of Texas independence presented the potential for further inflaming the slavery issue. As he had during the Arkansas statehood debate a year earlier, Morris did not raise antislavery objections to Texas recognition. When his Whig colleague from Ohio presented the petition from the Ohio State Anti-Slavery Convention to refuse recognition as long as Texas permitted slavery, Morris raised no objection when the petition was immediately tabled.[44] During the prior session of Congress, the administration's goal had been to defuse the issues surrounding Texas by postponing Senate action until after the 1836 elections.[45] After his initial enthusiasm for Texas independence, Morris supported the effort to defer the issue, ultimately joining Van Buren's supporters in opposing recognition. In early 1837, then, Morris's position on Texas appears to have been influenced at least as much by Jacksonian politics as antislavery.[46]

Petitions directed to the abolition of slavery in the District of Columbia, however, were an entirely different matter to Morris. Even before the session began, the actions of state legislatures revealed that petitions regarding abolition in the District of Columbia would continue to divide the Senate.[47] Although this issue did not arise in the Senate until late in the session, Morris was again the primary instigator of the debate. After Senator Tipton of Indiana had presented two petitions supporting abolition in the District of Columbia (although he professed to be "unable to perceive whence it is that Congress derives the power to interfere with slavery") and suggested referring them to the Committee on the District, Morris proposed that all such petitions be presented at the same time so that the question of their reception could be dealt with collectively. When the Senate consented to this approach, Morris presented six petitions (three from Ohio, one from Indiana, and two from Tennessee).[48]

Senator Buchanan (who also presented several petitions) moved that the petitions be handled as they had the year before; Morris objected. Although he had withdrawn his petitions and voted for Buchanan's procedure in 1836, he now argued that this method of handling memorials "made a mockery of [the petitioners] rights." In fact, he attributed the growth in organized antislavery in Ohio to how the petitions had been handled during the previous session. As an alternative, he suggested creating a special committee to be composed entirely of Southern senators to consider the petitions and prepare a report that would "reply to the arguments of the petitioners for the purpose of convincing them they are wrong in the impressing views they entertained." He would support printing a report that showed that "the course of the abolitionists was pregnant with much injury to the southern portion of the country . . . [and] the peace and harmony of the country." Reception and referral to a select committee eliminated the constitutional issue, but was nearly identical to the proposal of Henry Pinkney in the House, which had resulted in the adoption of the first gag rule. Although this approach had met with Van Buren's approval in 1836, it could not have been an approach sought by the abolitionists.[49]

Absent such a special committee, Morris wanted the petitions referred to the Committee on the District of Columbia. He proposed that this committee be instructed "to inquire into the power of Congress [to abolish slavery in the District]; into whether the slave trade in the capital consisted of slaves already there, or whether they were brought to this district for the purpose of sale; and also whether the power given to Congress to regulate commerce between the different states included the right to deal in slaves."[50] In short, Morris called for an investigation of Congress's relationship to slavery at a time when most members were trying to silence public discussion of the vexing subject. Although less than a year earlier he had concluded action on slavery in the District was inexpedient, events of the summer and fall had persuaded Morris to seek a public debate on the continued validity of that conclusion.

In retrospect, Morris appears to be either incredibly naïve or totally disingenuous in his suggestion to send the petitions to a select committee. For someone who had engaged in legislative politics and debate for three decades, naïveté seems unlikely. Certainly Morris was looking to put Calhoun on the defensive. But perhaps Morris was seriously trying to move the Senate beyond the question of the petitions to a reconsideration of congressional power over slavery. Eight years before, in the midst of an earlier petition campaign, Congress had adopted Morris's suggested special committee approach with a committee report on the expediency and constitutionality of abolition in the District. In the prior session, the Senate not only had appointed a select committee (chaired by Calhoun) to consider incendiary publications, but Virginia Senator John Tyler had argued for referral of Morris's petitions to the Committee on the District of Columbia so that he could obtain "an expression of opinion on the part of the Senate that it was not competent for Congress to interfere with the questions of slavery either in the states or in the District of Columbia." Moreover, after the Senate had voted to deny the prayer of the petitions in the last session, Daniel Webster had again sought to refer the petitions to the committee.[51]

In the spring of 1837, however, Calhoun had no intention of allowing a public discussion of congressional power over slavery. He believed that the petition campaign was "poisoning the minds of the people of the nonslave holding states, making them believe that slavery was sinful."[52] During the debate over petitions in the prior session, Calhoun had claimed that abolitionists were waging a war "of religious and political fanaticism . . . [upon slaveholders'] character" designed to "debase us in our estimation." The "insistence that slavery was a sin . . . assaulted the character and morality of slaveholders" and "engendered far more bitterness" than general claims that slavery was evil.[53] When Virginia's Senator Rives dissented from his view, Calhoun made "the most famous defense of slavery in American history."[54]

Prodded by Morris's persistence and Rives's refusal to agree on the merits of slavery, Calhoun explicitly rejected the notion of slavery as evil, which had been the consensus view, and articulated his vision of slavery as a positive good.

> I take higher ground. I hold that in the present state of civilization, where two races of different origin, and distinguished by color, and other physical differences, as well as intellectual, are brought together, the relation now existing in the slaveholding States between the two, is, instead of an evil, a good—a positive good. . . . I hold then, that there never has yet existed a wealthy and civilized society in which one portion of the community did not, in point of fact, live on the labor of the other. Broad and general as is this assertion, it is fully borne out by history.[55]

Calhoun's analysis explicitly grounded slavery in race and collapsed the distinction drawn by earlier Southern officials between the morality of slavery and its existence as evil. For example, during Virginia's legislature's debate over slavery following Nat Turner's uprising, most representatives, when they said slavery was evil, meant "not that slavery was a sin but that, like the Bank of the United States or the tariff, also described as evils, slavery had ill effects on white society." Indeed nearly three decades earlier, Georgia Congressman Peter Early explained: "A large majority of the people in the Southern states . . . do not believe it immoral to hold human flesh in bondage. Many deprecate slavery as an evil; as a political evil."[56] For Calhoun, slavery was neither a moral sin nor political evil.

At the conclusion of Calhoun's speech, Senator Tipton asked for a vote of the reception of the petitions. Senator Bayard then moved to table the motion. Morris asked for a roll-call vote on the motion to table. The motion to table passed the Senate by a nearly three-to-one majority.[57] Not to be deterred, Morris presented antislavery petitions on each of the following two days. He continued to present antislavery petitions throughout the remainder of the session,[58] finally stopping on March 2. The Senate adjourned *sine die* the following day in time for Van Buren's inauguration on March 4. In his inaugural address Van Buren reaffirmed his commitment as an "uncompromising opponent" of any effort to abolish slavery in Washington, DC, and added a promise to veto any bills that attempted to do so.[59]

Although one commentator has argued that Morris did not attract "general attention until 1838,"[60] his efforts had certainly not passed unnoticed. While the Ohio Anti-Slavery Society had largely failed to take notice of Morris's efforts in 1836, by the spring of 1837 it singled out Morris and John Quincy Adams for "their magnanimous exertions in behalf of the right of petition."[61] By the summer of 1837, not only did the leaders of the American Anti-Slavery Society value Morris's help in the Senate, they also recognized the possibilities inherent in having a United States senator openly identified with their cause. Henry B. Stanton, writing "solely in regard to Mr. Morris," told Birney that the senator "must come, if money and men can bring him" to the Society's national convention in 1837. He urged the editor of the *Philanthropist* "to leave no effort unemployed to persuade him to come." Stanton informed Birney that "Smith, Leavitt, Chaplin and Goodell" thought it would "be worth $25,000 to our cause to have [Morris] present."[62] Morris did not attend.

CHAPTER 4

The Absolute Creed of the Abolitionists

With the end of the Twenty-Fourth Congress and the inauguration of Van Buren behind him, Morris returned to Ohio. He found Birney once again in the midst of a controversy. Instead of the right to free speech and freedom of the press, the issues now involved the Fugitive Slave Law. In early March, a slave catcher had obtained a warrant from a Cincinnati magistrate and seized Matilda Lawrence, Birney's maid, as an escaped slave. Although trained as a lawyer, Birney thought it best to retain someone else to represent Matilda in an effort to prevent her return to slavery. He persuaded Salmon Chase (who had represented him a year earlier in a suit to recover damages for the mob's destruction of the *Philanthropist*'s press) to obtain a writ of habeas corpus to allow an opportunity to challenge Matilda's removal. The judge issuing the writ, however, scheduled the hearing for the next day, March 11.[1]

Chase had followed the articles appearing in the *Philanthropist* over the prior year and had spent time considering the Northwest Ordinance, but with only one evening to prepare, Chase relied heavily on Birney's arguments, which "built on ideas promulgated by Thomas Morris" in his Incendiary Publications speech.[2] Chase began by arguing that Matilda had not received the procedural protections of Ohio law, but he and "Birney were more interested in testing the constitutionality of the Fugitive Slave Act."[3] Chase's attack on the constitutionality of the Fugitive Slave Act closely followed the analysis Birney had laid out three weeks earlier in the

Philanthropist.[4] The constitutional argument drew heavily on the principle (which Morris had articulated in his Incendiary Publications speech a year earlier) that slavery could exist only as the result of state law and could not exist outside the state that created it, that the Fugitive Slave Clause did not empower Congress to adopt the statute, and that the Northwest Ordinance barred Congress from adopting the act.[5] The court found none of these arguments persuasive, and Matilda was returned to slavery.

The case ended a few days before Morris arrived in Ohio, but the controversy continued. Charles Hammond, editor of the *Cincinnati Gazette,* and Birney had carried on a debate in their papers over both Matilda's status and Birney's conduct as "harboring a fugitive." With the discussion continuing, Morris decided to weigh in on the constitutionality of the Fugitive Slave Law. Some of his friends in Clermont County (Morris may have instigated the petition)[6] had petitioned the Ohio General Assembly requesting the statute be amended to require jury trials in fugitive slave cases. But the committee to which their petition had been referred found it inexpedient and unconstitutional to legislate on the subject, deplored the increasing agitation of the abolitionists, and refused to "further fan the flame or contribute to the existing excitement" surrounding the issue.[7] The committee based its conclusion on the constitutional recognition of the slave trade and fugitive slaves.

Although Morris had acknowledged these same clauses in his report on the colonization society five years earlier, he now denied that they were determinative of the constitutionality of the Fugitive Slave Act. In a lengthy March 30 letter to the chairman of the committee, Morris laid out his constitutional argument in detail. Reiterating the position he had taken a year earlier in responding to Calhoun, Morris found "no recognition of [slavery] in the Constitution." As he had told the Senate, if the Constitution guaranteed slavery, the conclusion was "irresistible" that slavery existed "everywhere within the jurisdiction of the United States."
Morris, however, did not stop with denying the existence of a pro-slavery constitution. A few weeks earlier he had listened to Calhoun base his positive good argument on race. Morris denied that race could be used to establish a person's status as a slave: "The first great error into which you have fallen, is the presumption that a person of color found in Ohio, may be the slave of another man . . . The presumption however, is directly the reverse; it is that every human being found in the State is free; . . . color is not . . . evidence of property in man."[8] The Constitution did not recog-

nize persons as property, nor did it authorize the use of race to create a presumption of property.

He went a step further. Confronted in the Senate and at home with continued evidence of the reach and demands of slaveholders, Morris had begun to see the outline of an antislavery constitution. He argued "that instrument, instead of guaranteeing the continuance of slavery in the different states, in its whole scope and tendency, has evidently formed the design of terminating its existence at a not very remote period." More importantly, for the specific issue of the Federal Fugitive Slave Act, Morris argued that by virtue of the Tenth Amendment, Congress lacked the power to enforce the Fugitive Slave Clause so that not only was the law unconstitutional because of its lack of procedural safeguards (jury trials), it was an unconstitutional invasion of state sovereignty.[9]

Far from disapproving of the antislavery excitement, which worried the general assembly's committee, the senator thought "it [was] most fortunate for the cause of humanity, for justice, for the preservation of our own institutions, for the honor and dignity of the country, that this degree of sensitiveness . . . exist[ed] and [was] prevailing throughout the land."[10] He believed slavery was "constantly and continually an evil; an evil in all time, under all circumstances, . . . and evil without excuse, and without mitigation—the worst of all possible evils."[11] In 1836 Morris had withdrawn his abolitionist petitions and apologized for causing "agitation." Now, one year later, he actively sought confrontation. In his public letter to the committee chairman who had declined action on fugitive slaves, he said, "In addressing this paper to you, I am in hopes that your standing and character in society, will attract to it public attention, and cause it to be more generally read and considered than it otherwise would be, and I confess I am not without hopes to induce you to enter a controversy."[12] Morris had failed in his attempt to bring the Senate to debate slavery in the District of Columbia directly. As he returned home for the summer recess, however, he was still seeking to instigate a public debate. Events in the nation's economy, however, would force slavery off the front page and Morris to return to the Senate.

Van Buren had inherited not only the controversy over the antislavery petitions but also the consequences of the Distribution Bill and the *Specie Circular*. Although opposed by Jackson, the Distribution Bill had passed in April 1836 and required the federal surplus revenue to be distributed in four installments as "loans" to the states and deposited in state banks. To counter the inflationary consequences of this bill, Jackson issued the *Specie Circular* in the summer of 1836 requiring that purchases of government-owned land be paid for in specie. The result was a devastating credit squeeze, a precipitous decline in government revenues from the sale of public lands, and a dramatic reduction in the nation's money supply.[13] By the time Van Buren was inaugurated, the cotton market had collapsed, numerous banks had failed, and the financial Panic of 1837 had begun. In response, Van Buren called a special session of Congress to start September 4. At the opening of this session, he presented Congress with a comprehensive five-pronged plan, including the creation of an Independent Treasury, to deal with the panic.[14] Although Congress quickly approved the other four prongs of the bills, the proposal for an Independent Treasury bogged down in the Senate.[15]

The Jackson Administration had discussed an Independent Treasury plan in 1836 as a possible response to the deposit-distribution bill. The proposal called for federal funds to be deposited in "sub-treasuries" instead of state banks.[16] Faced with collapsing federal revenues and a banking panic, Van Buren now adopted the idea and pressed for its approval. Throughout the special session, Morris was a reliable vote in favor of the administration's plans. He supported the recommendation against re-chartering a national bank,[17] voted in favor of each of Van Buren's proposals, and followed Benton and Wright in defeating a revolt led by Senator Rives to retain the deposit system with state banks.[18] On October 4, he voted with Van Buren's supporters to pass the Independent Treasury bill in the Senate.[19] While supporting the president's economic program, during the special session Morris scaled back his efforts regarding anti-slavery petitions. Although throughout the summer petitions continued to be collected, during the special session Morris did not present any petitions directed at slavery in the District of Columbia and only three petitions directed at the possible annexation of Texas. Each of these petitions was quietly tabled without his objection,[20] but Morris could not escape the aggressions of slaveholders.

Early in the fall, while Morris was attending the special session of Congress, three men from Kentucky crossed the Ohio River and abducted Eliza Johnson, a Black woman, from her home near Ripley, Ohio. Although the men claimed she was a fugitive slave, they failed to comply with Ohio or federal law for the return of runaways. Upon Johnson being taken to Kentucky, the claimant (the sheriff of Mason County Kentucky) admitted she was not his slave. Nevertheless, she was imprisoned in Kentucky for two months. Johnson's friends from Ripley sought a writ of habeas corpus from the Kentucky Court to free her and attended the hearing to testify on her behalf. These witnesses reported being threatened and assaulted.[21]

When Morris landed in Ripley, Ohio, on his way home from the Senate's special session in Washington, he went to Ross's Hotel. There he met Alexander Campbell, a longtime friend and colleague, for dinner. During dinner they discussed the abduction and the events surrounding Johnson's detention in Kentucky. Their conversation was apparently overheard and reported in several Kentucky newspapers and repeated in the *Ohio State Journal*. According to these reports, Morris told Campbell that "war ought immediately to be declared against Kentucky; . . . and that every Kentuckian should be shot as soon as he sets foot on the Ohio side."[22] The newspaper reports set off a furor. Morris felt compelled to respond. On November 13 he sent a letter to Campbell, which he released for publication. Morris noted that "the idea of Ohio declaring war against Kentucky is . . . perfectly ridiculous." He was "not in the habit of indulging in expressions, such as shooting down men, on any occasion." Nevertheless, he told Campbell, "I shall never humble myself . . . so as to admit the right, in the remotest possibility, of any one to question me as to my particular expressions."[23]

After this nondenial denial, Morris turned to his views of the prior actions of "the slaveholding power."

> The first solemn reflection is the arrogance of the slave holding power in their efforts to prostrate the Constitution itself, and the freedom of speech and the press, by threats and violence; have we not seen it attempt to subject the mail of the United States to the most odious inspection, and the sacred seal of private correspondence liable to be broken by the rude hand of its power?—Have we not seen it attempt to prostrate the freedom of speech and the liberty of the press? Have we not seen and deplored its power in the whirlwind of the mob, and in the inflection of disgraceful stripes upon worthy and unoffending citizens? And above all, have we not seen it trample under foot and sacred and inherent right of petition?[24]

These attacks on civil liberties were bad enough, but the actions of Kentucky slave catchers persuaded Morris that "the slave-holding power is far more dangerous to the country than [he] ever anticipated; it is above the sovereignty of the states, if not that of the union. It will permit neither to recognize the colored person as a citizen enjoying certain rights."[25] The abduction of Eliza Johnson was simply part of the slaveholder's assault on liberty everywhere. This understanding persuaded Morris that resisting the slaveholding power required that Black, as well as white, Ohioans be recognized as "citizens" with civil rights.[26]

Morris then reemphasized the constitutional theory he had first articulated in attacking Calhoun's bill on incendiary publications. He denied that slavery was protected by the Constitution. "Were it otherwise," the supremacy clause of the Constitution meant "slavery exist[s], or may exist in all the states." More ominously, he had "not a doubt . . . [that] the slaveholding power . . . under color of the Constitution" intended "to establish itself in every state." If the South's interpretation of the Constitution was correct, Morris thought Ohio could no longer claim to be a "free state, because we have no inherent power in ourselves to be so, but depend entirely for that blessing on the slaveholding power."[27] Remarkably, after what must have been viewed by the slaveholders in Kentucky as a highly inflammatory response, Morris claimed that he not only "deplored" slavery, he also deplored "the agitation of the question." He simply was "not disposed to submit to the dictation of the slaveholding power, or to abridge the freedom of speech to the press, or the right of petition."[28] Thus, as Morris left Ohio to return to the Senate, he was in a most confrontational mood.

As the opening of Congress in December neared, the antislavery forces continued to urge more petitions. The *Philanthropist* called for one million signatures.[29] When Senator Swift from Vermont announced early in the new session that he had antislavery resolutions adopted by the state legislature to present to the Senate, Calhoun attempted to seize the initiative from the abolitionists. Van Buren's inaugural promises to veto any legislation directed at emancipation in the District of Columbia were insufficient. Before Swift could actually offer the resolutions, Calhoun intervened and proposed a series of resolutions defining the Southern position on the constitutional requirements for the protection of slavery. Calhoun's resolutions asked the Senate to endorse "a momentous restatement of the federal union; if taken seriously they would have changed the basis of American Federalism, and given the slave states a decisive predominance in the federal government."[30]

While Calhoun's demands for the protection of slavery had not changed, his political affiliation had. In a surprise move, during the special session, he had announced his support for Van Buren's economic program, and returned to the Democratic Party along with most of his followers. Calhoun's "move had a tremendous impact on . . . the Democratic party. . . . With Calhoun in the . . . fold the Southern identity of the party was secure."[31] Believing Van Buren needed his support for the Independent Treasury, Calhoun saw the opportunity to strike at the abolitionists. His "resolutions amounted to a manifesto intended to force senators to go on record and choose sides." His "goal was to confront the North with demands and to force public concessions from northern politicians in Congress."[32]

In response to the petition campaign, the South had begun "a full ideological reconfiguration of slavery." Calhoun's resolutions "articulated an especially coherent version of the new proslavery argument." The resolutions "together represented his entire political creed, encompassing his views on abolition, the Union, and the need to commit the federal government to the protection of slavery."[33] Instead of preventing Senate discussion of slavery, Calhoun now forced the issue and precipitated the debate. His resolutions were designed, in his words, to "test" the Senate's commitment to protect slavery by providing an opportunity "for the true friends of the union to come forward and show themselves."[34] To many Democrats, however, their new Independent Treasury ally was proving to be "rather a dangerous man. He [had] drawn [them] into an abolition debate unnecessarily which can do no good and may harm." Neither Northern nor Southern senators appreciated Calhoun's maneuver.[35]

These resolutions are justly famous for what they said; they are equally telling in what they omitted. Calhoun had failed to persuade his fellow senators that they could refuse to accept antislavery petitions. He now had "begun to reformulate" his arguments and adopted "drastic steps . . . to recall the Senate to its sense of obligation to the South."[36] While the resolutions claimed that slavery comprised an "important part" of the "domestic institutions" of the South, gone were the claims that specific provisions of the Constitution barred action on slavery in the District or the Territories. His argument was no longer textual but "essentially transconstitutional—an appeal to a southern version of higher law." Instead, it was "the solemn duty of the Government to resist all attempts by one portion of the Union to use [the Constitution] . . . to attack the domestic institutions of another."[37]

Calhoun asserted "that the intermeddling of any state, or states, or their citizens to abolish slavery in the District or any of the territories on the ground, or under the pretext, that it is immoral or sinful: or the passage of any act or measure of Congress with that view—would be a direct and dangerous attack on the constitutions of all slaveholding states."[38] Continued agitation risked the dissolution of the Union. Far from being sinful, Calhoun again argued slavery was "a great good."[39] In demanding that the federal government "resist" any effort to use the Constitution to attack slavery, Calhoun may have been "disgusted" by the failure of the House and Senate during the prior session to refuse to receive antislavery petitions,[40] but he was implicitly acknowledging the strength of Morris's critique of the pro-slavery constitution and his emphasis of the protection of the right of free speech, the right of petition, and a free press. Calhoun demanded that Congress resist its implications—not as violative of specific constitutional provisions—but out of a supposed theory of constitutional formation that created a duty to protect slavery and respect for the slaveholding state constitutions. Calhoun would never concede the merits of Morris's constitutional interpretation,[41] but his resolutions sought to evade, rather than rebut, Morris's constitutional claims.

Henry Clay saw what he believed to be Calhoun's effort to trap him between the North and South and damage his hopes for the Whig nomination in 1840. As a result, Clay proposed "his own resolutions, affirming his steadfastness and soundness on slavery."[42] Where Clay saw a personal political threat, Morris saw another demand for special treatment by the South. To him, Calhoun's resolutions posed a serious threat to the Constitution. In an entry in his diary, he recorded his view of Calhoun's resolutions:

> I am now a Senator in Congress from the state of Ohio, and have this day, in a small minority, been defending the liberty of speech, of the press, and the right of petition. Resolutions have been introduced declaring that we have no right—either political, moral, or religious—to discuss the institutions of any state with a view to effect a change in those institutions. . . . [T]hese Resolutions strike at all discussion of slavery in any of the states; these Resolutions are the most daring attempt against American liberty that has yet been brought forward in Congress since the foundation of the Republic, and as such I oppose them.[43]

The resolutions, coming on the heels of Eliza Johnson's kidnapping, pushed Morris beyond defending the abolitionist civil rights and toward endorsing their goals.

Morris composed his own set of resolutions, which followed Calhoun's, "with variations calculated . . . to protect the right of petition, the freedom of speech, and the liberty of the press" and introduced them the next day with the intention of using them as amendments to the ones already before the Senate. Although following Calhoun's format, Morris's resolutions struck directly at slavery. First, Morris reaffirmed his rejection of a pro-slavery constitution: "Resolved that domestic slavery, as it exists in the southern and western states, is a moral and political evil, and that its existence at the time of the adoption of the Constitution is not recognized by the instrument as an essential element in the exercise of its powers over the several states."[44] This premise led Morris to conclude that not only did abolitionists have a right to speak, all persons had a duty to seek the abolition of slavery:

> Resolved that it is the indisputable right of any state, and any citizen thereof, as well as the indispensable duty, to endeavor by all legal and constitutional means, to abolish whatever is immoral and sinful, and that Congress alone possess the power to abolish slavery, and the slave trade in this district or any of the territories of the United States; and the right of petition, of speech and of the press, to accomplish this object is not to be questioned, and that an act of Congress on this subject would be within its constitutional powers.[45]

When Morris's counterresolutions were read, Calhoun blurted out that they "displayed the absolute creed of the Abolitionist fully developed."[46] The Senate refused to print the resolutions.

Looking back, Thomas Hart Benton thought that Calhoun's "resolutions, and the debate to which they gave rise . . . constituted[d] the most important proceeding on the subject of slavery which has even taken place in Congress."[47] In that debate, Morris emerged as Calhoun's primary antagonist. He claimed that rather than protect slavery, it was "the duty of this Government to refrain from any attempt, however remote, to operate on the liberty of speech and the press." Calhoun had used the states' rights argument for the protection of slavery; Morris now turned to the defense of the abolitionists. The Constitution had "reserved to individuals, and to the states in their sovereign character, the full liberty of speech and to the press to discuss the domestic institutions of any of the states, whether political, moral, or religious; and . . . it would be the exercise of unauthorized power on the part of this Government, or any of the states

60   THE CREATION OF A CRUSADER

to attempt to restrain the same."[48] Over the next two weeks, Morris continued to assert that the South Carolinian's resolutions sought to destroy Northern liberties for the benefit of the slaveholding elites. He asked, "Why talk of attacks on Southern interests and Southern feelings?" He "did not believe that Southern rights existed antagonistic to those of any other region." He thought that the object of Calhoun's resolutions was that "free discussion on an important question" be "discountenanced" and "silenced." "This government," Morris contended, "was founded and has been sustained by the force of public opinion."[49]

Morris heard the echoes of the theoretical support for the nullification in the "compact theory" of the Constitution advanced by the resolutions and rejected Calhoun's understanding of federalism. "The Constitution of the United States did not distribute power among the states. It had derived all its power from the people of the states." More importantly, the claim "that slavery is recognized by the Constitution of the United States as an essential element in the distribution of its powers in the several states" was patently false. The Constitution "in no particular, or for any purpose, recognized domestic slavery as necessary for its action. It permitted or allowed this institution in the states, but it did not recognize or establish it." Morris again reminded the Senate that "it was the exclusive right of the states . . . to declare what property should be . . . , but "no act of this government should ever recognize the principle, that persons could under any circumstance be converted into property." Because "the word slave, or slavery, is not mentioned in the Constitution," Congress simply lacked the power to establish slavery anywhere. He did not stop, however, at denying the Constitution was pro-slavery. Indeed, "the framers of the Constitution intended that its whole moral power should operate in the extinction of slavery in all the states."[50]

Calhoun's resolutions had changed the nature of the debate. The demand for equality among the states went beyond the federal consensus prohibition against federal action against slavery in the states where it existed. The claim was "not that slavery as it exists . . . be sustained; . . . it is to be enlarged, extended, augmented, and made perpetual." Morris thought "the real object to be gained . . . by the passage of these resolutions [was] that Texas may be annexed to the Union in order to extend and perpetuate slavery." All of "this [was] to be done under the specious pretext of maintaining an equality of power between the slave holding and non-slave holding states."[51] To Morris, the Constitution as written was not pro-slavery; he

THE ABSOLUTE CREED OF THE ABOLITIONISTS 61

would not concur with Calhoun's effort to rewrite the document to make it so. Confronted with Calhoun's continued demand for special privileges for slaveholders, and the absence of any textual commitment to property in man in the Constitution, Morris found an antislavery constitution.

As Calhoun's recent biographer recognized, the debate over the resolutions was "vitriolic."[52] Certainly, the exchanges between Calhoun and Morris became more personal. Morris claimed that Calhoun had "thrown down the glove" and "asserted that none in the Senate could vote . . . against his [Calhoun's] views." For his part, Calhoun described Morris's resolutions as "irrelevant and offered by way of embarrassment." Morris responded "that the truth often embarrassed those who were in error, but this was their misfortune." He would "not be intimidated."[53] When Morris sought to eliminate the condemnation of "moral and religious" motivation for antislavery actions from Calhoun's resolutions, Calhoun responded by claiming that abolition "was nothing more than that fanaticism that had carried thousands of victims to the stake." Having equated abolitionists with the Inquisition, "it was impossible for him to consent to the suggestion of his colleague." Since "the South had been assailed upon the principle that slavery was wicked and immoral," he demanded the Senate condemn abolitionist action as based on the "pretext" of religion or morality.[54]

Calhoun's demand allowed Morris to turn Calhoun's prior remarks against him. During the debate a year earlier on the reception of petitions calling for the abolition of slavery in the District of Columbia, Calhoun had had a pointed exchange with Virginia Senator Rives.[55] Calhoun argued that slavery was "good" and asked Rives if he agreed. Rives, however, disagreed and said he thought slavery "a misfortune and an evil in all circumstances." Rives's refusal to acknowledge slavery as "good" triggered a telling response from Calhoun: "Surely if it was an evil, moral, social, and political, the Senator, as a wise and virtuous man, was bound to exert himself to put it down. This position, that it was a moral evil, was the root of the whole system of operations against it."[56] Calhoun's understanding of moral duty made acceptance of the language of his third resolution central to his purpose in pursuing his resolutions. Slavery had to be "good because you could not admit it to be evil."[57] This concession gave Morris an opening to challenge slavery directly.

Using Calhoun's admission to Senator Rives from a year earlier, Morris moved from simply protecting the petitioners' constitutional rights to endorsing their goals. Morris repeated his previous position that slavery

62   THE CREATION OF A CRUSADER

was "a moral and political evil, and its existence at the time of the adoption of the Constitution [was] not recognized as an essential element in its
powers." But echoing Calhoun's statement to Rives, Morris now went a
step further and claimed "that it [was] the indisputable right of any state,
or any citizen thereof, as well as an indispensable duty, to endeavor by
all legal and constitutional means to abolish whatever [was] immoral."[58]
Since slavery constituted a "moral evil," every citizen had an "indispensable duty" to work to abolish it by "all legal and constitutional means."
With this argument Morris moved from merely support of the abolitionists' civil rights to apparent support of their goals.

Morris's public protest in favor of individual liberties was not simply
a shield to conceal an antislavery argument. In responding to Calhoun's
resolutions, Morris returned to his distrust of Southern demands that he
described in the 1836 debate on incendiary publications. He viewed the
demands as coming not solely from Calhoun but from the slaveholding
states.[59] In Morris's mind, the Slave Power had emerged as the implacable
enemy of liberty. The senator from South Carolina had argued that abolitionist activity attacked Southern rights. But to Morris, this had the ring of
a demand for special privilege. As he had told his colleagues, he "did not
believe that Southern rights existed antagonistic to those of any other portion of the Union."[60] He opposed these resolutions because "they were par-
tial in their bearing."[61] Morris had come to the antislavery cause in defense
of personal rights against Southern attack. Rankin had not misunderstood
Morris when he called him a "republican in principle."[62] The political philosophy that led him to oppose any chartered or monopolistic institutions
forced him to object to Calhoun's resolutions.

The senator from Ohio, however, found little support for his position.
Gradually the Senate passed Calhoun's resolutions with only minor modifications giving its "assent to his view of the Constitution and its condemnation of abolition."[63] As he undertook the debate with Calhoun, "he knew
the prejudices that were against him and that his best friends would differ
from him."[64] Yet "he had wholly counted the cost and resolved to do his
duty."[65] While there would be a political cost, the debate also took a serious
physical and emotional toll on Morris. At one point, Daniel Webster felt
compelled to move (and the Senate approved) adjournment "in courtesy to
Mr. Morris" because "he was too indisposed to proceed with his remarks."[66]

After passage of the final resolution, Morris's Ohio Jacksonian colleague,
William Allen, offered a resolution saying that nothing in the resolutions

just adopted should be understood to interfere with the right of petition. For Morris, this was the height of hypocrisy. "We have been two weeks engaged in the examination of the resolutions. . . . And even at this last moment, my honorable colleague, who has defended and voted for them during the travail, comes forward with a kind of salve for all that has been said as well as done."[67] Nevertheless Morris acknowledged that "a late repentance is better than an obstinate perseverance in error."[68] Noting that he and Allen had "voted in opposition to each other, he thanked Allen for furnishing evidence . . . [Morris] had been correct in his views."[69] Whatever else these comments may have done, they could hardly have endeared Morris to Allen or Ohio Jacksonians.

Although he lost his struggle, the confrontation with Calhoun showed the degree of Morris's resonance to antislavery and earned him the respect of the national leaders of the antislavery effort. Morris's effort also reinforced the abolitionists' familiarity with his views and broadened their awareness of the significance of his constitutional theory. In addition to covering the debate as it unfolded, at the conclusion of the debate, the *Emancipator* reprinted Morris's November 1837 letter to Alexander Campbell in its entirety and said it was evidence that his opposition to Calhoun was "not the result of momentary impulse, but the fruit of thought, impelled and guided by deep and unmovable principle."[70]

After completing consideration of Calhoun's resolutions, the Senate returned to the subtreasury bill, which had become "the defining issue of party difference in Congress."[71] The president had renewed his call for an Independent Treasury in his Annual Message to Congress. The bill, reintroduced in December, now included both a specie provision and a "special deposit" section.[72] Senator Rives still opposed the entire Independent Treasury concept, and in early February he introduced a substitute bill. Clay and Webster pushed for a recharter of the National Bank. The Whig-controlled Ohio General Assembly instructed Morris to vote for the Bank. In the longest speech Morris had made to that point in his Senate career, he refused to follow the legislature's instructions.[73] On March 21, Rives's substitute was rejected 29 to 20, with Morris voting with Benton, Wright, and Buchanan to defeat the proposal.[74] A motion was made to strike the specie clause from the bill. Morris voted in favor of the amendment, which passed 31 to 21. This was the only vote involving the contents of the bill on which Morris deviated from the administration.[75] Two days later, Morris provided a critical vote in favor of the Independent Treasury

64 THE CREATION OF A CRUSADER

bill, which passed 27 to 25. On the most significant partisan issue of the session, he had remained a consistent supporter of Van Buren.

In the midst of the maneuvering on the Independent Treasury, Morris attempted a different approach to force the issue of slavery back before the Senate. He had tempered his initial enthusiasm for Texas independence, and throughout the debate surrounding recognition of Texas he had supported Van Buren's desire to defer consideration of the issue. He worked with Van Buren's forces to keep the issue out of the 1836 election and to delay action prior to Van Buren's inauguration. Only days before Jackson's term ended in March 1837, with Morris voting with Wright against the measure, the Senate had adopted Senator Walker's resolution supporting recognition of Texas. Possessed of the Senate's imprimatur, Jackson immediately recognized Texas as an independent nation.[76]

Southern senators now pressed for annexation. While Calhoun's resolutions were being debated, his South Carolina colleague William Preston introduced a resolution "to re-annex to the United States the territory of the State of Texas."[77] These efforts confirmed the fears of abolitionists and they continued to submit petitions against the annexation of Texas. These antislavery requests were received and immediately tabled without debate or reference to a committee. Confronted with this stone wall on the annexation of Texas, Morris decided to move beyond petitions.

While there was disagreement about the power of Congress to abolish slavery in the District of Columbia, there was no doubt about congressional power over foreign commerce or the international slave trade. Not only had Congress banned the importation of slaves into the United States, but it had also prohibited United States citizens from engaging in the selling of slaves from the United States to foreign countries.[78] Although "no one enforced the prohibition along the Texas/Louisiana border, neither before or after Texas independence,"[79] the recognition of Texas as an independent nation provided Morris with a vehicle to initiate a substantive discussion of congressional power over slavery.

On March 19, 1838, Morris introduced a resolution designed to precipitate that debate.

> *Resolved*, That the Committee on the Judiciary be instructed to inquire whether the present laws of the United States on the subject of the slave trade will prohibit that trade being carried on between the citizens of the United States and the citizens of the Republic of Texas, whether by land

or by sea; and whether it would be lawful in vessels owned by citizens of that Republic; and not lawful in vessels owned by citizens of this, or lawful in both, and by citizens of both countries; and also whether a slave carried from the United States into a foreign country, and brought back or returning into the United States, is considered a free person, or is liable to be sent back, if demanded, as a slave, into that country from which he or she in part came; and also whether any additional legislation by Congress is necessary on any of these subjects.[80]

The *Philanthropist* described this as "a very important resolution" and asked "what harm could the passage of such a resolution have done." Van Buren, "hoping to avoid renewal of the destructive sectional debate," wanted no further discussion of Texas slavery. The Senate had also had enough debate on resolutions directed at slavery. When the resolution was taken up the following day, the Senate overwhelmingly voted 32 to 9 to table it without debate.[81] Events in Ohio would prevent Morris from renewing his request in the next session.

By the spring of 1838 Morris had become committed to the antislavery movement. In the Senate he had acted as spokesman for the abolitionists. His efforts in this respect had been so consistent that the editor of the *Emancipator* gave him a perfect voting record on slavery-related issues in 1837 and 1838.[82] Yet he had not supported the abolitionists out of an intense hatred of slavery.[83] Rather, he had extended his long-held Jeffersonian civil liberty philosophy to the antislavery argument. "If I am an abolitionist," he told the Senate, "Jefferson made me so."[84] Morris repeatedly viewed the Southern demands for the protection of slavery as requests for special privilege and a denial of individual rights and had come to understand the Constitution as inherently antislavery.

He had not convinced his Senate colleagues of the correctness of his opinions. Although he had consistently supported the administration's economic proposals, the Senate's rejection of his now explicit defense of the abolitionists hinted at Morris's future. The risk in challenging Calhoun came from beyond the Senate chamber. By the time the Senate adjourned in July, the fall campaign in Ohio had already begun. The members of the general assembly to be elected in the fall could and would discard Morris for a less radical man.

CHAPTER 5

I Ask No Forgiveness

The petition campaign directed toward abolishing slavery in the District of Columbia had placed antislavery at the forefront of political debate. Congress's actions to restrain debate and refusal to receive the petitions convinced many abolitionists of the necessity of becoming active in the selection of their representatives. At first, abolitionists attempted to select the most acceptable candidates from among those proposed by the major parties by "interrogatories" seeking the candidates' views on antislavery. In the existing two-party system, however, the discussion of slavery had no place. The quest for support for abolitionists from among the two major parties would ultimately prove futile. The failure of Morris's reelection effort made this conclusion clear.

Van Buren had actively courted Morris's support of the Independent Treasury plan. When Morris had refused to follow the general assembly's instructions to support chartering a new United States Bank and to oppose the Independent Treasury, he had provided a crucial vote in support of the administration. There could be no doubt of Morris's commitment to Jacksonian economic policy.[1] At the same time, however, Van Buren had been "ruthlessly excising or suppressing candidates with antislavery or abolition feelings."[2] Prior to the adoption of the Seventeenth Amendment, senators were elected by the state legislature. During the previous two years, Ohio Whigs had gained control of the governorship and both houses of the Ohio General Assembly. As a result, for Morris to be reelected, Democrats had to regain control of the general assembly and then be persuaded to return Morris to the Senate. In the spring of 1838, the prospects for either event occurring did not appear promising.

Following the Whig triumph in 1837, the *Ohio State Journal* exclaimed: "Ohio is effectually purified from the taint of Vanocracy [Democrats]. She is Whig now at heart, and from the heart to every extremity."[3] In this flush of power, the 1838 Whig state convention severely censured Morris's course in the Senate. Claiming that Morris had "sustained the Administration in its recent course of misrule," the convention resolved that he had "misrepresented the State" by his "votes given on the Sub-Treasury Bill." These votes "violated all those sacred obligations" that senators had to follow "the will of a majority of the People fully expressed in sundry resolutions adopted and passed by the last General Assembly." This conduct was sufficiently egregious that the convention demanded Morris's resignation from the Senate.[4]

The Whigs continued their assault throughout the fall 1838 campaign. Describing Morris as "universally obnoxious" even to Democrats, the Whig press criticized him for campaigning on behalf of Democratic candidates for the general assembly.[5] For his part, Morris urged "the laboring classes" to vote; he feared "leaving this 'privilege' to non-productive classes" would "endanger the prosperity of the country." To Democrats, "let the battle cry be, no exclusive privileges, but equal and exact justice to all men."[6] Faced with the necessity of eliminating the Whig majority in the general assembly, however, Morris determined to do more than simply support Democratic candidates for the legislature.

Morris decided to meet both the Whig attack on his support for Van Buren's economic agenda and the Democrat unease with regard to antislavery head on. In response to the resolutions of the Whig state convention, he addressed a letter to the editor of the state Democratic Party paper, the *Ohio Statesman*. He defended his vote on the Independent Treasury bill at length, saying he knew of "nothing which the Government could allow of a more corrupting nature" than the plan supported by the Whigs.[7] Although the Whig censure had been directed entirely at his support for Van Buren's economic policy, Morris chose to make his actions in support of antislavery part of the fall campaign.[8]

In reviewing his conduct in the Senate, Morris said he had "advocated and voted, for the liberty of speech and freedom of the press . . . [and] contended for the right of petition as belonging to every reasonable being," and accused the Whigs of wanting to "confine [these rights] to a selected few."

68   THE CREATION OF A CRUSADER

He "opposed, and voted against, the further extension of slavery in every case in which [he] was permitted to do so by the Constitution," as well as "the Slave Trade between the different States and the Republic of Texas." He said, "the Whig Convention probably thought this trade an honest mode of turning a penny." Morris claimed the Whigs "viewed slavery with a very favorable eye, . . . [were] willing for its extension into every state in the Union, . . . [and] were in favor of the admission of Texas into the Union."[9]

Morris then went further than simply reviewing his actions in the Senate. He shared his views on the civil rights of free Blacks. In early 1837, he had told the chair of the general assembly committee recommending against providing jury trials in fugitive slave cases that "every human being found in the State is [presumed] free; . . . color is not . . . evidence of property in man."[10] Later that year, Morris condemned the "slave-holding power" for refusing "to recognize the colored person as a citizen enjoying certain rights."[11] He had reemphasized these points in his debate with Calhoun. "Color is no evidence of property; it does not therefore reduce a person to a thing; and a person in any state has the right to claim the benefit of the laws of such State."[12] Now he told Ohio Democrats "the right of petition belong[ed] to every reasonable being," and he "contended that all men are born equally free and independent and have an indisputable right to life, liberty and the pursuit of happiness." Morris thought this belief "was probably deemed my worst heresy" by the Whigs.[13] The language of the letter was taken directly from the bill of rights contained in the Ohio Constitution. These rights provided the foundation for Morris's argument surrounding Blacks' right to jury trials and civil rights contained in his 1837 letters. But Morris was not through telling Ohio Democrats that Black Ohioans were entitled to equal rights.[14]

A few weeks later, he told Ohio Democrats that "equal and exact justice to all men" was the key to electoral success.[15] Morris's phrase was one with which Democrats were familiar but unaccustomed to having applied to Blacks. Morris borrowed the phrase from Jefferson's first Inaugural Address. As his speech was winding down, Jefferson told his listeners that it was "proper that you should understand what I deem the essential principles of our government." First on the list was "equal and exact justice to all men." It was part of the "creed of [Jefferson's] political faith."[16] Morris had used it often in his efforts against monopolies, corporations, and elite privilege. He now applied it to Black Ohioans. In seeking reelection, Morris would deny neither his Jacksonian social and economic beliefs nor his antislavery actions in the Senate. Indeed, his Jacksonian fear of economic elites' claim to special privilege drove his opposition to the Slave Power and necessitated the extension of equal civil rights to Black citizens.

For Morris, Jacksonian opposition to the Money Power and opposition to the Slave Power were two sides of the same coin. As he had explained to a correspondent a few weeks before his letter to Samuel Medary at the *Ohio Statesman,* to "know the evil that besets us is the first step towards reformation," and then "ascertain the causes which have produced those evils."[17] The source of the evil he confronted was the desire for dominion over men, which led to a "love of ease and opulence" to live on the uncompensated labor of others. Morris thought "the desire to live upon the unrequited labor of others is acquiring a dreadful universality." The result

> is the slave holding power,—this Goliath of all monopolies,—that now brandishes his spear and threatens the overthrow of our most essential rights, and the most sacred of all our privileges. It defies even the Constitution, itself, to engage in single combat. It claims to be before and superior to that instrument which it contends has acknowledged its superiority, and has guaranteed its existence and perpetual duration. It imperiously asserts that it has converted men into property; and as a matter of course, any person, when he becomes a CITIZEN of the United States, has a right to the enjoyment and use of this species of property, in each and every state of the Union. It is upon this false position, that a person can be converted by law into a thing, that slavery rests its whole claim—a position at war with the Constitution of the United States, and which ought not to be sustained in our courts of justice.[18]

As evidence for this conclusion, Morris noted that the Fifth Amendment distinguished "persons" from "things,"[19] and claimed that "no one" during the revolution supported slavery; that no one at the time of the Adoption of the Constitution sought to enlarge its borders; and that the Ordinance of 1787 was a "rebuke" of the practice.

Despite the beliefs of the Founders and the provisions of the Constitution, "slaves [had] increased vastly in numbers and the power of the slave holder in an equal degree." From this position of strength, "the slaveholding power . . . asserts that the Constitution recognizes slavery . . . and the right of the slave holder to his slave is derived from that instrument."

> This is the first great and combined interest in this country which strikes at equal rights, but all other special and local interests have the same tendency when they claim peculiar or exclusive privileges. The monied interest is next to be feared, and whenever that or any other shall have acquired sufficient strength to induce or influence Congress to legislate for its special benefit, there will be an end to that equality of rights which the Constitution designed to establish for the benefit for all.[20]

Should the Slave Power succeed in distorting the Constitution, "it will then be no longer . . . the home of Liberty. It will be made its grave."[21]

The threats from the Money Power and the Slave Power then were indistinguishable. Nevertheless, Morris's support for civil rights for Black Ohioans in an appeal to Ohio Jacksonians was particularly remarkable. Although "repeal of the black laws [had been] the central focus" of Ohio abolitionists in the 1830s, "Democrats often adopted profoundly racist rhetoric to cement support from working-class whites."[22] During the session of the general assembly earlier that year, Leicester King had offered "a petition from Cincinnati African Americans seeking repeal of the black laws." Several Democratic senators "objected strenuously." They argued that Blacks had no right to petition, were not citizens, and their residence in Ohio was "only tolerated."[23] For Morris to refer to Ohio's Blacks as "citizens" entitled to petition and to reaffirm his commitment to "equal and exact justice" for all in a message addressed to Ohio Democrats is more than surprising.

In retrospect, Morris's decision to interject his antislavery/civil rights views into the campaign appears to have been the height of folly. Democratic editors, however, initially seemed to approve of the tactic. Morris's letter to Medary was published in Jacksonian newspapers across the state. The editor of the *Philanthropist* found this "a little remarkable," particularly the accompanying "laudatory comments" from papers "violent in their hatred of abolition." For its part, the *Philanthropist* thought the letter "must command the deep respect of every friend of man." The editor praised Morris's actions in the Senate as evidencing "sound sense and unflinching integrity." He believed it was "an honor to Ohio to be represented in Congress by such a man as Thomas Morris."[24]

Morris's effort to tie the Whigs to Texas annexation and the spread of slavery was calculated to appeal to Ohio voters in both parties and, although more problematic factually, appeared less risky. In January, while Morris was challenging Calhoun in the Senate, a select committee of the

Ohio General Assembly considered the question of Texas's annexation to the United States. The Committee concluded that "the annexation of the republic of Texas . . . [was] unjust, inexpedient, and destructive of the peace, safety, and well-being of the nation." In reaching this conclusion, the Committee noted that "annexation would be the grossest injustice to the non-slave holding states. It would, in a very few years, give the slave-holding interest a preponderance in the national government and expose all the great interests [of the North] now regarded by the South with extreme jealousy and aversion to the destructive influence of their hostile legislation." The report and resolutions were adopted unanimously in one house of the general assembly and without objection in the other. They were forwarded to a Whig congressman from Ohio for presentation to Congress. Although the House refused permission to read the resolution or the accompanying letter from the governor,[25] Morris's image of a Slave Power seeking to spread its influence throughout the country appeared to be gaining acceptance within both parties in Ohio.

Abolitionist numbers in Ohio had also grown dramatically in the two years since Morris had first presented petitions in the Senate. By 1838, there were 251 local Ohio antislavery organizations with over twelve thousand members—nearly double the number from 1836.[26] Even before his letter to *Ohio Statesman,* Morris had begun his campaign by appealing directly to Ohio abolitionists. He sent a letter describing his actions in support of the petition campaign to William Keys, which was read to the annual meeting of the Ohio Anti-Slavery Society. Although the Society's Executive Committee sought permission to publish the letter with its annual report, Morris apparently declined.[27] The letter was never published.

Morris was not finished with making his antislavery actions, and in particular his conflict with Calhoun, an issue in the campaign. In response to the editor's request, he also published his remarks in response to Calhoun's resolutions in the *Philanthropist.*[28] By juxtaposing his Senate remarks with the Whig Convention censure, he sought to reduce antislavery support for Whig candidates. The strategy was obviously fraught with danger. By emphasizing his belief in equal rights and his defense of abolitionists' right to petition and to speak, Morris risked Democratic support should they regain control of the Ohio General Assembly.

Events in the fall, however, seemed to play into Morris's hand. John B. Mahan, a neighbor of Morris in Clermont County and active in the underground railroad, was abducted from Ohio. He was taken to Kentucky in

September 1838 and charged with aiding escaped slaves. The Democratic press immediately charged that the Whig governor, Joseph Vance, was complicit in Mahan's arrest. The *Ohio Statesman* claimed that Vance's "object was to gratify the dark spirit of slavery with which the moneyed aristocracy are deeply imbued."[29] Stung by the charges, the Whig press went so far as to accuse Morris of staging Mahan's arrest for political purposes.[30] Perhaps more importantly for Morris, the incident appeared to confirm his narrative of the Southern threat to Northern liberty. His debate with Calhoun seemed to have foreshadowed the events of the fall. Although the Democrats never explicitly tied Morris's Senate reelection efforts to the Mahan episode, their support for resistance to slaveholder demands encouraged Morris and the abolitionists.

In the spring of 1838, the American Anti-Slavery Society had concluded that local societies should interrogate candidates for office. The national organization recommended that abolitionists vote, "irrespective of party," only for candidates supportive of the antislavery position as reflected in their responses to the questions.[31] A year earlier, the Ohio Anti-Slavery Society had recommended that abolitionists "adopt means for ascertaining the sentiments of candidates" without suggesting how this was to be done. With the fall elections for the Ohio General Assembly determining Morris's future in the Senate, the Ohio society unanimously endorsed the proposal to question candidates directly.[32] The *Philanthropist* had begun the year by reminding its readers that "the antislavery cause takes precedence in the minds of its adherents of all party objects" so that "no political action of theirs can be right or expedient which conflicts with its claims." In the summer, the paper again reminded abolitionists that a failure to "take their principles" to the polls would bring "dishonor to themselves . . . and injure the cause to which they are pledged." The editor also severely criticized the Whig press for attacking Morris as an abolitionist. By the fall, the *Philanthropist* had all but endorsed Morris and urged support for Democratic candidates for the general assembly.[33]

As the results of the statewide canvass became known in late October, it was obvious that the Democrats had regained control of the general assembly. More importantly for Morris, much of the state's press attributed the outcome to the electorate's desire to see him reelected.[34] Because stump speakers and partisan editors had made it clear that the contest for the general assembly in 1838 was primarily for the right to choose the next senator, most observers thought Morris's candidacy had swayed antislavery

Whigs to vote for Democrats.[35] One contemporary source estimated that Morris's candidacy had changed twenty thousand votes from the previous year.[36] While this was undoubtedly an overstatement, his candidacy clearly appeared to have had an effect on antislavery Whigs. A correspondent to the *Philanthropist* from Belmont County believed "a very large number of Whigs stayed home from their high respect of Morris," and he "had reason to believe that for the same cause" many voted for the Democratic candidate for the general assembly.[37] Thus when the Democrats won a sweeping victory, Morris's strategy of tying the Whigs to the Slave Power and the annexation of Texas appeared to have been successful.

Much of the Whig press agreed with the *Philanthropist*. In an issue that carried reports of hundreds of Whigs staying away from the polls, the *Ohio State Journal* gave its view of the election:

> We attribute our loss in that department [the general assembly] to the abolitionist. That party at this time holds the balance of power in a number of counties of the state, sufficient to decide the party complexion of the Legislature. They can give the government to the Whigs or the Tories, as they may themselves decide. In the late contest they threw their weight into the scale against the former and secured the triumph of the latter. Their objective in doing so was to secure the reelection of Thomas Morris, an abolitionist of the strictest faith, and, withal, the Tory incumbent of a seat in the National Senate and a candidate for reelection. We are well satisfied that the course pursued by the abolitionists changed the result in a sufficient number of counties to give the Assembly to the [Democratic] Administration.[38]

Although a recent study of the election returns found "no substantial evidence . . . to show that Ohio abolitionists abandoned their primarily Whig loyalties for the doubtful policy of supporting Democratic candidates,"[39] the perception that Morris had influenced the election outcome was widespread. Particularly within antislavery circles in southern Ohio, the Mahan case and Morris's reelection effort convinced "many contemporaries . . . that abolitionism had indeed played a critical role in the Whig defeat."[40] In responding to Calhoun, Morris had said that if he did "not represent the sentiments" of his constituents, there was a ready "correction at hand." In fact, he told the Senate, he "courted the expression of [the general assembly] judgement upon me."[41] Morris believed that the election results vindicated his actions in the Senate.

74   THE CREATION OF A CRUSADER

The success of the Democrats, however, did not assure Morris's reelection to the Senate. The prospect for Democratic support remained uncertain. The augurs did not bode well. Although he had consistently supported Jackson's economic programs and the expungement of his censure, when Jackson stopped in Cincinnati in March 1837, on his retirement journey back to Tennessee, a "huge mob assembled." Morris, however, was nowhere to be found. He was the only prominent local Democrat not invited to the reception.[42] Following the 1838 election, the state Democratic paper, the *Ohio Statesman,* also immediately distanced itself from Morris. A few weeks earlier the paper had sought abolitionist votes, but the editor now claimed that neither the Mahan case nor abolitionists had cost the Whigs "a single vote."[43]

In Washington, he had clearly fallen into disfavor with his Jacksonian colleagues in the Senate. For example, during his first four years in the Senate, he had been elected to the Manufactures, the Agricultural, and Judiciary Committees. When the Senate organized following Van Buren's inauguration, however, Morris lost his seats on the Manufacturers and Agricultural Committees. Instead, he was relegated to chair the Committee on Pensions.[44] Despite his support of Van Buren's economic plan, Morris's antislavery actions had taken him outside the Democratic mainstream. In particular, in his response to Calhoun's resolutions, Morris moved from supporting the right of petition to supporting the goals of the abolitionists. Although during the fall campaign he had chosen to emphasize his conflicts with the Whigs and Calhoun, Morris was the only Democrat to vote against Calhoun's resolutions. In particular, Senator Allen, his Ohio colleague whom Morris had attacked publicly, voted to support each resolution.[45]

In the national arena, Martin Van Buren had moved to calm the South and organized his administration around Southern planters and Northern republicans.[46] Van Buren had made it clear in his inaugural address not only that he opposed abolition in the District, but that he abhorred the continued agitation supporting it.[47] Most Ohio Democrats viewed cooperation with the South as sound political strategy and had no intention of allowing Morris to damage this coalition. The prospects for Morris's reelection by the general assembly were dubious at best. Although his initial opposition to Calhoun on petitions and incendiary publications was within the range of acceptable Democratic behavior, his continued efforts to force a debate on the merits of slavery were not. Moreover, many Ohio legislators were virulently racist. For example, Thomas Buchanan, the Democratic state legislator from Morris's home county, had "declared that Negroes have no more right to petition than dogs."[48] Certainly the senator's belief in "equal and exact justice" for all did not meet with much favor in his eyes. Yet with the Democrats now in control of the general assembly, men such as Buchanan had the responsibility of selecting the next senator from Ohio.

The local antislavery societies realized the problems Morris would encounter. Many of the groups began to petition their representatives in the general assembly to support him. The *Philanthropist* urged that such action not be taken, however, arguing that "such petitioning would be certain to defeat its own object."[49] Commenting editorially on the race for the Senate, the paper claimed to be "indifferent." Despite the editorials, the editor was not indifferent; rather, he felt an open endorsement of Morris by the antislavery societies would be a liability. Already Southern Democratic papers were calling for Morris's defeat.[50] Official antislavery support for him would only cause more clamor. Nevertheless, the *Philanthropist* could not follow its own advice. On the eve of the general assembly's meeting to elect a senator, it said the election "about to take place will decide . . . whether Ohio is to be a free, sovereign, independent state, or a mere appendage to the slave holding South." The editor told his fellow citizens that "it should afford particular joy that it was . . . a senator from Ohio . . . [who] stood forth singlehanded as the champion of human rights . . . when so fiercely assailed by the advocates of eternal slavery." Only by "bowing their necks to the yoke" and displaying "a spaniel like fidelity to the slave-holder" could the general assembly fail to reelect Morris.[51]

Conscious of the press reports of the reason for the Democrats' return to power, Morris decided to take the contest to his critics. On November 23, 1838, he wrote, "To the People of Ohio and Members of the General Assembly" at the suggestion of "some valuable friends" to explain his views. Six days later, just before departing for Washington, he gave the same address to a group of his political friends in Cincinnati. Both statements were published in the *Cincinnati Daily Gazette* and reprinted in the *Emancipator*.[52] He made no apologies for his antislavery views or his actions in the Senate. As he had done in his letter to the *Statesman* in June, Morris began by directly attacking Calhoun's constitutional and positive good arguments. He had "always believed slavery to be wrong in principle, in practice, in every country and under every condition of things!" Taking direct aim at Calhoun's positive good argument, Morris said slavery was "so radically wrong, that no time, place or circumstances can palliate it or give it even the appearance of being right; and that American slavery [was] the most obnoxious of its kind, a libel upon our republic institutions and ruinous to the best interest of our country."[53]

Morris noted that he had "repeatedly asserted that the framers of the Constitution . . . intended that its whole moral power should operate to the extinguishment of slavery." Morris insisted that the Constitution did not guarantee the existence of slavery, nor did Congress possess the power to determine what was property. The Constitution simply did not recognize that persons could be property. As a result, only the states could determine the nature and extent of property rights.[54]

Not only was there no constitutional guarantee of slavery, slavery was "at war" with the "great fundamental truths" contained in the Declaration of Independence.[55] Nevertheless, since slavery was a creature of state law, Congress had no "power to free the slaves in the different states." He also continued to "have great doubts" that Congress could deny admission to a state on the grounds that it recognized slavery and so would continue to "go for admission" as he had done in the case of Arkansas.[56]

Congress, however, was not entirely without power to act on slavery. Morris had "no doubt" that "Congress can prohibit the existence of slavery in the territories," and more importantly, "ought on all occasions to exercise this power." Although "an anomaly in our republican institution and dangerous . . . to the sovereignty of the States," Congress also had the power to legislate on any matter for the District of Columbia. The only question was "ought Congress to exercise such power and abolish slavery in the District"?[57] This was the issue that had confronted Morris in 1836. He now believed "that the time will come, and is not far distant, when Congress will abolish slavery in the District," but he rejected Clay's notion that residents of the District must agree before the action could occur. Rather, a representative was "bound by the will of his constituents and the people of the District are by the Constitution made subject to that will." Morris, the states' rights Democrat, felt "a strong aversion to the principle that Congress should exercise any power on the right to individual property." He was also "well aware, that should Congress abolish slavery in the District, it might be attended with injurious consequences to some of the states . . . a circumstance which Congress ought, if possible, to avoid." Nevertheless, "these are matters of expediency which . . . must sooner or later give way." Abolition in the District, then, was not a question of consent or power, but as he had concluded in 1836, "expediency."[58]

As he returned to Congress, then, Morris was hardly an advocate for immediate emancipation in either the District of Columbia (where Congress had the power), or in the territories (where Congress had the power), or in the states (where Congress lacked the power). It remained "with the states where it exists to abolish it."[59] Nevertheless, he believed "it to be the duty of every man, in whatever situation he may be placed, to use his moral power to obtain that highly important and beneficial consummation." Once slavery was abolished, Morris believed "the negro entitled to all those rights to which man is endowed by his Creator." These natural rights included life, liberty and property, but did not include social or political rights.[60] The Jacksonian, who had once believed that colonization was the only realistic approach to free Blacks, now thought they were entitled to the natural rights of all Americans. The *Emancipator,* in reprinting the speech, thought that Morris was "generally . . . correct in this matter."[61] The Ohio Democratic caucus thought otherwise.

Even though the *Ohio Statesman* denied that the Democrats' majority in the legislature was attributable to Morris's popularity, public perception was otherwise and his removal presented the Democrats with a problem of some delicacy. Morris's primary opponent for the Senate seat was Benjamin Tappan, the brother of New York abolitionists Arthur and Lewis Tappan.[62] Tappan had known Morris for over thirty years. He had collaborated with Morris during the judicial impeachment effort thirty years earlier and shared his radical hard-money views.[63] The two men had contended for the Senate seat in 1832. Although each had thirty votes apiece in the initial caucus vote, when the third-place candidate threw his support to Morris, he was elected.[64] When Jackson made a recess appointment of Tappan to the Ohio District Court Judgeship in the fall of 1833, Morris actively supported Tappan's confirmation in the Senate. When he failed to be confirmed, Morris blamed not only the Whigs but also his former protégé Thomas Hamer.[65]

When the general assembly convened in December, the Democratic caucus appointed a committee to question prospective candidates. The committee was comprised of Thomas Buchanan (who had already expressed his feelings in regard to the right to petition), John Brough, and David Tod, who had already pledged to support Tappan.[66] The committee nevertheless propounded three questions to each of the candidates. The first two of the three questions addressed to the candidates concerned their position on basic party programs (Are you in favor of the Independent Treasury Bill? Are you a supporter of the leading measures of the present

78 THE CREATION OF A CRUSADER

administration?). These questions Morris answered succinctly and in the affirmative. Morris remained in the mainstream of Jacksonian thought on each of these issues.[67]

On the final question, however—Are you for or against modern abolitionism?—Morris responded at length. He began by saying that he was "opposed to slavery in all its forms; and against its further extension in our country." He believed "Congress [had] no power over it as it exists in the states," but neither did Congress have "the power to create a system of slavery where it does not exist." He reiterated his earlier statement that Blacks "ought to be protected in and enjoy their natural rights, but [he did] not believe that it would be good policy, or promote the safety of the country, the happiness of ourselves or the negro race, to admit them to the enjoyment of equal political or social privileges." He did "hold that citizens . . . have an indisputable right to speak, write or print on the subject of slavery as on any other subject," and that the right of petition was "inviolate on all subjects and above the power of the law."[68] His response was entirely consistent with his address and speech two weeks earlier in Cincinnati.

The committee's question, however, had been phrased in terms of "modern abolitionism": "I have thought it best to answer your third interrogatory as I have done, because a direct answer might be liable to misconception or misunderstanding. As to what modern Abolitionism is; as it is represented by many, I believe it entirely wrong, but whether that representation be correct or not, I do not pretend to say."[69] Morris's answer is not as coy as it might appear. His address reaffirmed the position he had taken two years earlier in his speech on Calhoun's incendiary publications bill. The Constitution did not promote or protect slavery; it was entirely a matter of state law. Slavery existed only where created by positive law. The thrust of the Constitution, augmented by the Declaration of Independence, pointed to the abolition of slavery. Congress had the undoubted power to abolish slavery in the District of Columbia and prohibit it in the territories. By 1838, these positions had become orthodox for abolitionists.

In contradistinction to most abolitionists, however, Morris continued to believe that Congress could not refuse to admit a new slave state. Nor did he yet believe that action on slavery in the District was obligatory. He continued to believe it was within the discretion of Congress, although he expected eventual abolition. Finally, he rejected (as did most abolitionist leaders) Alvan Stewart's theory of congressional power to abolish slavery in the states and continued to subscribe to the federal consensus. Moreover,

"Modern abolitionism" had become almost a term of art. Democrats used it to encompass "abolition's national scope, its openness to female participation, its foreign connection, and its involvement in other aspects of reform."[70] In effect, "modern abolitionism" equaled Garrisonianism. Morris did not subscribe to those views. If that was the definition of an abolitionist, Morris said he was not one. Ohio Democrats were not persuaded.

Benjamin Tappan had sought a Senate seat since 1832 and had been actively campaigning throughout the fall of 1838.[71] Although in his correspondence with his brothers he had criticized abolitionists, Tappan had frequently expressed his opposition to slavery. Some in the Democratic caucus were concerned enough about Tappan's views on abolition to oppose his election.[72] Unlike Morris, however, Tappan had responded to the committee's questions by condemning abolitionists and agreeing not to attack slavery while in the Senate.[73] A few weeks later, Tappan confirmed his opposition to "modern abolitionism" and assured his brother "that the democratic party in Ohio . . . [had] not mistaken their man."[74] Upon learning of his brother's election in place of Morris, Lewis Tappan wrote: "To tell you the honest truth I should have preferred to have heard that you had become a deacon of a church."[75] When Tappan's agreement to not introduce antislavery petitions in the Senate became public, the Whig press claimed that Tappan was "an abolitionist, equally with the ostracized member," but that he had surrendered his principles to the "debasing power of party drill."[76]

After Tappan's election, Morris initially thought the party had made a mistake. "Morris and many of his friends . . . and all of the abolitionists in the southern parts of our state endeavored by every means in their power to make the People believe that [Tappan] was much more enthusiastic in favor of abolitionism than T. Morris."[77] Morris acknowledged his defeat was "a rebuke for the course [he had] as a Senator taken . . . and the opinions [he had] expressed on the subject of Abolition, but he knew Tappan well" and "he was a more strenuous opposer of slavery." Indeed, Morris recalled that Tappan's opposition to slavery had been "urged against him when he was a candidate for District Judge."[78]

Morris's surprise appears genuine and reveals much. The Whig paper in Morris's home county thought that Morris had been "bamboozled" by his "crafty associates." When Van Buren needed his support for the independent treasury, the Ohio "Regency" had "flattered" Morris "into the belief that he could command the support" of the party.[79] His apostasy from the

Jacksonian line was not opposition to slavery. Morris's belief that slavery was "an evil" and that Congress had power over it in the District did not take him outside of Jacksonian orthodoxy. Indeed, the *Washington Globe* reprinted much of Morris's November 23 public address defending his antislavery actions in the Senate as evidence of his Jacksonian bona fides.[80]

Rather, Ohio Democrats no longer found Morris acceptable because of his defense of abolitionist agitation and his attacks on the South.[81] The central fact about slavery in the second American party system was that national parties and slavery agitation were mutually exclusive. "Compromise and conciliation, rather than confrontation, were the accepted operating principles" of both national parties.[82] In Ohio, "the vast majority of Democrats agreed that slavery was an evil in the abstract," but that it "was a distant question best dealt with by those in the locality where it existed." Their opposition to slavery "was not based upon its unjust treatment of blacks in the South, but rather upon its threat to the free labor system of the North." As a result, they "saw no inconsistency in attacking blacks and abolitionists as vigorously as the institution of slavery itself."[83]

Presenting antislavery petitions and defending free speech was acceptable. Decrying slavery without condemning abolitionist agitation, and dismissing the threat to disunion while attacking the Slave Power, violated the party creed. Jacksonians simply "did not consider slavery a legitimate political issue; they interpreted antislavery demands as disguised efforts to provoke disunion."[84] As a result, they "tried every device to prevent it from becoming an issue of importance in the Northern States."[85] Morris's surprise at Tappan's selection reveals both his failure to grasp this Jacksonian understanding of the consequences of abolitionist agitation and how far he had departed from it.

Ohio Democrats hoped to quiet abolitionist ferment within the state party, but their rejection of Morris only served "to drive him further along the abolition road."[86] Morris took his rejection by the Ohio legislature bitterly. The suspicion and distrust of the South, which he had long harbored, surfaced again. Upon learning of Tappan's selection, he penned a strong letter to the editor of the *Ohio Statesman*. In it he aggressively defended his course in the Senate and expressed his concern over the growth of Southern power. "I ask no forgiveness," he said, "for my antislavery sins." He told fellow Democrats that "it has, perhaps been my misfortune to love and respect the Constitution of my country and the rights of the people under it, more than an administration or majority." His entire course had been guided by a desire "to preserve the constitutional rights of man." Morris believed that "the power of slavery here [Washington] is tremendous—its march is onward." This power sought such extensive privilege on the behalf of slavery that he could not yet see "any ray of hope for [the slave] until public opinion shall become more united and vigorous in his behalf."[87]

Convinced by the election returns that his course had been approved by the people of Ohio,[88] Morris had to look elsewhere for an explanation of his defeat. Southern newspapers' demands for his rejection by the general assembly provided him with an answer. The *Alabama Beacon* had called Morris "a self-willed fanatic" and expressed disbelief that "this opinionated individual is to weigh against the whole undivided Administration party in the Senate."[89] Already suspicious of Southern demands for orthodoxy on the slavery issues, his defeat confirmed his fear of the Slave Power. During the weeks following his defeat, Morris grew increasingly bitter toward the South. He became convinced that "like the grave, this Slave Power cannot be satisfied."[90] But its attacks now went beyond general moves against the Constitution and rights of expression.

Morris was certain that the Slave Power had been responsible for his defeat. Subservient Ohio representatives, he said, "have been able by the slaveholding power to strike me down."[91] The general assembly's "subservience" to slaveholders appeared to be confirmed within a few weeks of Morris's defeat. In the aftermath of the Mahan saga, Kentucky sent "commissioners" to the Ohio legislature seeking, in the recollection of one participant, "to make freedom in Ohio worse . . . than slavery." The general assembly responded by reaffirming the state's Black Laws, reasserting the denial of Black Ohio residents' right to petition the general assembly, resolving that any attempt to interfere with slavery by congressional action was unconstitutional, and adopting the Fugitive Slave Law of 1839, "the most comprehensive state law on recapture it would ever produce." Although Ohio had adopted a fugitive slave law during Morris's first term in the general assembly, and he does not appear to have ever sought its repeal, the adoption of the new statute at the request of the Kentucky commissioners confirmed that the Slave Power now controlled the Ohio General Assembly.[92] The Democrats rejected not only Morris but his call for "equal and exact justice."

In the weeks following his rejection, the senator came to view the Slave Power as "more powerful and dangerous to the peace and prosperity of the country than banks or any other interest that has ever existed among us."[93] Although in 1834 he had called the bank a "curse,"[94] he now claimed that the Slave Power was "more powerful and dangerous" than any bank. He viewed the Slave Power as the quintessential threat to liberty and opposed it as a special interest. Accustomed from his constant struggles against banks and corporations to think in terms of monsters and to use the rhetoric of conspiracies, Morris applied these concepts to Southern slave owners. The earlier demands from the South to quiet the abolitionist crusade had awakened the senator's concern for personal liberties. His striking parallel of the slave interest with the bank interest illustrated his essentially Jeffersonian motivation. When he perceived the Southern attack as being aimed directly at himself, however, his fears solidified into an understanding of the South as an aggressive, unified Slave Power.

CHAPTER 6

The Beacon Fires of Liberty

As a career politician, Morris found himself in an anomalous position. While abolitionists discussed methods to join politics to antislavery without a sacrifice of principle, Morris had to blend antislavery to politics to maintain his principles. Morris created the Slave Power to accomplish this task. His dramatic reply to Henry Clay in the Senate provided the impetus for the emerging third-party movement and justified political antislavery. In the development of the conviction of the need for third-party action, Thomas Morris's experience was crucial; in the implementation of that conviction, his leadership was vital.

After his return to Washington, Morris learned of his defeat for reelection and the general assembly's passage, at the request of a delegation from Kentucky, of an enhanced fugitive slave law and adoption of "a raft of resolutions affirming the black laws and repudiating all forms of antislavery action" and denying Black Ohioans' right to petition.[1] Morris attributed all of these actions to the influence of the Slave Power on Ohio Democrats. Writing to the editor of the *Philanthropist* in early January, Morris conveyed his views of the members of the General Assembly:

> If the Legislators of the free states will obey, with trembling submission, the behests of the slaveholding power; if they will tamely submit to be taught their course of action by official agents from the slave states; if they will not protect their own peaceable citizens from the midnight violence of the

THE CREATION OF A CRUSADER

slave-hunter and slave-dealer: they are unworthy of the confidence of a free people, tyrants themselves in heart, enemies to human liberty, and traitors to the Constitution and freedom of the country.[2]

Morris can hardly be said to have "accepted his ouster graciously."[3]

On January 10, in the course of presenting a petition from Brown County, Ohio, seeking the repeal of congressional acts establishing slavery in the District of Columbia, he addressed the Ohio General Assembly's decision to not receive petitions from Blacks. After reporting that he had asked Southern senators whether their states allowed such petitions (and being advised that they did), Morris turned his attention to the character of the Ohio Democrats who had adopted the resolution. He said, "he had no language to express his feelings with regard to such men," but went on to describe them as "a class of small politicians, who, like insects, have sprung from the corrupt and agitated waters of party spirit and party drill; mere summer flies, who buzz round the circle of power, and draw a precarious and short lived existence from the putrid mass of prejudice, which interest has created to keep the colored race in bondage."[4] He thought these men "politicians who would make the lacerated back of the trembling slave a hobby to ride into office."[5] The general assembly's actions made Morris "more and more convinced that it is necessary for the peace of country, and for the equal justice for which government was instituted, even independent of regard for the slave himself, that slavery should come to an end."[6] For Morris, the destruction of slavery had become a political imperative.

The more Morris reflected on his defeat, the more certain he became of the alliance between the Money Power and slavery. He had observed the "billing and cooing between these different interests for some time" and "during the first week of the session" told his private friends . . . that these powers were forming a union."[7] This combination threatened the free states:

> Thousands of those laborers have fled from the northern states, on account of the oppression of monopolies, and the monied aristocracy there; and from the slave states, because there degraded to the condition of the colored people, by the monopolist of the human flesh, the large slaveholder and aristocrat of the South. Constant and unceasing vigilance is necessary, to prevent the same aristocracy and the same system of slavery from taking root and spreading in the states in which they not now are.[8]

As he had warned in 1836, "Slaveholders insist that slavery is a part of the Government and . . . that by the Constitution, the slaveholder can work his slaves in each and every state in the Union, and that no state can deprive him of this right." Morris thought that if this view of "slavery were confined to the slave states only," he would not be as concerned. Unfortunately, Ohio had "a class of politicians who love slavery as a system and would extend it throughout the Union." He explicitly included in this class of politician Thomas Buchanan and John Brough, who had served on the committee that posed the abolition question to Morris.[9]

With his term nearing its end, Morris sought an opportunity to explain again the threat posed by the slaveholding power and the political necessity of its destruction. Recalling the debates surrounding Calhoun's resolutions a year earlier, on February 6, 1839, Morris "submitted a resolution directing the Judiciary Committee to inquire into certain matters pertaining to the institution of slavery in the States and Territories." The resolution asked the Judiciary Committee to consider three questions: (1) whether the right of petition includes requests directed at the abolition of slavery; (2) whether Congress could abolish slavery in the District and the territories; and (3) whether Congress could restrain the exercise of any right that questioned the justice of slavery or tried to weaken or abolish it in the states.[10] A correspondent to the *Emancipator* described the resolutions as "an unusual dose of abolitionism," and that "some symptoms of uneasiness were manifested" by other senators during the reading of the resolution.[11] In essence, Morris's resolution asked the Senate to reject the position it had adopted in approving Calhoun's resolutions the year earlier.

Immediately Senator Hubbard from Michigan objected, stating that "he could not believe that the Senate would . . . discuss the agitating question at this period of its session," and asserting that "it was matter of policy, if not duty, to let this whole subject alone." A senator from Alabama asked to move that the resolution not be received, but was ruled out of order. The resolution was then tabled.[12] Morris's attempt, however, provided Henry Clay with an opportunity he had been seeking. With the election of 1840 on the horizon, Clay faced a conundrum with regard to slavery. To secure the Whig nomination for president, he needed to improve his position in the South while quenching the growing abolitionist sentiment for political action. Early in his career, Clay had supported abolition in Kentucky. By the time he had become Speaker of the House, however, he had given up on abolition. In December 1816, he presided at the organizational meeting of the American Colonization Society. Clay ultimately became president of the Society, making himself vulnerable to attacks from both Calhoun and abolitionists.

Clay could hardly have escaped the implications of the fall election in Ohio for Whig prospects in 1840. The widespread losses were almost universally attributed to antislavery Whigs deserting the party in an effort to reelect Morris to the Senate.[13] Clay had concurred in this assessment of the cause of the Whig defeat in Ohio.[14] The failure to reelect Morris led to increasing calls for the creation of an antislavery third party. The executive committee of the New York State Anti-Slavery Society debated such a move at its January 1839 meeting. Perhaps alerted to the New York discussions and aware of the Ohio results, Clay acted.[15]

Prior to delivering his February 7 speech, Clay had consulted with several colleagues, including Sen. William Preston of South Carolina. Preston thought the speech would offend persons on both sides of the slavery issue. In response, Clay supposedly noted that he believed his position was correct, and that he "had rather be right than be President." As one of his biographers observed, however, "actually he would rather be both right and president." Later Clay would claim that this speech cost him the 1840 Whig nomination, but "Clay knew what he was doing" and made the speech "after full deliberation," with the intent of offending the radicals on both sides of the issue.[16]

Clay chose to use antiabolition petitions to attempt to improve both his position with Southern Whigs prior to the 1840 Presidential Campaign and to remind Northern Whigs of the imperative to support the party. On February 7, 1839, the day after Morris submitted his proposed resolutions, Clay presented petitions from various citizens of the District of Columbia requesting Congress to refrain from abolition, saying, "there were insuperable obstacles to emancipation."[17] A few months earlier, Clay had told James Birney that "never, in my life, was I in favor of the immediate emancipation of slaves." Indeed, he believed the abolitionist organization had "thrown back fifty years" the prospect of ending slavery.[18] He now made the same argument in the Senate.

Clay deprecated the introduction of the slavery issue into politics and contended that "it was inexpedient, if not unconstitutional, to abolish slavery in the District of Columbia." He claimed that "the abolition of slavery must be left to the workings of Providence in the future of the next hundred years."[19] Although Morris had used almost identical language in 1836 to explain his position on abolition in the District,[20] it now seemed to Morris that Henry Clay, an old political opponent, had capitulated to the Slave Power in his quest for the presidency. This conclusion was supported by Calhoun's immediate outburst in support of Clay's argument and shared by others in the North.[21] Calhoun's endorsement of Clay's speech confirmed Morris's suspicions "that new moves ha[d] taken place on the political chessboard and new coalitions [had] formed . . . settling and disposing of the rights of the country for the advantage of political aspirants."[22]

That evening, "scarcely anything was talked about throughout the city [Washington] but the great speech" of Clay. The belief that Calhoun would continue the discussion on the next day increased the excitement and speculation. The galleries were packed early in anticipation of the debate, but instead the Senate considered the reception of Morris's resolution, presented two days earlier. Senator Hubbard of Michigan, for the express purpose "of getting rid of the resolution," moved to table it. Senator Buchanan, however, encouraged Hubbard to withdraw his motion momentarily. In Buchanan's view, "fair play is a jewel; and . . . the Senator from Ohio had a right to be heard, and to reply to the remarks that were made yesterday." Senator Hubbard responded that "fair play" was not an issue, and that Morris should, "in imitation of the example set" by Clay, offer a petition and then speak. Hubbard reminded Morris that he enjoyed this privilege.[23]

This response, patronizing and demeaning as it was, angered Morris. First, he was "very much obliged" to learn from Hubbard that "he had the same right as any other Senator to express his opinion. . . . He supposed that he ought to return his profound thanks for this precious privilege." But he was not done. In the words of the *Congressional Globe,* he "proceeded to comment on the course of Senators with much severity."[24] Although not reported in the *Congressional Globe,* a correspondent to the *Emancipator* said that Morris "dropped the remark that if any tyrant in Europe should treat petitions as Congress had done, he would be dethroned."[25] He was immediately gaveled out of order. When he asked if it was his language that was out of order, the chair simply reminded Morris that the motion to table was not debatable. The motion to table the question of printing the resolution was then adopted by a closely divided Senate.[26]

The next day, February 9, following the strategy adopted by Clay and recommended by Hubbard, Morris presented petitions from several states (including two from New York signed by Arthur Tappan) seeking "the abolition of slavery in the District of Columbia, the suppression of the trade in slaves between the States, and praying that no state may be admitted in the Union whose constitution tolerates slavery." He then spoke "at great length and with much warmth in support of the objects of the petitioners."[27] The speech was not only the longest he had ever delivered in the Senate but the most important speech he made in his life. In many respects, it was the valedictory of his political career.

Since that January day in 1836 when Calhoun had challenged the reception of the antislavery petitions Morris presented, he had been considering "the place of slavery in the Constitution the framers produced." Some commentators today believe that the "Constitution enacted mechanisms that empowered slave holders politically, which would prevent the national government from becoming an immediate, or likely impediment to the institution. . . . This made the Constitution nominally neutral but operationally proslavery."[28] After three years of debate and thought, however, Morris had concluded that the Constitution was the antithesis of proslavery. Only the distortions of the Slave Power could make the Constitution proslavery.

Throughout his speech the senator was taunted with "loudly whispered curses" from the gallery. One young man was so upset by Morris's assault on slavery that he "literally gnashed his teeth" at the senator.[29] Despite the crowd's response, Morris persisted in his attack on Clay, Calhoun, and the Slave Power: "The aristocracy of the North, who by the power of a corrupt banking system, and the aristocracy of the South, by the power of the slave system, both fattening upon the labor of others, are now about to unite in order to make the reign of each perpetual." He told his audience that "the cotton bale and bank note have formed an alliance." In replying to Clay, Morris hoped "to drive from the back of the Negro slave the politician who [had] seated himself there to ride into office for the purpose of carrying out the object of this unholy combination." To Morris, the "power behind the throne, greater than the throne itself . . . [was] the power of SLAVERY," which was "aiming to govern the country, its Constitutions and laws."[30] The North had to defend itself against the attack of the South. The aggressive nature of the Slave Power compelled the free states to concern themselves with slavery.

Morris believed that the "Slave Power [was] seeking to establish itself in every State in defiance of the Constitution and the laws of the States within which it [was] prohibited." In order to achieve this goal, the Slave Power claimed "parentage from the Constitution." If Clay was right, "it is slavery then, not liberty, that makes us one people."[31] Morris denied the claim. In what became "most vital precept of antislavery constitutionalism,"[32] Morris melded the Declaration of Independence with the Constitution: "The Senator says that it was the principles of the Constitution which carried us through the Revolution. Surely it was; . . . It was the principle that all men are born free and equal. . . . It was for the natural and inherent rights of man they contended. It is a libel upon the Constitution to say that its object was not liberty, but slavery, for millions of the human race."[33] For Morris, the absence of the words *slave* or *slavery* from the text of the Constitution was not to "shroud" the founders' "hypocrisy,"[34] but because the document was antislavery. As he had told his colleagues a year earlier, "the framers of the Constitution intended that its whole moral power should operate to the extinction of slavery in all the states."[35]

Morris thought Clay had concluded "that the evil of slavery is incurable" but found "consolation . . . , in the midst of this existing evil, in color and caste." In other words, the Constitution did not guarantee slavery. Instead, "it is color, not right and justice, that is to continue forever slavery in our country. It is prejudice against color which is the strong ground of the slaveholder's hope."[36] But as Morris had argued two years earlier in commenting on the Fugitive Slave Act, "slavery has no just foundation in color; it rests exclusively upon usurpation, tyranny, oppressive fraud and force. These were its parents in every age and country.[37]

Clay had urged that slaves, as property, were governed by the Commerce Clause. Returning to his understanding of slaves as persons for purposes of the Constitution, Morris thought Clay's "argument is a non-sequitor. Unless the honorable Senator can first prove that slaves are proper article of commerce. We say that Congress have power over slaves only as persons, but cannot make them property."[38] The absence of any recognition of property in man not only meant slavery was not guaranteed by the Constitution, but also that Congress lacked power to make any person property.

Morris noted that at the "conclusion of the argument made by the Senator from Kentucky," Calhoun was "filled not only with delight, but with ecstasy." His reaction removed "all doubts" about the alliance of slavery with the Money Power. As a result, Morris returned to the Slave Power's threat to Northern liberty: "I am not now contending for the rights of the negro, rights which his Creator gave him and which his fellow-man has usurped or taken away. . . . I am endeavoring to sound the alarm to my fellow-citizens that this power, tremendous as it is, is endeavoring to unite itself with the moneyed power of the country, in order to extend its dominion and perpetuate its existence."[39]

But Morris's argument had gone beyond the encroachments of the Slave Power: "To say that I am opposed to slavery in the abstract are but cold and unmeaning words . . . I, sir, am not only opposed to slavery in the abstract, but also in its whole volume, in its theory as well as practice."[40] Although early in his career he had endorsed colonization, Morris now rejected it:

> It is not necessary now to enter into any of the benefits and advantages of colonization; the Senator [Clay] has pronounced it the noblest scheme ever devised by man; he says it powerful but harmless; I have no knowledge of any resulting benefits for the scheme for either race. I have not a doubt as to the real object intended by its founders; it did not arise from principles of humanity and benevolence towards the colored race, but a desire to remove the free of that race beyond the United States in order to perpetuate and make slavery more secure.[41]

Far from supporting colonization, Morris recalled his efforts and resolutions in the Senate. Only two months earlier he had denied supporting "modern abolition"; he now welcomed the designation *abolitionist:* "If those resolutions are Abolitionism, then I am an Abolitionist from the sole of my feet to the crown of my head."[42]

Morris steadfastly denied any intention to use anything but moral force to halt the Slave Power. His definition of moral action, however, struck directly at Clay's feared electoral consequences of abolitionist actions. Morris argued that "the ballot-box [was] the great moral lever in political action," and called on abolitionists to take their principles to the polls. Clay had opposed bringing antislavery ideas into politics, but Morris replied that the only one who feared the ballot box was a "tyrant; he who usurps power and seizes upon the liberty of others" and characterized Clay's speech as "the language of a stricken conscience seeking for the palliation of its own acts by charging guilt upon others" in an effort "to cast suspicion upon the character of their opponents in order to draw public attention from themselves."[43]

In the midst of the assaults on liberty by the Southern slaveholders, however, Morris thought he discerned a "sure sign of the final triumph of universal emancipation." He had "endeavored to warn [his] fellow-citizens of the present and approaching danger, but the dark cloud of slavery is before their eyes, and prevents many of them from seeing the condition of things as they are." But he was convinced "that cloud, like the cloud of summer, will soon pass away and its thunders cease to be heard. Slavery will come to an end." Earlier he had told his constituents that the slave's hope rested on Northern public opinion. As he closed this speech, his last in the Senate, he told his colleagues that he intended to change public sentiment. "I hope," he said, "on returning to my home and my friends, to join them again in rekindling the beacon fires of liberty upon every hill of our state, until their broad glow shall enlighten every valley."[44] He had resolved to take his case to the people. If the leaders of Ohio's Democratic Party were under the influence of the Slave Power, he would circumvent their power. His defeat had not shaken his Jeffersonian faith in the people. As he had written earlier to a Cincinnati friend, "Past experience [the struggle to recharter the Bank] has taught us that when liberty and the Constitutional rights of our citizens, . . . have been stricken down in Legislative Assemblies they have found support in the country."[45]

Morris's speech had an electric effect upon Northern abolitionists. Most antislavery papers published the entire text, and thousands of copies were printed in pamphlet form.[46] The American Anti-Slavery Society printed the entire speech as an "Antislavery Examiner," along with Theodore Weld's "Slavery as It Is," and circulated it across the North.[47] Garrison thought Morris "deserves something better than a statue of gold" for the speech. As the *Liberator* observed, the speech was printed not only in the antislavery papers but also in the *Congressional Globe,* which would "of course be circulated through all the Southern States."[48] Morris had achieved what the incendiary publication effort had failed to accomplish—to deliver an antislavery message to Southern opinion leaders.

Morris's reply to Clay came at a time when his rejection by his party had heightened his influence and prominence in the antislavery movement. After his reelection defeat, he became a martyr to the cause. The *Philanthropist* said he had been "laid on the altar of slavery as a peace offering to the South."[49] More importantly, in his speech he had used the concept of the Slave Power to justify political action on the part of the abolitionists:

> We who are opposed to and deplore the existence of slavery in our country are frequently asked, both in public and private, what do you have to do with slavery? It does not exist in your state; it does not disturb you! Ah, sir, would to God it were so—that we had nothing to do with slavery, nothing to fear

from its power, or its action within our own borders. . . . But this is not our lot. . . . it is our friends, our rights, our privileges, the safety of our friends, as well as the sovereignty of the states that we are now called upon to protect and defend. The slave interest has at this moment the whole power of the country in its hands.[50]

His recognition of the aggressive Slave Power had driven Morris to embrace abolition. Only by destroying the source of its power could the country be saved from the Slave Power.

Since the South had launched this assault on personal rights from a position of power in the government, the North had to strike at her there. The most direct method of doing this was to gain control of the federal government: "The ballot box is sufficient to correct all abuses. Let me, then, proclaim here, from this high arena, to the citizens, not only of my own state, but to the country, to all sects and parties who are entitled to the right of suffrage, TO THE BALLOT BOX: Carry with you honestly your sentiments respecting the welfare of your country. . . . Fear not the frowns of power. It trembles while it denounces you."[51] This coupling of the Slave Power concept with political action riveted the idea in the jargon of antislavery. His "Slave Power thesis transformed slavery into a political threat, . . . one with potentially disastrous outcomes for the North's farmers and workers."[52]

To the antislavery movement, Morris had given an effective, cohesive argument with which to answer their opponents. Not only had he explained the antislavery nature of the Constitution (the absence of any right to property in man; the lack of power in Congress to establish slavery anywhere; the use of the Declaration of Independence to inform the meaning of the Constitution), but he had provided a political justification for utilizing the antislavery Constitution to attack slavery. The Slave Power "soon replaced the three-fifths clause as the symbol of southern power." This thesis, which was "absent from the early Federalist attacks on slavery and the Missouri debates . . . was a far more sophisticated and complex formulation." Morris had given abolitionists the ability to "argue that slavery was not only morally repugnant, it was incompatible with the basic democratic values and liberties of white Americans."[53] Thousands of copies of the speech were printed in pamphlet form and distributed for free by abolition societies across the nation.[54] The *Emancipator* reported that he had "effectually answered Mr. Clay as far as argument [was] concerned."[55] A correspondent to the *Philanthropist* was "astonished at the power with which [Morris] came down upon his antagonist."[56] The speech took the antislavery argument beyond a righteous appeal to the nation's conscience and grounded it in political action. A historian of the early political antislavery movement thought Morris's speech "might have stood as the basis for all political action from that time until 1860."[57]

A commentator on the relationship of civil liberties to the antislavery struggle has claimed that the concept of the Slave Power did not emerge until 1845.[58] After the senator's reply to Clay, however, with its vast circulation in the antislavery press, the Slave Power "became permanently lodged in the national debate."[59] Salmon Chase spoke for a host of others when he credited Morris with having first shown him "the character of the Slave Power."[60] But beyond awakening the North to the existence of the Slave Power, Morris's speech spurred political antislavery activity. Indeed, William Birney later remembered the Ohioan's speech as the "trumpet call" to political action.[61] Those who picked up the concept were leaders in the third-party drive. Within four months of his reply to Clay, a national antislavery convention debating political action declared there was "no doubt that the SLAVE POWER [was] now waging a deliberate and determined war against the liberties of the free states."[62]

The idea of a third party had been discussed in private correspondence earlier, but after this Senate debate, the idea burst into public view.[63] In general, the antislavery leaders accepted the federal consensus and agreed that they could not attack slavery in the states where it already existed. Thus a political party could actually do little to abolish slavery outside the territories and District of Columbia. But Morris had presented political action as a necessary response to the Slave Power. The vague suspicion of the South had existed in abolitionist circles for some time,[64] but not until this Senate debate did the antislavery men recognize the political possibilities of a Slave Power argument. Eventually it formed "the basis of a platform for the . . . political grouping that became the Liberty Party." His reply to Clay, coming immediately after his "martyrdom" by Ohio Democrats, fixed the concept of the Slave Power in abolitionist rhetoric. "By the summer of 1839, assaults on the Slave Power saturated abolitionist publications."[65]

What Morris had done in his speech was to begin to change the symbolic definition of political reality. The Slave Power began to replace the Money Power as the symbol of the age.[66] Although "there is still so much to be learned about direct continuities between various movements" using a conspiracy rhetoric,[67] Morris's image provided a direct link between the Jacksonian war on the Bank and the antislavery attack on Southern power. He began his Senate career contending against Henry Clay and the Money Power; he ended it struggling with Clay and the Slave Power. Morris recognized his transitional role. As he told a Cincinnati friend:

> I have been with you in opposition to the power of concentrated wealth; to banks and systems that band together men in sustaining any particular or private object by which they can operate on and control the legislation and government of the country, I have said to you, that immediately after the settlement of the Money question, there was one of far more importance which the people must decide—the question of equal rights and civil liberty, in opposition to which would be arrayed the whole force of the slaveholding power: An interest, which private, local, and arrogant in its nature, has united together more persons for selfish purposes, and is more powerful and dangerous to the peace and prosperity of the country than banks or any other interest that has ever existed among us.[68]

The attack on civil liberties now came from a new quarter. When Morris filtered his perceptions of the South through the screen of Jacksonian imagery, the Slave Power emerged. Within a decade, large numbers of Northerners would accept this definition of national political reality. When viewed through the prism of Morris's antislavery Constitution, the solution to blending abolitionism with politics was to make Southern power, not the slave, the issue.

CHAPTER 7

A Rotten Branch to Be Lopped Off

Although Morris remained in the ranks of the Ohio Democratic organization, his efforts in the Senate made him a "folk hero to the men who formed the Liberty Party" and propelled him into the forefront of the antislavery movement.[1] All across the North, and particularly in Ohio, local abolitionist societies passed resolutions commending Morris. In early May, the annual meeting of the American Anti-Slavery Society also offered its praise, calling him "a voice which they cannot but hear and must respect."[2] The Democratic Party, however, wished to remain a national organization. With this goal in mind, the subject of slavery had to be handled in a way satisfactory to the South. Morris's ideas on slavery were not acceptable to the South, and his position within the party had become tenuous. He would not go quietly.

A few weeks prior to his 1839 reply to Clay, Morris had written Bailey: "I am more and more convinced, that it is necessary for the peace of our country, and for that equal justice for which government was instituted, even independent of any regard for the slave himself, that slavery should come to an end."[3] As a result, Morris had concluded that "resistance to slavery is our duty. It is both a religious and political duty; and the only question is, how shall we best discharge that duty?" While he believed that "we must do it with much forbearance and suffering," we should "carry with us our opposition to slavery into all the social circles of life, talk of it there as it is; protect ourselves against [slavery's] blighting influence in the discharge of our political duties; . . . [and] bestow our suffrages upon no man . . . who will . . . break down the rights of the citizens in the free states to feed the monster slavery."[4] It took Morris only a few weeks to embark on this task.

With the expiration of his term, Morris returned home from Washington and spoke to an overflow crowd at the Hamilton County courthouse in Cincinnati.[5] He continued his attack on the Slave Power and targeted the draconian state fugitive slave law adopted by the Democrat-controlled general assembly earlier that year. Morris's primary audience for the event were members of the local Democratic Party. He chose to announce the meeting only in the local Democratic paper; no mention was made of his plan in the *Philanthropist*. Morris defended his actions in the Senate and "recited the impact of the slavery-power on the liberties of the nation." He paid particular attention to "subservience of the legislature to the dictation of Kentucky" in adopting the Ohio Fugitive Slave Law. Describing Morris's delivery as "perfectly calm and deliberate, almost to a fault," the reporter said "that the boldest passage's . . . containing sentiments which Abolitionists themselves . . . have not generally insisted on" were the best received by the Democratic crowd.[6]

In particular, Morris concluded "that Ohio, under the federal constitution, was not bound to deliver up runaway slaves."[7] In a subsequent letter to the editor of the *Philanthropist*, Morris elaborated on the basis for his conclusion. His analysis had been largely previewed two years earlier in his letter to Senator Smith and in Chase's Matilda argument. He argued that Ohio had the right "as a sovereign State . . . to provide by law the mode and manner of determining a claim to any article of property." In his view, because the Fugitive Slave Clause was located in article IV of the Constitution (not article I) and contained no grant of enforcement power to Congress, the Tenth Amendment barred Congress from compelling state officials to participate in returning escaped slaves. As a result, "neither Ohio nor . . . [any] other State, was bound by the operation or force of any foreign laws to deliver up any runaway slave." Any such law "was unconstitutional; and in violation of the reserved rights and sovereignty of the States."[8]

In reaching the conclusion that Congress lacked the power to compel state officials to enforce the Federal Fugitive Slave Law, Morris (the state's right Democrat) was anticipating Justice Story's analysis three years later in *Prigg v. Pennsylvania*.

The clause is found in the national Constitution, and not in that of any state. It does not point out any state functionaries, or any state action to carry its provisions into effect. The state cannot, therefore, be compelled to enforce them; and it might well be deemed an unconstitutional exercise of the power of interpretation to insist that the states are bound to provide means to carry into effect the duties of the national government nowhere delegated or entrusted to them by the Constitution.[9]

The *Emancipator* described Morris's speech as "the beginning of the fulfillment of [Morris's] promise . . . [to] go home to Ohio and light up the beacon-fires of liberty." The editor recommended that Ohio abolitionists "call for the delivery of his lecture at every principal point of influence in the State."[10]

The *Emancipator* was particularly impressed by the favorable reaction of local Jacksonians to Morris's constitutional views: "If we mistake not, slaveholders will yet have cause to repent that they ousted Thomas Morris from office and thus furnished him the leisure for advocating more extensively and effectively antislavery doctrines and measures. Mr. Morris had energy and influence enough to work a great change in his party."[11] Indeed, what intrigued abolitionists most was Morris's apparent ability to attract Democrats to their cause.[12]

Morris, who took seriously his commitment to gather grassroots support for his defense of civil liberties, spent the summer and fall of 1839 defending abolitionist John Mahan from criminal assault charges[13] and lecturing on the "encroachment of the Slave Power."[14] Strictly abolitionist organizations, however, did not comprise all of his audiences. At one point he conducted a weeklong debate in Clermont County with a Democratic state senator and representative who approved the strengthened Ohio Fugitive Slave law and denied the right of Black Ohioans to petition the general assembly.[15]

Morris's continued antislavery activities angered the main body of Ohio Democrats. His debating Democratic officeholders and attacking the party-sponsored "Black Laws" certainly did not help the fall campaign.[16] Nevertheless, throughout the fall of 1839 canvass, the state Democratic press avoided attacking Morris. Since their success the previous year had been attributed largely to him, the Democrats were reluctant to attack the ex-senator. Instead, they attempted to justify their stringent anti–Black Laws by claiming that the abolitionists wanted to flood Ohio with free Blacks.[17]

98   THE CREATION OF A CRUSADER

After appealing to the prejudices of the state's citizens, the Democrats tried to link the Whigs with the abolitionists.[18]

Morris, however, remained active in Democrat politics in Ohio. In particular, he remained a committed "hard-money" advocate and an inveterate foe of banks. The Democrat governor, William Shannon, was not. When the governor's annual message to the general assembly in December 1839 supported banks, the *Cincinnati Advertiser* called for a public meeting on December 12. Morris addressed the meeting "to explain [his] views on the subject of banking, and point out the mistaken positions and unsoundness of the Governor's . . . and the fallacy of his arguments." The meeting then adopted resolutions recommending that Shannon not be supported for reelection.[19]

Shortly after the December 12 meeting, Hamilton County Democrats held a convention and elected Morris as a delegate to the state nominating convention to be held in January. In Morris's view, his actions regarding Shannon and the Ohio banks triggered the decision at the party's annual state convention to expel him from the party. As soon as the Cincinnati proceedings were known in Columbus, "The bank friends of Gov. Shannon convened together in order to devise the best means to avoid the force . . . of the meeting and secure Gov. Shannon . . . the nomination for re-election." Based on friends' reports, Morris believed he "was viewed with a kind of 'holy horror' by [Shannon's friends]," and they agreed that the charge of abolitionism was the best way to have Morris "and others most obnoxious to the . . . views of the Governor . . . lopped off the democratic party." All of this confirmed for Morris "that the bank power and the slave power are endeavoring to unite their forces to rule the country."[20]

The resounding Democratic victory in the fall 1839 elections cleared the stage for an attack on Morris. Whatever may have been his impact in 1838, obviously he was not necessary for Democratic electoral success in Ohio. Indeed, his antislavery speeches made the charges of a Whig-abolitionist alliance dubious.[21] Thus, as preparations began for the annual state Democratic convention in January 1840, his Democratic opponents moved to force Morris out of the party. Five days before the opening of the convention, Representative Flood introduced the following resolution into the general assembly: "In the opinion of this General Assembly the interference of citizens of one state, in the internal regulations of another, is highly censurable and improper, and we view the unlawful, the unwise and unconstitutional interference of the fanatical abolitionists of the North with the domestic institutions of the southern states as highly inimical, and that is a duty obligatory on all good citizens, to discountenance the abolitionists in their mad, fanatical and revolutionary schemes."[22] These resolutions were then included on the agenda for the state convention.

This move by Democrats in the general assembly prepared the way for the party's convention action on Morris.[23] The Ohio Democratic leadership intended to make antiabolitionism a litmus test of party orthodoxy. On the opening day of the convention, the *Ohio Statesman* supported the Black Laws and attacked Morris. The editor claimed that Democrats had refused to reelect Morris because his "abolition tendencies had endangered the repose and safety of the Union by encouraging war upon the compromise of the Constitution in the Senate of the United States."[24] On the first day of the convention, Thomas Hamer, a bitter enemy of Morris, was elected chairman and, with Morris not in attendance, the convention moved quickly through discussion of bank charters, corporations, and the currency, and nominated Shannon for a second term.

The next day, Flood introduced resolutions similar to the ones he had presented to the general assembly. The new resolutions said that efforts to abolish slavery in the District of Columbia by "organized societies in the free states are hostile to the spirit of the Constitution and destructive to the harmony of the Union." The resolutions concluded that "political abolitionism . . . is only a device for the overthrow of democracy" and "no sound democrat will have part or lot with them."[25] Although these resolutions were greeted with "rounds of applause" from the delegates, Morris rose and attempted to defend the abolitionists. Immediately the members of the convention began to hiss and cough, but he would not yield; with the aid of only one supporter, he stubbornly continued. At the conclusion of his speech, a representative from Montgomery County (Dayton) suggested a method of dealing with Morris. After prefacing his remarks with a general assault on the abolitionists, this delegate described Morris as a "rotten branch that should be lopped off." The convention greeted this remarkable announcement with loud shouts of "Agreed! Agreed! Turn him out of the party!" In the view of at least one Democrat newspaper, "the course taken upon the abolition question was certainly the correct course."[26] Thus amid general joy at being rid of the abolitionist curse, Thomas Morris was read out of the Ohio Democratic Party.

Ohio Democrats had moved to establish party orthodoxy on the slavery question. The national party leadership viewed Southern votes as essential to their retaining power and, with the presidential elections rapidly approaching, wished to calm Southern fears. When the *Ohio Statesman* talked of the compromise on slavery in the Constitution, it merely accepted the Southern pro-slavery constitution argument, an argument that Morris denied. There was no longer any room for antislavery views in the Ohio party. With his ouster, Ohio Democrats entered the fall elections unencumbered in their attacks on the abolitionists. Morris must either "disavow" his principles and "join with the rank mass of servility in doing homage to the slaveholder," or "separate [himself] from them."[27] Rather than surrender his view of the Slave Power, Morris decided to look for a new political home.

As historians have often noted, free Blacks occupied an anomalous position in antebellum America; they were "a third element in a system made for two."[28] In some respects, political abolitionists found themselves in a similar position. Neither of the two national parties could permit antislavery to become part of their party platforms and still retain their Southern members. Consequently, they tacitly agreed to keep discussions of slavery out of politics. That such discussions occasionally crept into the political arena deeply disturbed national figures and generated reactions such as Clay's speech in 1839. The Democrats' refusal to return Morris to the Senate had awakened many abolitionists to the futility of working within the existing structure; his dramatic reply to Clay had given the movement a political imperative. Political abolitionists began to debate the necessity of withdrawing from the existing two-party system and establishing their own political organization.

Western antislavery activists had long supported the idea that the suffrage should be used for their cause. Initially they had attempted to question the various candidates about their position on slavery, but this practice had proven unsuccessful. The most disheartening experience among Ohio abolitionists had been the rejection of Morris by the legislators who most believed owed their election to his influence.[29] By the spring of 1839, the *Philanthropist* advised its readers to "retire from the contest and leave the dough-faced politicians to fight their own battles."[30]

Not all antislavery partisans believed the solution could be found by withdrawing from the contest. Instead, some of those men, impressed by Morris's reply to Clay, with its endorsement of taking abolitionist principles to the ballot box, proposed making independent nominations.[31] At the annual meeting of the American Anti-Slavery Society in May 1839, the merits of political action were debated at length without reaching a definitive conclusion. Instead, the meeting issued a call for another meeting to be held in Albany, New York, for "The thorough discussion of those great principles which lie at the foundation of the abolition enterprise . . . and of the measures which are suited to its accomplishment . . . especially those which relate to the proper exercise of suffrage by citizens of the free states."[32] The *Emancipator* urged the Albany meeting to "devise and adopt. . . . such political measures as are necessary, first to resist the encroachments of slavery upon the rights of the free, and secondly to adopt wide and effective constitutional measures for hastening and aiding the abolition of slavery itself."[33]

In late July 1839, the convention met in Albany. Birney had urged Morris to attend the convention, and Morris had written Charles Denison of his intention to come.[34] He told Denison he was "well pleased that such a convention has been called," and that unless something was done to arrest the progress of the Slave Power, "we shall soon find ourselves, even in the free states . . . governed by the will of the slave-holding interest."[35] The state of his "health and domestic affairs," however, prevented him from attending. Instead, he sent a letter to the convention in which he reminded the delegates that "moral power must operate by means to make it effectual." "Political action is necessary," he said, "to produce a moral Reformation in a nation; . . . surely the ballot box can never be used for a more noble purpose than to restore to any man his inalienable rights."[36] Morris stopped short, however, of advocating independent nominations. In the summer of 1839, he still thought of himself as within the Democratic Party.[37] Thus the calls for political action in his letter should probably be understood as invitations to join his faction of Democrats.

Morris's letter presented something of a conundrum for abolitionists like Garrison, who opposed political action. In March, Garrison had said Morris deserved more than "a statue of gold" for his reply to Clay,[38] a reply that justified abolitionists taking their principles to the ballot box. The influence of Morris's ideas within antislavery circles was now too great for Garrison to ignore. Garrison decided to print the former senator's letter to the Albany convention and then attack his political assumptions: "[Morris] assumes that political action is necessary to produce a moral reformation in a nation. This is to reverse the order of events. Moral reformation is necessary to produce enlightened conscientious, impartial political action."[39] Kraditor argues that Garrison's objection to Morris's position was one of "expediency, not principle."[40] Whether Garrison's concern was merely tactical or principled, Morris's influence had grown to the point that his views could not be ignored. The ex-senator's prominence was such that some leaders of the third-party effort believed that he should be the abolitionists' candidate for president.[41] Morris's continued affiliation with the Ohio Democratic Party ruled out that possibility.

The Albany convention debated the possibility of making independent nominations or forming a new political party for three days, but the idea failed to win majority support. The advocates of separate political action (at this point led principally by Myron Holley) had to settle for a resolution, which called on "every abolitionist who has the right to vote . . . to use his right."[42] Holley and his supporters did not give up. The Executive Committee of the American Anti-Slavery Society called a special meeting in the early fall at Cleveland on the Western Reserve to again discuss political action. This time the vast majority of the delegates were from Ohio. Once again Birney encouraged Morris to attend and believed he would be there.[43] For whatever reason, Morris did not go to Cleveland. Instead, most of the delegates were Whigs from the Reserve, and the presidential aspirations of Ohio's William Henry Harrison were on their minds. After two days of debate, the idea of independent political action was again rejected.[44]

The antislavery organizations in Ohio had consistently opposed the creation of a third party. In May 1838 the society had unanimously adopted a resolution stating that it was "opposed to every measure that looks towards a separate political organization" because among other things, "it would render our motives suspect" and "corrupt their ranks by filling them up with selfish and unprincipled adventurers."[45] The opposition was led by Gamaliel Bailey, editor of the *Philanthropist,* who was also a Harrison supporter. Although trained as a doctor, Bailey had briefly edited the *Methodist Protestant* in Baltimore. He subsequently relocated to Cincinnati and became friends with many of the leaders of Lane Seminary. Under their influence, he participated in the establishment of the Cincinnati Anti-Slavery Society in 1835. When Birney moved the *Philanthropist* to Cincinnati in the spring of 1836, Bailey was named assistant editor of the paper. When Birney left Cincinnati to become corresponding secretary for the American Anti-Slavery Society in New York, Bailey became the editor. By late 1837, he had become the leading spirit of the Ohio State Anti-Slavery Society.[46]

Bailey had editorialized against any "measure that looks towards a separate political organization" and called the idea of separate nominations "wrong in principle and inexpedient."[47] He had not changed his mind by the time of the Cleveland meeting: "To this project we have always been strenuously opposed, and we have seen nothing as yet to change our minds."[48] After the results of the convention became known, Bailey triumphantly reported that "this must be taken as a clear indication of the sentiments of the abolitionists of this state on the project of forming a separate political party. As a body, *they are opposed to it.*"[49]

Holley refused to give up after his defeat at Cleveland and organized another meeting at Warsaw, New York, on November 15, 1839.[50] At this gathering the advocates for separate political action finally had their way. The meeting nominated James G. Birney for president and Julius LeMoyne for vice president. The lengthy string of conventions had made the lack of consensus within antislavery ranks on the advisability of creating a third party obvious, however, and both men promptly declined.[51] In Birney's case his decision was also based on his "personal sensitivity." As he explained in a letter to Holley, Birney had not seen in any abolition newspaper "the slightest commendation of his nomination." Instead, several leaders of the political action movement had informed Birney that they thought Morris (or perhaps William Jay) would be more effective.[52] But the men pushing for a third party simply would not let the idea die. Throughout the winter they argued for their ideas in the antislavery press.

In Ohio, Bailey actively worked to stop the movement. Following the Cleveland meeting, he published a list of eight reasons he opposed independent nominations. He feared it would divide abolitionists, bring unprincipled office seekers to the antislavery ranks, alienate abolitionist clergymen, and that the major parties would combine to crush the movement. As a result, no party based on a single idea could succeed or survive.[53] Despite the opposition, the third-party evangelists succeeded in arranging still another convention to discuss the matter in Albany, New York, in early April 1840. Without one representative from the Northwest and almost half of the delegates abstaining, the Convention, by the slenderest of majorities, again nominated Birney for president. This time Birney accepted the nomination, and the smoldering debate over political action burst into flame.[54]

Bailey continued to oppose the movement. He urged support for Harrison throughout the spring, at one point telling Birney that he was "sorry— deeply sorry" that Birney had been nominated and with astonishing naïveté claimed that Harrison's election would cause Democrats "most likely to reinstate Tom. Morris and begin to manifest a most ardent attachment to free principles."[55] Bailey "completely dominated" the Ohio Anti-Slavery Society meeting at Massillon in May 1840, which again rejected the idea of independent nominations.[56] A month later, however, Bailey abruptly changed his mind. Perhaps influenced by Harrison's earlier statements in favor of slavery and critical of abolitionists, Bailey first recommended that Ohio abolitionists not vote, or if they must vote, cast their ballot for Birney.[57] Not until July 7 did Bailey recommend voting for Birney.[58]

Following the April convention in Albany, the American Anti-Slavery Society met in May in New York City. When Abby Kelly, a Quaker feminist Garrisonian, was seated on the business committee, the Tappans and their supporters walked out. That evening, thirty anti-Garrison leaders, meeting at Lewis Tappan's home, formed the American & Foreign Anti-Slavery Society and adopted a constitution he had prepared weeks earlier. The new organization's constitution explicitly denied women voting power in the association and shunned political action. In the words of Bertram Wyatt-Brown, "the new Society began as a museum of old abolitionists." Not only had the Garrisonians refused to follow, but many of the leaders of the push for a third party distanced themselves from the new organization as well.[59] Although he was not present, Morris's national prominence caused the leaders of the new organization to name him to the Executive Committee.[60]

Throughout this infighting among abolitionists, Morris had not spoken publicly on the independent nomination question. By September 1840, however, when Ohio antislavery forces again met (this time outside Cincinnati in Hamilton County) to consider again their response to the Birney's nomination, he had decided to support the new organization. In what the *Philanthropist* called "the strongest speech we have ever heard from him," the ex-senator urged "support of the resolution recommending Birney." According to the press report, "He demonstrated the absolute necessity of resorting to consistent, single-eyed political action for the overthrow of slavery and denounced the policy of doing nothing. As a free citizen he was bound to vote, and to vote right, and called upon every free citizen not stay home, but to go to the polls and vote for liberty."[61] Although Morris admitted supporting Van Buren's "general policy," he lashed out with the "severest denunciations against the pro-slavery subservience of both him and his party."[62] Convinced that the Democrats would never reject the Slave Power, Morris cast his lot with the third party.

Historians have attributed the outcome of this convention to several men. Birney's son thought Joshua Leavitt, a representative of the New York abolitionists, was "the efficient cause" that changed the minds of the delegates.[63] Undoubtedly the presence of the editor of the *Emancipator* and a nationally recognized leader of the third-party movement aided those supporting Birney. Leavitt, however, spoke only in support of the general resolution that characterized slavery as "the paramount political question." The resolution passed overwhelmingly with only three dissenting votes. Given the closely divided vote on the support of Birney, it is unlikely that Leavitt's speech (which focused on the economic consequences of slavery and the Slave Power with which Ohio abolitionists were already familiar) supporting a noncontroversial resolution significantly impacted the outcome.[64] For his part, Leavitt, after reporting that support for Birney's nomination passed by three votes, noted only that "the elite of the Ohio Abolitionists was at the convention, and the elite of the elite goes with us fully," and that Bailey had been converted.[65]

Bailey's conversion to independent nominations was crucial to the outcome of the meeting. Despite his long-standing support for Harrison coupled with his basic Whig sympathies, by September 1840 Bailey was ready to support Birney.[66] He served as chair of the arrangements and publicized the call for the Hamilton convention in the *Philanthropist*. He also led the convention's business committee, which prepared the resolutions in favor of Birney and political action.[67] As the debate unfolded, Bailey also made a significant tactical contribution to the outcome of the convention. Morris had been scheduled to speak at another meeting on the evening of the first day of the convention. When he asked if the convention would adjourn early that day so he could fulfill his commitment, the opponents of the Birney nomination attempted to use the request as an opportunity to regroup and defeat the resolution supporting Birney's candidacy. Bailey realized the opening Morris had created for the opponents and quickly persuaded Morris to break the speaking engagement and remain at the convention.[68]

Beyond the successful maneuver to avoid the long recess, Bailey's most critical contribution to the convention's decision to support Birney was his selection of the location of the meeting. Regardless of the speeches and efforts of the leaders, most of the delegates who attended both the Massillon and Hamilton conventions voted as they had in May. The difference in the outcome was the presence of a new group: the antislavery Democrats who came with Morris. These supporters proved to be "the decisive element in reversing the balance of forces that had prevailed at the Massillon meeting."[69] Thus locating the convention outside the Western Reserve Whig stronghold, thereby allowing Morris and rank-and-file

Southern Ohio antislavery Democrats to attend, proved decisive. Leavitt, in his report of the convention, specifically recognized the presence and consistency of these "gentlemen" with the "ex-Senator as their head."[70]

In the days leading up to the Hamilton Convention, Bailey had explicitly sought to attract Democrat support. Three weeks prior to the meeting he had published a letter from Morris describing the events leading to his being read out of the Democratic Party in January. The letter was critical of Van Buren's record on slavery and the Ohio party's position on banks and currency.[71] Bailey's stated goal in publishing the letter was to influence Democrats to renounce their party. More than a third (22) of the votes (the final vote was 57 to 54 in favor of supporting the Birney nomination) cast to reverse the decision made at Massillon came from Hamilton County attendees, many of whom, as Leavitt acknowledged, followed Morris. Bailey's early biographer acknowledged this, although he then attempted to give the editor credit for swaying the convention.[72]

In reality most of the members of the Hamilton convention had attended the meetings in Cleveland and Massillon. Few changed from the way they had voted earlier. Those who did change were probably more influenced by the views of Morris, whose "long experience as a politician" in Ohio entitled "his judgement to much consideration."[73] Undoubtedly Bailey's change of heart and Leavitt's support gave impetus to the meeting, but the decision to move into the political arena in 1840 to further antislavery would not have occurred without the presence of Morris and the disenchanted Southern Ohio Democrats who agreed with him at the Hamilton meeting.[74] His prominent role in the creation of the Ohio Liberty Party provided the Whig press with the opportunity to tie the new party to Morris's hard-money views. To them, it seemed clear that "the Locofocos and the ultra abolitionists of Ohio [had] formed a coalition to oppose Harrison."[75]

The Whig attacks on the Hamilton convention's decision to support Birney persuaded Morris and Bailey that a defense of the convention's actions was needed. Three weeks after the convention, Morris led a public meeting at the courthouse in Cincinnati to "explain and justify the proceedings of the convention" and describe "the reasons which induced it to adopt the resolutions" in support of Birney.[76] Bailey, in covering the courthouse meeting, then defended Morris. Noting that "a few persons are fond of charging [Morris] with a sinister design" in his actions, Bailey said Morris had "always been an antislavery man" even "before there were any modern abolitionists to back him." After his defeat for reelection to the Senate, Morris was given "the brand of abolitionist" and "proscribed by the leaders" of the Democratic Party. Bailey claimed Morris no longer took any "part in the political movements of either party," but neglected "no opportunity of . . . vindicating the character of abolitionists . . . [despite] the groundless suspicions to which his position may subject him." To Bailey, such suspicions "evince as little sagacity as generosity."[77]

Starting late and with little political experience, the Liberty Party in Ohio had no chance of success. Morris made several speeches in the two months following the Hamilton convention, and Bailey moved the *Philanthropist* behind the Birney nomination, but they could not overcome the din of "Tippecanoe and Tyler, too."[78] Birney's departure to attend the World Antislavery Convention in England, and his stay there throughout the campaign, certainly did not aid the Liberty effort, but his presence at home would not have made much difference.[79] Veteran political observers had never seen such excitement. Samuel Medary, the editor of the *Ohio Statesman,* thought "every man, woman and child preferred politics to anything else."[80] Caught up in the surge of partisanship generated by torchlight parades and hard cider, few people heard the weak voice of the Liberty men.

As the votes were counted, it became clear that Harrison and the Whigs had won a sweeping victory. The antislavery candidates, attacked by some of their former allies within the Whig Party, polled only 903 votes, or .3 percent of the total cast in Ohio.[81] Bailey, basing his conclusions on correspondence with abolitionists across the state, reported "that a majority on our ticket was composed of democrats."[82] The men who would later lead the Liberty Party in Ohio—Salmon Chase, Leicester King, and Edward Wade—were kept all in the Whig ranks by the prospect of winning the national election. The burden of the Ohio campaign had fallen almost entirely on Morris, who had spent the fall "enlightening the minds of his Democratic friends on the antislavery question."[83] Thus in crediting former Democrats with casting the bulk of Liberty votes, Bailey was probably correct. Regardless of the prior affiliation of their voters, the new party had failed to attract support even among acknowledged abolitionists. Less than one in twenty of Ohio's abolitionists supported Birney.[84]

Morris believed that it required "very little sagacity and foresight to discover that cause" of Harrison's success. The reason for the outcome of the election was clear: "the consolidated action and influence of the slave power in the country." Morris thought Harrison was committed to slavery as a matter of "principle," and that the Slave Power would use his support to "attempt to force an acknowledgement of the justice of its bloody code from the freeman of this country." Convinced of its dominance, he felt that the Slave Power would "spurn all restraints and bid defiance to every principle of justice and law that obstruct[ed] its onward progress." The election of 1840 fit into that pattern of events that Morris had seen for the past two years: his defeat for reelection, the Senate's endorsement of Calhoun's resolutions, Clay's capitulation to the South, and his own ouster from the Democratic Party. Although he remained "certain that the principles of justice and right [had] a strong and lasting hold on the hearts of a vast majority of the American people, he was just as convinced that the Slave Power was a growing and continuing threat."[85]

CHAPTER 8

A Torrent of Eloquence and Argument

Morris's speech to the Senate in February 1839 had given impetus to the national third-party drive. The treatment he had received from the Democrats had confirmed for Ohio abolitionists the impossibility of working within the two established parties. He had directly spurred the organization of the Liberty Party in Ohio with an impassioned speech at the critical September 1840 Hamilton convention. To the nascent Liberty Party, Morris had given vitally needed political experience and leadership. Most of the men who traveled with him on his early stumping tours were ministers—moral agitators, not politicians.[1] The political experience and prominence that had entitled "his judgement much consideration" in the formation of the Ohio Liberty Party gave him a prominent role in leadership of the organization.

Morris spent much of the fall of 1840 speaking on behalf of the Liberty Party ticket. As the campaign began to wind down, he started thinking about the future of political antislavery. While he remained certain the abolitionists would "eventually free us from the curse of Slavery, . . . correct information as to the operation and effect of this system of wickedness upon our moral as well as political condition [was] yet needed in many parts of the country."[2] Drawing on his experience in the Senate, in late October Morris proposed that "each state choose a delegate to attend at the City of Washington during the next session of Congress." This group would collect information on slavery, as well as monitor the actions of Congress and public men and report to their states. In effect, he was proposing the creation of an antislavery lobbying operation in the capital. He asked Bailey to seek reaction from other antislavery societies.[3]

The reaction to Morris's proposal was immediate and positive. The *Philanthropist* reported nearly unanimous support from around the country. Leavitt at the *Emancipator* was particularly enthused by the plan. In their enthusiasm, however, supporters lost sight of Morris's goal. He had recommended a single representative from each state to inform and lobby; proponents seemed to understand the proposal as creating a shadow Congress with apportioned delegates and, apparently, a policy-making agenda. Morris tried to bring the discussion back to his simpler proposal, but the misplaced understanding of his recommendation and imminent convening of Congress caused the idea to be shelved.[4]

Leavitt, however, realized the merit of Morris's original idea. Less than a month after announcing it was too late to implement the plan for the current session of Congress, Leavitt went to Washington. Over the next five years, Leavitt, occasionally joined by Theodore Weld, established the "Abolitionist Lobby" and worked to represent antislavery. His "lobbying efforts provided party members and others valuable information concerning congressional actions relating to slavery" as well as mobilized "an antislavery insurgency in the House of Representatives which ultimately succeeded" in eliminating the gag rule. His biographer concluded that Leavitt's efforts constituted "one of his most important contributions to the cause."[5]

Following their defeat in the fall, the Ohio antislavery forces wasted little time in reorganizing and strengthening party operations. The Hamilton convention in September had accepted the necessity of an independent nomination in the presidential race. No nominations for any state office, however, had been made. Within weeks of the presidential election, Western Reserve third-party supporters met at Akron and nominated Morris for governor.[6] Several other county societies urged that a state convention be held to confirm the decision made at Hamilton to make independent nominations. By early December the State Executive Committee called for a meeting in Columbus on January 20, 1841. In calling the convention, two goals were stated: (1) "reestablish harmony and confidence among Abolitionists," and (2) "to agree upon some rational, effective plan of antislavery political action." In particular, the meeting would consider whether they should nominate candidates for "Governor, members of Congress, and members of the General Assembly."[7]

Two weeks before the state convention in Columbus, a large meeting in Cincinnati was held to discuss the congressional gag rules and slavery in the District of Columbia. The meeting was not called by Liberty Party supporters but "men unconnected with abolition societies, and whom we [Bailey] are far from regarding abolitionists, controlled the meeting and its measures." In the words of the *Philanthropist,* the leaders "were substantial citizens . . . [of] whom it were ridiculous to charge with visionary notions or excessive enthusiasm."[8]

Although the weather was not encouraging ("a sleety dripping night"), the courthouse was full. The meeting selected a Business Committee, which reported several resolutions that concluded it was "the duty of Congress to take immediate measures for the total prohibition of Slavery and the Slave Trade in the District of Columbia," and that the gag rules "violat[ed] one of the most sacred provisions of the Constitution" and "ought forthwith to be rescinded and abandoned."[9] Following the report of the resolutions, the chair of the Business Committee spoke in support. He was followed by the pastor of the First Congregational Church of Cincinnati. He objected to the measures because "it would agitate the South, and interfere with its rights." The meeting then "called for" Morris to speak. He "spoke with great earnestness and force . . . going over the whole ground." Following Morris's speech, the meeting unanimously approved the resolutions directed at the gag rule, slavery, and the slave trade in the District.[10]

The meeting's call for the immediate abolition of slavery in the District of Columbia was significant, but Bailey did not think it went far enough. The resolutions failed to recognize that "the federal government is wielded by the slave-power, and the policy and politics of the nation controlled by its despotic will." Not only did the meeting fail to recognize the reach of the Slave Power, but the participants' "church-connections with slaveholders, their business relations to the South, [their] silence . . . on the subject of slavery in the states, and [their] unthinking opposition . . . [to] abolitionism," gave "countenance and support to the practice of slave holding."[11] Bailey's Slave Power language had been learned from Morris, but his critique of the national government was not likely to sway an audience made up predominantly of Whigs who had just elected Cincinnati resident William Henry Harrison to the presidency.

Bailey was unable to attend the state Liberty Party convention two weeks later in Columbus but gave explicit instructions about its organization. More importantly, the week before the delegates met, he editorialized in favor of early nominations. He hypothesized that the other parties might add these candidates to their own tickets out of self-preservation. Noting that he had seen many abolitionists "for whom under no circumstances would I vote," Bailey concluded that abolitionists should only nominate "candidates of good moral character, fair repute, and sound understanding." With these admonitions, the delegates gathered in Columbus.[12]

The meeting lasted nearly three days. The organizers had sought the use of the Ohio House of Representatives chamber for its evening meetings, but the House refused. As a result, all sessions were held at the courthouse with a standing room–only crowd, which included several state senators and representatives. The first day proceeded with debate only on a resolution declaring that slavery was using the power of the federal government "to extend its domination and advance its interest at the expense of the interests of free labor" and "operated most injuriously on . . . the free states and on the domestic and foreign policy of the nation." The resolution was adopted after a "thrilling and splendid" speech by Morris in support.[13]

The next day several additional resolutions were presented. They all passed easily until the tenth, which recommended that "Abolitionists nominate candidates for office in all places where they are not perfectly assured that one or both parties will nominate candidates for whom they can . . . vote before the nominating convention of these parties have acted." The debate continued until after dark. Finally, "just before the adoption of this resolution, Mr. Morris poured upon [the meeting] such a torrent of eloquence and argument as [the secretary of the convention] had seldom heard equaled." According to the report of the meeting, Morris's speech "was followed with a deafening call for the question." The resolution calling for the nomination of a full slate of Liberty Party candidates was adopted 118 to 16.[14] Morris, at Bailey's suggestion, was also scheduled to deliver the featured evening address. Before a packed house, Morris delivered "one of his best efforts, and with overpowering force, demonstrated the tyranny of slavery over this whole nation." Not all his listeners, however, were so favorably impressed. During his speech, "several fellows of the base sort" threw "rotten apples and the like" at Morris.[15]

The first few weeks of 1841 had been a heady time for Morris. His speech describing the predations of the Slave Power had been well received by nonabolitionists in Cincinnati. He had helped shepherd the decision to create the Liberty Party through the Columbus convention and again had his attack on the Slave Power enthusiastically received (at least by abolitionists). The rotten apples he had dodged the last night in Columbus, however, foretold worse things to come.

Although Liberty Party support was almost nonexistent in Montgomery County,[16] Morris stopped in Dayton on his return to Cincinnati following the Columbus convention. Two years earlier, after Morris's reply to Clay, a group of Dayton citizens "attached to both political parties" had written Morris to compliment him on "the honest and independent course" he had followed while in the Senate. The writers were particularly impressed by Morris "firmly maintaining the honor and dignity of your state against Southern aggression and Northern servility." They asked Morris to select a time to speak in Dayton on "these important questions."[17] Morris had responded by thanking them for the invitation, and assuring them of his "efforts against the monstrous demands of the slave-holding power."[18] Although he promised to let the group know when he could come to Dayton, he apparently had never set a time. Morris decided to take advantage of the opportunity now.

The Montgomery County courthouse had been reserved and handbills were posted announcing that Morris would speak. Upon his arrival at the courthouse, he found a mob intent on preventing him from speaking. The mob took over the meeting, read a series of resolutions "denouncing abolition and any attempt Mr. Morris might make to speak." Others "stood upon the clerk's desk . . . calling for that damned scoundrel that had come there to make a disturbance." For his own safety, he remained in the crowd, away from the podium, and ultimately left without being recognized. Foiled in their plan to assault Morris, the mob rampaged through the home of a Black Dayton resident. When the local newspapers attributed the mob's actions to the agitation of the abolitionists, Morris responded publicly. Although the mob resulted from local bigotry, Morris always attributed the hostility to Southern instigators. He believed the mob was the result of "the influences of the slaveholders, no matter whether they reside in the slave states or amongst us." In short, "the slave power has commanded it, and the mob in Dayton are its executive officers." For him, the Dayton experience was simply another example of the Slave Power's influence.[19]

Morris, however, was not content to simply blame the Slave Power for the mob; he decided to remind his readers of Black Ohio residents' right to equal and exact justice.

I contend that the constitution of this state, as well as common justice and humanity, secures to the black person in Ohio ALL THE RIGHTS which belong to the white man except those expressly taken away by the constitution itself; that the establishment of justice was the first and primary object of the instrument, . . . [and] that ALL MEN ARE BORN EQUALLY FREE AND INDEPENDENT.[20]

To Morris, "all of these important rights are as fully and forcibly secured to the colored as the white man." For him, Ohio's Black Laws were not only unjust, they were unconstitutional by virtue of the Ohio constitution's bill of rights. As he had often stated before, "it is not color, but slavery which disgraces and injures the black man."[21]

Following the January state convention, Morris devoted himself to strengthening Ohio abolitionists' commitment to political action and establishing effective local political units. He spoke at numerous local meetings and helped to bring several new members into the party.[22] Tyler's succession to the presidency aided the recruitment of additional supporters. Many antislavery Whigs could not back a slaveholding president and joined the ranks of the Ohio Anti-Slavery Society.[23] By the time of the state society meeting in the summer of 1841, the *Emancipator* found "the revolution in sentiment among Ohio abolitionists since last fall . . . surprising." Indeed, "the great mass of the abolitionists present . . . were in favor of the independent political action."[24]

Morris's influence within the Liberty Party and demand for him as a stump speaker was solidified by the action of the first truly national (that is, Northern) Liberty convention. The convention met on May 12, 1841, in New York City to make nominations for the 1844 elections. Delegates from thirteen Northern states (including three from Ohio) were present. After deciding unanimously to proceed with nominations, the convention again nominated Birney for the presidency. The delegates then selected Morris as their vice presidential candidate. In explaining why the convention had abandoned Thomas Earle (the 1840 vice presidential nominee) and selected Morris, the *Emancipator* noted that "many . . . thought it material that the North West . . . be represented" and "some were influenced" by the thought of Morris presiding over the Senate. Moreover, after Birney's strange performance in the preceding election, many of the more practical delegates wanted someone with political experience on the ticket. The convention also adopted a plan of organization for the Liberty Party, appointed a central committee, and resolved to meet again in two years.[25]

In an address issued to explain the party's views, the delegates drew heavily on Morris's ideas. As a point of departure, the convention found "the government of the United States, as a matter of existing fact, is under the control of the slave power." After cataloging a long list of consequences (particularly relating to slavery's ties to the Bank of the United States), the address declined to take positions on tariffs, independent treasury, or public lands. Instead, the address claimed that all political parties had "paramount objects" and identified the Liberty Party objects as "emancipation—abolition—human freedom." The delegates concluded "that by the abolition of slavery . . . (or at least by the overthrow of the ascendancy of the slave power)," the economic turmoil of the past several years could be ended.[26]

At the same time that the national party was gathered in New York, the Hamilton County antislavery organization met outside Cincinnati. Over three hundred people gathered to nominate candidates for local offices and to hear Morris speak. He picked up where he had left off in his February letter to the mayor of Dayton: "We live in a country where much is said of Constitutional liberty—of equal and exact justice to all men," and then asked "is justice meted out to the slave and is this the land of the free for the poor oppressed negro?" In response to the claim "that the Constitution of the United States countenances slavery," Morris thought, "as well might it be said that it countenances murder." He believed that "the slave is not degraded because he is black." Instead, the slave was degraded because to Calhoun and others, the "slave and labor have alike been considered beneath the white man." Slavery had contaminated "every stream of justice and social rights." He would not vote for anyone who was "not willing to let the oppressed go free."[27]

When news of the New York City nominations reached Ohio, the *Philanthropist* was enthusiastic: "We need not say that we shall sustain this nomination. This our friends might know from our past course. We are glad that the movement is made at the early period. . . . The nomination will serve as a standard around which to rally the friends of Universal Liberty."[28] This enthusiasm carried over to the anniversary meeting of the Ohio Anti-Slavery Society three weeks later. Although the delegates decided not to discuss the Liberty Party during the society meeting, a party convention met immediately upon the adjournment of the anniversary session and overwhelmingly resolved to "sustain the nomination of James G. Birney and Thomas Morris as candidates for the President and Vice-President."[29] Morris participated in both meetings, spoke frequently, and offered a resolution recommending antislavery nominations in all Ohio Senate and Representative races. In the resolution, Morris reiterated his call for "equal and exact justice" for all and articulated his understanding of the Liberty Party's principles. Any candidate nominated by the party was committed, "if elected, in all of his official acts [to] use his influence and give his votes in opposition to slavery, in favor of equal rights and the establishment of impartial justice to all men." The resolution was adopted unanimously.[30] Throughout the remainder of his life, Morris never deviated from this understanding of the goals of political antislavery.

When he returned to Cincinnati following the summer antislavery meetings, Morris found that John Brough, one of the state legislators who had worked to defeat Morris and adopt the anti–Black laws of 1838 and was now editor of the Democratic *Cincinnati Enquirer,* was whipping up "resentment toward free Black people and white abolitionists" by running "articles claiming that the city's commercial fortunes were being damaged by its growing reputation as a haven for enslaved people seeking freedom."[31] Finally, on August 10 he published an article "complaining that the city was 'overrun with free blacks' who took jobs from 'white citizens' and lived by plunder when they were not working."[32]

The next day, Morris began his part in the fall campaign of 1841 by publishing a lengthy address "To the Democratic Portion of the People of Ohio." He told the Democrats the "aim of Democracy "is equal and exact justice to men of all climes and colors," and that "slavery [was] the most heinous offense against justice that man can possibly commit." Support for slavery and failure to apply the equal justice standard to free Blacks struck at the freedom of all.

> My first principle of democracy is, "ESTABLISH JUSTICE." This is declared to be the chief end and object of our Constitution; and if we do not this, in equal and exact measure to all men, our government is a mockery. He that will not do justice to a black man, will do injustice to a white man if he can make gain by the act; and he that will not do justice where it is most required, and will not endeavor to establish it where it is most trodden down, will never do justice in lesser matters.[33]

Morris thought it clear that "the slave power in our country degrades labor," and that "Negro slavery as it exist[ed] in the United States [was] at war" with Democratic principles. With the nation still feeling the effects of the Panic of 1837, he blamed these monetary problems on the failure of the Slave Power to repay their debts to Northern banks. Saying that there were "thousands if not tens of thousands in Ohio" who felt as he did, Morris urged the Democrats to oppose slavery "by every legal and constitutional means."[34] The *Emancipator* reprinted the entirety of Morris's address on the front page of its November 4, 1841, edition. With the lack of a presidential race to stir party loyalty, Liberty leaders felt they had a chance to win converts from the existing major parties.

Morris's prior prominence within the Ohio Democratic Party made him the ideal person to further an emerging view among national Liberty leaders that Jacksonians were potential fertile ground for third-party converts. The party's focus on human rights and equality fit well with the Liberty Party's attack on slavery. Morris's appeal had made the necessity of extending "equal and exact justice" to Blacks explicit. While the majority of professed abolitionists were Whigs, many Liberty leaders found the Whig position on slavery "hypocritical and deceptive, making empty gestures toward the abolitionists while standing behind the slave interests in supporting the gag laws in Congress." In retrospect, these beliefs were naïve, but Morris's transformation appeared to provide some prospect of success. Launching the fall campaign in Ohio with a direct appeal to Democrats made sense.[35]

Morris followed his published appeal to Democrats by attending a joint Indiana-Ohio political antislavery meeting in Eaton, Ohio. His speech at Eaton "demonstrated the fearful results of the reckless encroachments of the Slaveocracy, its destructive influences on the liberties of the American people . . . and the danger of [it] uprooting and overturning our republican institutions." In reporting to the *Philanthropist,* the president of the meeting thought it "but sheer justice . . . to remark, that judging from the plaudits, that [Morris's] speech carried conviction to all present. Indeed, it surpassed any political speech [he] ever heard."[36]

From September until early October, Morris traveled and spoke constantly for the Liberty Party. At county conventions, torchlight marches, and courthouse meetings, he assailed the Slave Power and attributed the plight of the country to their political ascendency. The continual requests for Morris from Liberty Party leaders, not only in Ohio but adjoining states

118   THE CREATION OF A CRUSADER

as well, illustrated clearly his position of influence and leadership.[37] These efforts exhausted Morris; by the beginning of October, he was ill and confined to bed.[38] Despite the labors of the new party, most voters remained in the ranks of the major parties. The Ohio Liberty Party did, however, manage to increase its total vote to 2,748, an increase of 300 percent.[39]

As the campaign ended, Morris received an inquiry from Bailey. A Philadelphia correspondent had asked Bailey to sound Morris out on the prospect for mounting a constitutional challenge to slavery in the District of Columbia. Morris had his reply published in the *Philanthropist*. Before turning to the specific question asked, Morris announced, "my opinion has long been settled, that by the constitution of the United States, Slavery by the legal force and fair construction of those instruments, is forever abolished throughout our country."[40] As he had told Ohio Democrats considering his reelection to the Senate in 1838, while Congress had no power over slavery in the states, Congress did not have "the power to create a system of slavery where it does not exist."[41] The question of slavery in the District of Columbia, then, was an easy one:

> It seems to me to be a clear position, that the Constitution of the United States, gives to the Supreme Court jurisdiction in all cases where the liberty of a human being is violated or restrained. Negroes by the Constitution of the United States, are not recognized as property, but as persons, as human beings, as men; and as such cannot be made property by any acts of Congress. If this be so, and it seems to be self-evident, then the Supreme Court has jurisdiction, derived from the Constitution, over the question of Slavery, not only in the District of Columbia, but throughout the United States, in all places over which Congress has exclusive power of Legislation.[42]

The senator, who five years earlier had found it inexpedient for Congress to abolish slavery in the District, now concluded that slavery was unconstitutional there. The question was no longer Congress's power to abolish slavery but its power to establish it. As Chase would later tell Lewis Tappan, "all practically important constitutional positions for antislavery men . . . are the logical consequences of this."[43]

Morris had told the Senate in 1836 that the Constitution did not recognize slaves, only persons, and that slavery could exist only as a result of positive state law. As a result, Congress had no power to enact slavery. The linchpin of his constitutional argument was the absence of any recognition in the Constitution of the possibility of property in man. These views had become antislavery dogma. Morris, however, had continued to think about the consequences of the Fifth Amendment on congressional power regarding slavery. By 1841, he had concluded that not only had Congress not been given any power to make men property, but the Fifth Amendment's prohibition on congressional action taking away a "person's" liberty affirmatively barred any congressional action creating slavery.[44] The act of Congress in 1801 continuing the laws of Virginia and Maryland in the District,[45] to the extent they created slavery, were therefore unconstitutional. On the eve of the Ohio Liberty Party Convention, the *Emancipator*, in sharing Morris's views, announced to abolitionists across the nation that slavery in the District was "unconstitutional."[46]

Salmon Chase had first become associated with antislavery during the riots surrounding Birney's efforts to publish the *Philanthropist* in Cincinnati. He had represented Birney in litigation arising from the riots and later in claims regarding the fugitive slave Matilda.[47] Although he was identified with Birney, Chase consistently denied holding any "abolitionist" views and remained active within the Whig Party in southern Ohio. As Morris and Bailey were preparing for the September 1840 Ohio Hamilton County antislavery meeting, which supported Birney's nomination, Chase refused Bailey's request to sign the call for the meeting and told his friends that he was "not willing to take part in the third-party movement."[48] He supported Harrison in 1840,[49] and ran as a Whig candidate for local office in Hamilton County in 1841. Although he subsequently claimed to be "one of the first who took an active part in organizing the Liberty party in Ohio," not until his defeat in the fall 1841 local election, Tyler's succession to the presidency, and the extremely violent Cincinnati race riots in September did Chase decide to join the Liberty ranks.[50] By November 1841, he was publicly calling (along with Morris) for a state Liberty Party Convention.[51]

Chase joined the Liberty Party because he felt that it had a chance of ultimate electoral success.[52] If this were to be the case, the party would obviously have to expand its base of support dramatically. Chase believed the quickest method of doing this was by toning down the party's rhetoric of abolitionism and "purging the Liberty Party of its abolitionist label."[53] To achieve his goal, Chase enlisted the aid of Gamaliel Bailey. Chase and Bailey had become friends and knew each other "very well" before Chase joined the Liberty Party. They shared an "intense religiosity" and "a penchant for learned discussion," which had drawn them together.[54] Bailey had initially "hoped the Liberty Party would draw Chase . . . into abolition-ism. Instead . . . Bailey . . . moved away from immediatism and assumed [views] similar to Chase's in the linking abolitionist goals to non-abolitionist political means."[55] By now Bailey thought of himself as the "independent tribune" of all the antislavery people in Ohio. This position resulted from the departure of Ohio Garrisonians from the Ohio Anti-Slavery Society and Bailey assuming the proprietorship of the *Philanthropist* from Birney's son.[56] Bailey maintained working relationships with both organizations and the Liberty Party.

Following its gains in the fall elections of 1841, the Ohio Liberty Party met in late December to nominate a candidate for governor in 1842. The December 1841 Ohio Liberty Party Convention was again held in Colum-bus with more than two hundred attendees (including "the leaders of both parties who were anxious lookers on")[57] and proved to be "the defining event in Ohio Liberty Party history."[58] The convention nominated Leices-ter King, a former Whig state senator and judge, for governor.[59] Chase and Morris were appointed to the Business Committee, which drew up the resolutions to be adopted by the convention. Chase was charged with writing the party's platform and address, while Morris composed a memo-rial to the state legislature, "setting forth the past policy of the state in re-gard to the subject of slavery [that is, the Fugitive Slave Law and the Black Laws] and praying for such legislation as may be deemed necessary."[60]

Bailey had consistently sought to keep the state abolition society and the Liberty Party separate. To some extent, this effort was the result of self-interest, but Bailey also felt there was a principled basis for the separation. Abolition sought the elimination of slavery across the nation, including within the states where it already existed. Because Congress lacked the power to abolish slavery in the states, however, political action could not achieve that goal. Only moral suasion could be used to achieve abolition.[61] By the late fall of 1841, Chase had come to agree with this view of the ap-propriate reach of political action.[62] In his hands this generally accepted proposition of the federal consensus and Morris's constitutional theories became the basis for the Liberty Party's platform.

Chase's address drew heavily on Morris's understanding of the local, positive law basis for slavery (which Chase had previously used in the Matilda case), the need for equal justice, the absence of congressional power to establish slavery, and the abuses of the Slave Power. Emphasiz-ing that the Constitution "no where recognizes the idea that men can be the subjects of property," the address argued that "the Constitution found slavery, and left it, a State institution—the creature and dependent of State law."[63] This insight, articulated by Morris first in 1836 in responding to Calhoun's Incendiary Publications Bill and repeated on scores of occasions in the intervening five years, became "the constitutional and political heart of the Liberty position."[64]

The address acknowledged no power over slavery in the states but (echoing Morris's reply to Clay) claimed that political action was necessary nevertheless: "Because SLAVERY HAS OVER LEAPED ITS PRESCRIBED LIMITS AND USURPED CONTROL OF THE NATIONAL GOVERNMENT. It is strictly a State institution, but it has arrogated to itself a national character. . . . [I]t has unwarrantably assumed control of the general government . . . for its own purpose."[65] "This power thus hostile to free institutions, free labor and to freedom itself, is the Slave Power." In words taken from Morris's Jacksonian principles, Chase concluded that the Slave Power had "established an Aristocracy in the country, constituted the slaveholders a privileged order," and "prostituted the energies and resources of the nation to the vilest of purposes, without constitutional authority."[66]

From these principles, Chase drew what seemed to be the logical conclusion. The political solution to this problem was "the absolute and unqualified divorce of the government from slavery."[67] At the same time the address proposed repealing (1) the "oppressive laws which degrade the black man"; (2) securing "to every man a speedy and impartial trial by jury in all cases where life or liberty shall be in question"; (3) and securing "to the whole population of the state, the benefits of general education; a sound currency; an adequate market; and an economical . . . state government."[68] What the address did not seek was emancipation of any slave. In emphasizing the threat of the Slave Power, the Ohio address resembled the address adopted by the New York City nominating convention, but in denying any interest in abolition, the Ohio platform appeared to discard the "paramount objects" of the Liberty Party.[69] In Bailey's words, the address explained "the essential difference between . . . political antislavery action, and organized abolitionism." Although abolitionists supported the party, the party should not be abolitionist.[70]

The words of the address—powerful and eloquent—came from Chase's pen. The ideas came from Morris. To outside observers, this seemed clear. The Democrat *Cincinnati Enquirer* recognized "the talented character of the Convention," but "lament[ed] that Mr. Morris' powerful mind should be devoted to so poor a cause."[71] A correspondent to the *Philanthropist* complimented several convention speakers but said that "among these addresses . . . those of Messrs. Morris and Lewis were particularly distinguished for power and eloquence."[72] The Whig *Cincinnati Republican* noted that Morris had "been a prominent leader in the Loco Foco ranks" but was "now the nominee of the abolition papers for the office of Vice President." The editor was convinced that Morris was "the ruling spirit" of the Liberty Party and "entitled to the paternity of the Convention."[73] Chase and Bailey may have orchestrated the convention, but the press viewed Morris as "the head of political abolition in Ohio."[74]

The years 1839 through 1841 marked the high tide of Morris's influence on the antislavery movement. Morris had gained national recognition with his reply to Clay, and his rejection by his party made him a martyr to the abolitionists. By linking the concept of the Slave Power to the rest of contemporary political rhetoric, Morris began a redefinition of sectional political reality that would reach its conclusion in the 1850s. He provided the antislavery movement with an effective argument with which to respond to its critics and spurred the move into the political arena. In making the Slave Power and not the slave the issue, Morris had outlined the method that later politicians would use to blend antislavery with political success. The South's perceived attack on civil liberties and on himself as the defender of those liberties drove Morris from antislavery to abolitionism. This journey toward radicalism, combined with the stubborn determination to be heard and the strict devotion to principle, which had given him national reputation, would prove to be no match for the younger, more nuanced politicians now joining the Ohio Liberty Party.

CHAPTER 9

Independent Opinions and Ultra Doctrines

During the first two years of the Liberty Party's life, Thomas Morris had given it leadership and was credited by those outside of the organization with being the prime mover in its development in Ohio. Morris's place in the Ohio Liberty Party leadership, however, did not remain unchallenged for long. To a degree, Morris's influence on the early political antislavery organization stemmed from the dearth of other experienced politicians within the Liberty ranks. The efforts of the third party to win converts and the disenchantment of many antislavery Whigs with the administration of John Tyler brought increasing numbers into the Liberty fold. Some of them—Salmon Chase and Leicester King, for example—were veteran political workers. These new recruits recognized the political liability of radical abolitionist demands and attempted to moderate the party's message to broaden its appeal. As historian Dwight Dumond observed, Morris "was far in advance of Chase and other political antislavery men in Ohio in courage and ability, though not so shrewd a politician."[1] The remaining three years of Morris's life would be spent in a factional struggle with these more pragmatic politicians for leadership of the Ohio Liberty Party.

Although the *Emancipator* commented on the "perfect unanimity and great cordiality" of the December 1841 Ohio Convention,[2] the combination of Chase, Bailey, and Morris within the same party structure would not permit cordiality to continue. Chase was "deeply and conscientiously religious, but he was openly vain beyond belief." In his "personality deep religious conviction intertwined with inordinate ambition and self-regard." Those who knew him well found him "insincere, selfish and intriguing." Indeed, one noted that "political intrigue, love of power, and a selfish and boundless ambition were the striking features of his life and character." Chase's vanity was legendary; many thought it his defining characteristic. On his death, his Supreme Court brethren chose "pride of opinion" as the trait that best described Chase.[3] Upon his arrival in the Liberty Party ranks, these traits almost immediately led to conflict with Morris and Birney.

Several years later, William Birney explained the background to the dispute between Morris and Chase: "Mr. Chase, Whig, and Mr. Morris, Democrat, both aspired to lead the Liberty party in this region. The men are almost totally different in character. Neither will consent to follow. That is the only point of similarity, perhaps, in the mental structure of the two. Mr. Morris was for pushing ultra doctrines. Mr. Chase thought moderation would better insure success."[4] In short, Chase sought to bring to the "one-idea" program of the Liberty Party a more politically pragmatic approach.[5] Neither shared leadership nor Morris's increasingly radical understanding of the Constitution fit in Chase's plan.

Chase and Bailey saw Birney's nomination as an impediment to the Liberty Party's political success. Birney and Morris had been nominated at the party's national convention in May 1841, but by the time of the Ohio Liberty Party state meeting in December, neither man had formally accepted the nomination. Birney had been distracted by moving from New York to Saginaw, Michigan, and may have been concerned about the Liberty Party's increasingly egalitarian posture. He had supported Clay against Jackson and traced "the ascendancy of the slave power" to Jackson's presidency.[6] Whatever the reason for Birney's delay, it provided Chase with an opportunity to implement his strategy toward increased moderation. A few weeks prior to the meeting in Columbus, the Indiana State Liberty Convention had recommended "assembling a National Convention of Delegates . . . for the purpose of adopting a declaration of sentiments in relation to the questions of national policy." In reporting the resolution, the *Philanthropist*, although earlier endorsing the actions of the New York nominating convention, now said "that the convention for nomination which met in New York last spring, could hardly be called a national anti-slavery convention."[7] Bailey hoped another convention would be called.

The Indiana State Liberty Convention recommendation said nothing about revisiting the selection of Liberty Party nominees. The resolution, however, provided a vehicle for Chase and Bailey to move against Birney. At the Columbus meeting, they persuaded Morris to offer a broader resolution: "That this Convention concur with the Convention of Indiana, in recommending that a National Convention of the friends of Constitutional Liberty, be held at Cleveland, Pittsburg, or some other central and convenient place, at which any vacancy, which may occur, in the nomination of President and Vice President, made by the Convention held at New York, in May last, may be supplied, and such other measures adopted as may promote the speedy triumph of Constitutional Liberty."[8]

A second resolution, also targeted at Birney, authorized the Ohio Liberty Party Central Committee to "fix the time and place of holding this Convention." Soon after the Ohio meeting, Chase wrote to Birney asking him to decline the Liberty presidential nomination. After noting that Morris had not yet accepted and "did not wish the nomination, if any man more likely to strengthen the cause could be selected," Chase told Birney that "all regard your election . . . as impracticable." Chase favored the substitution of John Quincy Adams, William Seward, or William Jay (all Whigs) on the ticket.[9]

Unknown to Chase, Birney had sent his acceptance of the nomination on January 10, 1842. In his acceptance letter, Birney had indicated a "cheerful acquiescence in the substitution of another, when one shall be found that will be more serviceable," but to Eastern abolitionists, Chase's suggestion to look outside the Liberty Party ranks for a nominee appeared to be an attack on abolitionist principles.[10] They urged Birney to ignore the request. Alvan Stewart, who as chair of the national Liberty Party Executive Committee was angered that the Ohio Convention ignored the national committee, told Birney "that on consultation with friends I beg that no consideration on earth may induce you to yield or resign your nomination, in consequence of an unregulated spirit which inhabits a few bosoms in Ohio." He believed Birney's withdrawal "would destroy us and political action."[11]

Joshua Leavitt was even more direct. Referring to Chase as "a raw recruit" who had been "worshipping the Log Cabin" while the Liberty Party was formed, Leavitt noted that Chase had "taken hold" in Ohio and was "much impressed with the idea that all that had been done needs undoing."[12] For the time being, Birney rejected the proposal entirely. To him, it seemed "strange . . . that any abolitionist conversant with our cause could have thought . . . of going outside our ranks for candidates for any office. Out of our ranks, all public men are of the Whig or Democratic party. How can they be abolitionists?" In short, Birney did not believe the party should nominate anyone not committed to abolitionism and found none of Chase's suggested alternatives "more serviceable."[13]

In an effort to overcome Birney's insistence that Liberty Party candidates be abolitionists, the Ohio leadership attempted to enlist the aid of the Massachusetts Liberty Party. On February 9, they sent a letter enclosing the proceedings of the Ohio Convention to Leavitt and asked that it be shared with the Massachusetts party's annual convention meeting in Boston. The letter explained "that we regard as the proper end of the Liberty Party the deliverance of the government from the control of the slave power; not the emancipation of slaves in the slave States." The letter recommended leaving "to philanthropists the work of promoting the general cause of abolition, . . . but let us beware of seeming to desire to use political power to effect emancipation in the States." Any other course would "excite distrust and jealousy, and alienate many who would be disposed to cooperate." The letter warned that "a different course, taken elsewhere, shall operate unfavorably upon us."[14] Claiming that the letter arrived too late, Leavitt did not present it to the convention, nor did he make its contents public. Not until June, after being pressed by Bailey, did Leavitt publish the letter in the *Emancipator*.[15]

To Eastern party leaders, the letter proposed "an almost revolutionary change in the party's policy."[16] This was certainly the goal of Chase and Bailey and the letter's language was theirs. Perhaps chastened by Birney's response to his request to step aside in favor of a nonabolitionist politician, Chase did not sign the letter; the signatories were Morris, William Birney, Bailey, and Brisbane—all recognized abolitionists who had been with the Liberty Party since the campaign of 1840. In all likelihood the letter was drafted by Chase or Bailey,[17] but they hoped the apparent endorsement of their view by acknowledged Ohio abolitionists would mute the potential criticism that Ohio's position was the result of new leaders and contrary to the goals of abolitionists.[18]

By the time of the letter, Morris had concluded that slavery was unconstitutional in the District of Columbia and the territories, but he still subscribed to the federal consensus that Congress could not reach slavery in the states—a view that he had held for years and which did not conflict with his views on the necessity of abolition.[19] The letter's description of what was politically possible was consistent with the federal consensus and his constitutional understanding. Since 1836, the political problem, as Morris saw it, was the power and demands of the Slave Power. Because he thought of the issue as political, he would not have understood the absence of an endorsement of moral suasion and immediate abolition as "revolutionary." Within a few months, however, his understanding of the consequences of Chase's "moderation" would lead to a split. By the time Leavitt published the letter, Morris had moved beyond its sentiments and was pressing "ultra" doctrines with regard to Congress's power to abolish slavery in the states. Regardless of Morris's views, Leavitt's reluctance to publish the letter signed by Morris evidenced his concern about both its content and Morris's influence.

On the same day as the letter to Leavitt, Bailey editorialized in support of the position articulated by Chase in the Ohio Liberty Party's resolutions and address. Arguing that "the great duty of antislavery men is to make their cause as little exceptionable as possible," Bailey asserted "the primary object of the Liberty Party is not the extinction of slavery in the States; for we at the North have no political power to legislate for its abolition." He then placed the call for a new national convention on a ground unrelated to replacing the nominees; "we shall insist on the propriety of holding a National Liberty Convention . . . with a view to define precisely the objects and measures and principles of this Liberty Party."[20] The effort to move the Ohio party away from its identification with immediate abolition was evident but not universally endorsed. A few weeks after the *Philanthropist* published the convention proceedings and Bailey's editorial, a correspondent wrote to dissent. The writer observed that "the abolitionist goes out to redeem the negro," but the Liberty Party "views slavery chiefly as it affects the white man."[21]

Birney was well aware of the effort not only to replace him but also to temper the abolitionist identification of the party. Later in the spring, Birney had an opportunity to confront Chase directly. In April Birney returned to Cincinnati to visit his son, handle some business concerns relating to real estate he owned, and engage in a speaking tour. On the evening of April 22, Chase hosted a dinner at his home for Birney and local Liberty leaders. Birney strongly objected to what he saw as the move away from abolitionism toward a more moderate stance for the party. Although actively pursuing just that goal, Chase and the others disingenuously agreed.[22] Perhaps to assure himself of Chase's bona fides in proclaiming agreement with him, Birney asked Chase to write to Gerrit Smith and explain the Ohio Liberty Party position.[23]

Birney's choice of Smith to be the recipient of Chase's explanation is revealing. Smith was the leading radical abolitionist in western New York.

128   THE CREATION OF A CRUSADER

He believed the Liberty Party should "be a holy biracial revolutionary vanguard that could not concede slaveholders had rights."[24] He was the author of an "Address to the Slaves" adopted by the New York Liberty Party Gubernatorial Nominating Convention in Peterboro on January 19, 1842. The address encouraged slaves to flee and argued that they were free to take (steal) items necessary for their escape.[25] The address caused an immediate sensation within the Liberty Party. Eastern leaders and the *Emancipator* appeared to endorse Smith's views.[26] Bailey, in the *Philanthropist*, criticized the idea severely. Smith and Bailey would engage in a heated public debate for several months.[27] Birney could hardly have picked a person less likely to be persuaded by Chase than Gerrit Smith.

Three weeks after his meeting with Birney, Chase wrote Smith. After telling Smith that he was gratified to be corresponding "with one whose character [he had] long been accustomed to admire," Chase assured Smith that "whatever slight differences of opinion" might exist between them, he did not doubt the Eastern Liberty party's "integrity of purpose." Chase was "disposed to let them choose their own mode" of acting, trusting "that Time and Experience will show what plans are wisest."[28] Chase first explained the need to keep the political actions separate from religion and then turned to the goals of the Liberty Party: "The allegations against us of an intention to interfere with slavery in the states by the exercise of physical or political power prejudices against us many worthy and sensible people, who think the Constitution authorizes no such interference. We ourselves are almost unanimous in this opinion."[29] He urged that the party "direct all the energies of our political action against the unconstitutional encroachments of the Slave Power" and against "slavery itself wherever it may exist without Constitutional sanction." Chase then explained what that meant: "When I say that we are against slavery wherever it exists without constitutional warrant I mean that we are against Slavery in the District of Columbia, in Florida & on the seas; in short we hold that no man can be constitutionally held as property in this country except in states where the local constitution maintains Slavery."[30] Chase had not only accepted Morris's conclusion that slavery was unconstitutional in any area under Congress's control, he defined that theory as the appropriate limit of Liberty Party policy.

Chase believed "that these views find ready access to the minds of thousands—many of whom are averse to identifying themselves with Abolitionists in name." He was "not anxious" that party members take on "any other name than that of Liberty Man." He thought "these views worthy of being adopted everywhere," and that "action upon them [would] accomplish all that the most sanguine abolitionist [could] reasonably hope from the action of the political party."[31] In effect, Chase and Bailey thought the Liberty Party should focus on attracting the votes of persons similar to those who had attended the January 5, 1841, Cincinnati meeting ("substantial citizens . . . whom it were ridiculous to charge with visionary notions"). The attendees at the meeting opposed both abolition and the Slave Power. At the time Bailey had criticized the attendees for not going far enough; now he and Chase thought the Liberty Party should go no further.[32]

If Chase hoped his letter would reassure Smith, he was mistaken. Writing three months after Chase's letter and one month after Leavitt published the letter from Morris, Smith responded publicly: "Ohio abolition can amuse itself with a new-fangled Liberty Party, whose selfish scheme it is to keep but its own neck from under the yoke of slavery. Ohio abolition (shame on it!) can, through its mouthpiece, *The Philanthropist,* tell the wretched, starving, fugitive slave, that it is immoral for him to pick up a loaf of bread, which is not legally his own."[33] Bailey, angered that Smith had responded publicly rather than write privately to the offending "Ohio abolitionists," described Smith's response as "sheer . . . misrepresentation." Although Ohio abolitionists remained committed to "the overthrow of slavery," Ohio Liberty Party members differed from those in the East. Ohio "would measure political action against slavery by the political responsibilities and powers of the free States." As Bailey had written in February, the Liberty Party's object was "the abolition of unconstitutional slavery" and the redemption of "the administration of the Government from slaveholding rule."[34]

In his quest to remove Birney from the top of the Liberty Party ticket, Chase did find one New York ally—Lewis Tappan. Chase had handled the Tappan brothers' legal matters in Ohio since Birney had moved to New York in 1837. He now sought to enlist Lewis Tappan in the cause.[35] When Tappan learned that Chase and Bailey "were thoroughly dissatisfied with Birney," Tappan was "overjoyed." Tappan agreed that "too radically antislavery an interpretation of the Constitution would only alienate the people." When Chase confided that "warm, ardent, uncompromising men," committed to "unconditional and immediate emancipation," had initially organized and led the Liberty Party, Tappan agreed. "To achieve success with voters, however, a more moderate approach was required." Encouraged by Chase, Tappan wrote John Quincy Adams, John Jay, and William Seward in an effort to persuade one of them to accept the Liberty Party nomination.[36]

In the midst of these maneuvers designed to reduce the party's identification with abolition and to replace Birney with a more prominent Northern politician, the party's nominees were attacked as coconspirators in league with British agents to destroy the Union. The belief that abolitionists were in league with the British to destroy the Union had become widespread among Southern defenders of slavery and manifested the same "paranoid style" of thinking as the abolitionist focus on the Slave Power.[37] On January 24, 1842, Henry Wise, a congressman from Virginia, addressed the Birney and Morris nominations on the floor of the House of Representatives. In his view, Joseph Sturge, a British abolitionist who had visited the United States, advised abolitionists to focus on the presidential election in 1844. Birney and Morris "had been set up by the British societies to be their candidates for President and vice-president." The nominations had been "in prompt response to the advice of this foreign agent."[38] Where the Liberty Party saw the Slave Power, slaveholders saw a British plot.

Despite the turmoil surrounding the presidential ticket, the Ohio Liberty Party conducted its first gubernatorial campaign. In late February, the *Philanthropist* began issuing appeals for "Action! Friends, Action!"[39] By early summer, plans had been made for a series of rallies throughout the state and Morris was on the stump.[40] On the Fourth of July, he participated in a large southern Ohio Liberty rally at Mount Pleasant. From early August through mid-September, King, Lewis, and Morris spoke in a series of sixteen meetings in every corner of the state. When other speakers dropped out to rest, Morris continued "with unabated vigor." The reports of these events cheered antislavery observers. The Liberty speakers addressed crowds of eight hundred at Columbus, one thousand in Clark County, and seven hundred at Bellefontaine.[41] Clearly, support for the Liberty cause had progressed rapidly from its tiny beginnings in 1840.

The issue in Ohio in 1842, however, was not slavery but currency and banks.[42] The Liberty Party thus tried to tie slavery to local finances: "The Liberty men propose a sound currency, extended markets for labor, and the reestablishment in their just authority of the original principles of the Constitution in regard to personal rights. They believe that sound and adequate markets cannot be had, until the causes which have given us a disordered currency and insufficient markets shall be removed. Among the causes, they regard slavery as the chief."[43] In short, the party in Ohio had adopted an economic understanding reflective of Morris's hard-money wing of the Democratic Party.[44] Given the Whig background of all the other leaders (Chase, Bailey, King, and Lewis), Morris's influence on the Ohio party's platform is evident. The message did not differ in substance on economics from his address to Ohio Democrats in 1841. The Ohio Liberty Party leadership not only adopted Morris's Slave Power theory and constitutional limitations on the power of Congress to establish slavery but also came to share his views of monopolies, paper money, and corporate privilege.[45] Beyond economics, Ohio Liberty leaders adopted Morris's understanding and articulation of Black civil rights and his demand that civil rights be part of the Ohio party's goals. When asked during the campaign about the rights of Black Ohioans, Leicester King (a former Whig and now the Liberty Party's candidate for governor) replied, "equal and exact justice to all men irrespective of color or condition is regarded by me as a sound maxim of free democracy."[46]

The presence of additional experienced political leaders in the ranks, the vastly improved organization, and the years of preparatory labor increased the effectiveness of the Liberty Party argument. The party's total vote in the governor's race—5,405—nearly doubled the statewide total from a year earlier. As one historian has noted, although the third party was again defeated, it now seemed to possess a balance of power within Ohio politics. The two major candidates for governor had been separated by less than thirty-five hundred votes. In an era of evenly matched major parties, the control of only a small portion of the votes might have given the abolitionists influence on the outcome.[47]

Although the party failed to elect any of its candidates for state office, in at least one aspect the election was a victory for antislavery and a vindication of Morris. A year earlier, at the request of the Liberty Party state convention, Morris had drafted and presented to the general assembly a "memorial" (petition) praying for changes in state laws regarding slavery.[48] With the Democrats back in control of the general assembly, the 1839 Fugitive Slave Law, adopted at the request of Kentucky in the aftermath of Morris's defeat for reelection, was repealed. The repeal's draftsman told the House "the law . . . was passed at the insistence of the State of Kentucky, but since . . . that state had sent agents here to interfere in our domestic concerns, he thought it nothing but justice to let them take care of their own negroes."[49] Three years after his defeat for reelection and two years after his expulsion from the Ohio Democratic Party, Democrats in the general assembly accepted both Morris's critique of the Slave Power's influence in the adoption of the 1839 law and his argument that Ohio was not required to assist in the return of fugitive slaves (endorsed by the *Prigg* decision) was now accepted even by Ohio Democrats.

All was not harmonious, however, between Morris and his colleagues. As William Birney reported to his father, by the summer of 1842 Chase and Morris were in a struggle to lead the party in Ohio. Chase and Bailey agreed that moderation was the way to electoral success; Morris did not. Although Chase had assured Birney of his support for the Liberty Party's commitment to abolitionism, he and Bailey continued to work to distinguish the party from abolitionism. Morris thought otherwise and was increasingly shut out of the pages of the *Philanthropist* and roles on business committees at party meetings.[50] Eastern leaders, however, believed they had persuaded other members of the Ohio leadership to "not favor the over-wise fancies of Chase and Bailey" and of "the propriety of a firm and cordial support of our present candidates."[51] Chase and Bailey did not give up.

Possessing the balance of power between the Democrats and the Whigs in Ohio was not synonymous with electoral success. As Chase told Lewis Tappan, "If the Liberty party perseveres in its present course as adopted in some states with Mr. Birney as a candidate, it will, I fear, become extinct."[52] In spite of Chase's pressure, Birney and his supporters refused to cooperate. The Ohio lawyer appeared stymied. He decided to adopt a different approach to force the calling of another national Liberty Party Convention and orchestrate a reconsideration of Birney's nomination. If Birney would not resign, perhaps Morris could be forced to withdraw his name. This would necessitate the calling of a new convention to replace him and give Chase and Bailey a chance to have Birney removed by the convention.

At the 1841 Ohio Liberty Convention, Morris hinted to the delegates that he would step aside if a more suitable person could be found. His motivation for this announcement is unclear. It may simply have been a conventional response. Birney, in accepting his nomination two weeks later, expressed a similar sentiment. Morris's health may also have played a role. By the time of the convention, he was sixty-five years old, and the exertion of the fall campaign had forced him to decline invitations to speak outside Ohio and to convalesce in bed. Birney's actions may also have influenced Morris. Birney had initially declined the nomination in 1840, and then after accepting it, spent the summer and fall in Great Britain. His delay in accepting this nomination may have been thought to indicate a reluctance on Birney's part to serve. In any event, accepting the vice presidential spot before the nominee for the top spot had accepted may have seemed untoward. Finally, Morris's awareness of Chase's plan to ask Birney to decline and convene a new nominating convention may have contributed to his delay in accepting the nomination.

After Birney accepted the presidential nomination, Morris continued to hesitate responding to the offer of the vice presidential spot on the ticket. Deferring his response until Birney acted is understandable, but Morris's further delay is puzzling. Perhaps he was waiting to see if Chase could persuade Birney to change his mind. Whatever may have been Morris's thinking, his inaction allowed the proponents of a second nominating convention justification for their continuing efforts. As a correspondent to the *Emancipator* noted, one of the reasons urged for the need of a second convention was that since Morris "has not accepted the nomination, and may not, we ought to call a convention to nominate another." The writer argued that if Morris did decline, "though no one expects it, and all would deprecate it," the party could at that point hold another meeting. "But to call for one for that purpose before he declines, would be virtually, asking him to do so."[53]

Beyond its strategic utility in replacing Birney, the idea of removing Morris from the ticket greatly appealed to Bailey personally. Writing to explain the developments in Ohio to his father, William Birney said, "[Bailey's] jealousy of Thomas Morris, Esq. has not only led him to omit publishing the Liberty party ticket, but has shown itself in our committee meetings in sharp words and constant collisions."[54] Morris's decision to decline the nomination would not only give the Ohio group the opportunity to substitute a more viable candidate for Birney but would also solidify control of the Ohio party by Chase and Bailey.

To the chagrin of these advocates of political pragmatism, Morris had grown increasingly radical in his abolitionist demands. At the Ohio Liberty Party Convention in December 1842, Morris articulated his radical political position more clearly. The address (again drafted by Chase) accepted Morris's views on the absence of congressional power to establish slavery but reaffirmed the absence of power to abolish slavery in the states.[55] Morris, however, told the convention "thousands of human beings are held, unconstitutionally, in bondage under the laws of our American Congress.

... He did not believe that there was any warrant for such legislation in the Constitution; he was sure there was none in the moral code which was at the foundation of all law."[56] Although a year earlier the convention had promised no interference with the recovery of fugitive slaves, Morris again denied "the monstrous proposition that 'what the law makes property is property" and encouraged slaves to escape by saying, "no slave ought to be content with his condition. . . . He could not blame the slave for desiring to escape from bondage, nor could he blame those who aided their escape. To charge such persons as criminals was to offend common sense and common justice"[57]

Although some historians have placed Morris in the ranks of the movement to remove Birney, and viewed his declining the vice presidential nomination as evidence of his participation, Birney's biographer did not.[58] When the proposed alternatives to Birney are considered, Morris's involvement becomes highly doubtful. John Quincy Adams had bitterly opposed Jackson, and Morris had campaigned strenuously against Adams. William Jay was the privileged son of a prominent Federalist and opponent of Jefferson. William Seward was the political enemy of Van Buren and a proponent of economic policies that Morris abhorred. Chase's efforts at identifying alternatives to Birney appeared directed toward creating a "united Whigs and abolitionist" political enterprise.[59] Morris would not have cooperated with two of his rivals within the Liberty Party to support any of these men. Instead, Morris acted in response to Chase and Bailey's increasing power in Ohio. After Morris announced his intentions, William Birney wrote that lack of support "by the party paper of his own place of residence" had forced Morris to withdraw his name.[60] Morris's withdrawal may have been sought by Chase and Bailey as a way to further their goals, but it was not a result of cooperation.[61]

When politically attacked, Morris seldom conceded the field to his opponents. Indeed, the evidence suggests the ex-senator viewed his declination as a means of circumventing Chase and Bailey's influence in Ohio and reasserting his own leadership. Throughout his political career, he had consistently believed that popular opinion was on his side. When he failed with the people, he blamed the Slave Power (that is, his defeat in 1838 and the Dayton riots).[62] The tone of his rejection of the vice presidential nomination was strikingly similar to the conclusion of his reply to Henry Clay. Just as he had intended to take his case to the people then, he now sought the support of the Liberty rank and file.

He told the 1842 Ohio Convention that he "prized" the Liberty nomination "beyond any office which either of the other parties could bestow." But "in view of the rapid progress of the party . . . he had come to the conclusion to decline [the nomination] in order that another convention representing the greater numbers that now . . . compose the Liberty party might have an opportunity to act upon it."[63] The convention then adopted a resolution calling for a national convention in the summer to select a new candidate. Although actively working to convince Morris to decline, Bailey wrote to Birney to inform him of the situation: "Morris has declined with the expectation, I doubt not, of being renominated."[64]

Bailey's assessment of Morris's expectation was probably correct. Two weeks before Bailey's letter to Birney, Morris wrote to further explain his decision. He reiterated that the "nomination was not only unsought, but unlooked for." Nevertheless, he viewed "it as the highest honor ever conferred" on him. He recognized, however, "that many men far more able and worthy" than he was had "of late been added to the [Liberty] ranks." As a result, he "thought it due to the cause, and to the country, to afford an opportunity . . . to review the nomination."[65] As Bailey suggested, Morris then left the door open to renomination: "I would not have taken the step which I have had I not fully understood that a General Convention of Liberty men from all the states would be held. . . . When that convention shall have met, they may dispose of my name as they shall judge best."[66] The prospects for his renomination appeared good. Bailey's sympathetic early biographer acknowledged that within the Liberty Party, even in Ohio, Morris's position on issues was probably more popular than the ideas of Chase and Bailey.[67] Renomination by a new convention would provide Morris the opportunity to vindicate his positions and aid his struggle against Chase and Bailey for leadership of the Ohio party.

Morris had adopted a similar approach earlier in his career. Following the failed impeachment attempt directed at Ohio Supreme Court justices, the general assembly had expanded the number of seats on the court by one. Morris was elected to fill the seat and served for a year. The general assembly (in order to address the incumbency of other statewide officials) passed a "sweeping resolution" that ended the terms of all officials and necessitated reelecting the Supreme Court. This time, Morris was not chosen. He blamed former governor Thomas Worthington (who had instigated the impeachment effort) for withdrawing promised support. Morris then sought reelection to the Ohio House and attempted to use that position to recover his judicial seat. The effort ultimately fell a few votes short in the general assembly but demonstrated Morris's belief that he could overcome betrayal by political colleagues by direct appeal to perceived supporters.[68]

The continued attempt to oust Birney angered his Eastern supporters, and they lashed out at all the Cincinnatians. In a lengthy letter urging Birney not to do the "bidding of a clique of Cincinnati lawyers," Joshua Leavitt outlined Eastern opinion of Morris: "I would have supported him zealously, because I respect him and believe him honest, and because he took a bold stand in the Senate and I would like to see him preside there." Although he had previously focused his anger on Chase and Bailey, Leavitt now linked "Morris and the Cincinnatians" together. Leavitt's ire at Chase carried over to the ex-senator. "Mr. Morris has seen fit," he said, "after keeping our nomination two years in his hands, to reject it. My mind is that it should stay rejected, and we look among the Atlantic states for our candidates." Yet, Leavitt was puzzled. "With regard to Morris' course," Leavitt could not "fathom any deep design."[69]

Observers in Cincinnati, however, thought they understood the motivation behind Morris's action—frustration with Bailey. They believed Bailey's "jealousy of Thomas Morris . . . not only led him to omit publishing the Liberty party nomination but has shown itself . . . in sharp words and constant collisions." Bailey told Birney's son that he thought Birney the best candidate, "but that he disliked Mr. Morris."[70] Whatever may have been his motivation, Morris's withdrawal necessitated the new nominating convention Chase and Bailey had sought. The Ohio Liberty Party Convention again ignored the national executive committee and issued a call for a new convention. When Leavitt criticized the effort, Bailey defended the action by suggesting a process of state-by-state nominations.[71]

Chase appeared largely indifferent to Morris's candidacy once he had withdrawn. Chase may have viewed Morris's rejection of the vice presidential nomination as simply a means to an end—replacing Birney on the Liberty ticket. Although Chase worked diligently to recruit someone to replace Birney, he never suggested an alternative to Morris. Chase may well have concluded "that Morris' political career was finished" and viewed him simply as, at best, a "collaborator."[72] For Bailey, however, the effort to remove Morris from the ticket was personal,[73] and he continued his effort to discredit Morris prior to the Albany Convention.

With the growing signs of disillusionment with Morris appearing in the East as a result of his withdrawal, Bailey moved to put the final touches

INDEPENDENT OPINIONS AND ULTRA DOCTRINES   137

on the destruction of his "friend." In the same letter in which Bailey suggested that Morris hoped to be renominated, he told Birney:

> You know I never concurred in his nomination. He does not believe in admitting free colored people to the right of suffrage—how will that suit the Liberty men of the East? Besides, he is not of good report among them that are without. I feel sorry, extremely sorry, to be obliged to appear in any way opposed to his nomination. He is my friend—and I have found him very kind in many things; and I admire the independence with which he forms his opinions and the boldness with which he utters them. But, I cannot shut my eyes to the fact that his nomination is injuring our cause in every place where his is personally known. He is not obnoxious on account of his abolitionism, but on many other accounts, and has always been so.[74]

Bailey then told Birney that he, too, because of his opposition to universal white male suffrage, was "not the most eligible candidate that could be selected."

In choosing to attack Morris for his supposed views on Blacks voting, Bailey was hoping to take advantage of Eastern Liberty Party leaders' suspicion of the Ohio Liberty Party. At the conclusion of his public dispute a year earlier with Gerrit Smith over encouraging slaves to escape, Bailey had published a letter from Smith. In reiterating his charge that the program of the Ohio Liberty Party was a "selfish scheme" that "professes no hatred of slavery" but only "wishes to divorce the Government from slavery," Smith alluded to Morris's statements at the end of the 1838 senatorial campaign as one of the reasons "for suspecting that there may be some unsoundness in Cincinnati abolition." Smith told Bailey, "With all our admiration of the skill and bravery with which he has fought for liberty, we cannot forget the letter of Nov. 23d, 1838, to the People of Ohio, &c, in which your honored neighbor advocated the shocking doctrine of excluding the colored men from society and political power."[75] Far from being random, Bailey was well aware of Morris's potential vulnerability in the East on this issue.[76] Whether motivated by "jealousy" of Morris or a genuine belief that Morris's radical views were "obnoxious," Bailey made the tactical decision to "privately" remind Eastern leaders of Morris's prior position.

Bailey's allegation raises a host of questions. For over a year he and Chase had been engaged in an effort to move the Liberty Party away from abolition and toward a focus on the Slave Power and the containment of slavery.

The persons they sought to attract (nonabolitionists) were highly unlikely to support Black suffrage. Indeed many, if not most, Ohio abolitionists rejected Black suffrage. The constitution of the Ohio Anti-Slavery Society specifically rejected voting rights for Blacks. As a result, "Ohio Liberty leaders did not openly advocate granting blacks the suffrage."[77] Even more curious, William Jay (Bailey's preferred replacement for Birney) also opposed Black voting.[78] Absent Bailey's personal animus for Morris, then, it is difficult to believe Bailey found Morris's views on suffrage (whatever they were) disqualifying.

On the shaky basis of the accusations in Bailey's letter, however, historians have accused Morris of opposing Blacks voting and called him "a staunch foe of black suffrage."[79] Yet Bailey's indictment was full of inconsistences and contradicted by contemporary sources. Although Morris undoubtedly shared the prevailing prejudices of his time on Black inferiority,[80] by the time of Bailey's letter, Morris had overcome his earlier objections and was willing to accept Black voting. Indeed, Birney thought so. In responding to Bailey, Birney acknowledged that he was aware that Morris had once been opposed to Blacks voting,[81] but thought Morris "had relinquished it." Birney agreed that "Morris's renomination . . . would meet with few advocates as long as he is opposed to the doing away with color as a ground of civil rights or privileges." If Morris opposed civil rights for Blacks, he would not "find a single advocate for his recommendation."[82]

The absence of contemporary evidence for Bailey's claim is striking. Some commentators cite the astonished replies of Lewis Tappan and Birney to Bailey's accusation as further proof of Morris's bias.[83] In actuality, however, the letters of these two men expressed amazement at Bailey's revelation. They did not substantiate it. Indeed, the fact that this statement shocked the Eastern Liberty Party leadership (individuals extremely concerned with the maintenance of correct principles) casts further doubt on its validity. Even Bailey's earliest biographer, while accepting his opinion of Morris, found no direct evidence to support the editor. Instead, he argued that Morris's belief that the riots in Dayton in the winter of 1841 were caused by Southern slaveholders forced Bailey to doubt the sincerity of Morris's racial views.[84]

While the editor was undoubtedly correct in asserting that the Dayton disturbances had their origin in the prejudice of the local citizens, Morris's failure to perceive this as the central cause did not prove his own racial bias. Rather, it simply reflected his paranoia of the South. He believed that the attitudes and institutions of Ohio were being perverted by the Slave

Power. Just as his defeat in 1838 had resulted from foreign dictation, so outside agitators had instigated the Dayton riots. "The dark spirit of slavery has hoodwinked justice," he said, "and left her eyes open only to see the faults, supposed or real, of the black man; while a public press under the rod and influence of the slave holding power, in order to raise an injurious prejudice has" denounced Blacks.[85] Since Morris believed this to be the case, his logic carried him to the conclusion that the removal of the Southern influence would provide the solution to most of Ohio's citizens—not Morris's—racism.

Like "every state that entered the Union between 1800 and the Civil War [Ohio] limited the suffrage to white men."[86] In making his allegations against Morris, Bailey ignored several statements of Morris supporting voting and equal rights for Blacks. At least as early as 1841, Morris had commented favorably on Blacks voting. In his appeal "To the Democratic Portion of the People of Ohio," he had reminded his fellow citizens, "You will see that under the Ordinance of 1787 Negros were not denied the right of suffrage, nor were they ineligible as representatives . . . Negroes therefore had the right to vote, and if my information be correct . . . did vote for members of the Ohio Constitutional Convention. I then resided in Clermont County: we had but two or three colored men in the county at the time, and they voted."[87] Earlier that year, Morris told the Ohio Liberty Party summer meeting that they should only support a candidate committed, "if elected, [to] use his influence and give his votes in opposition to slavery, in favor of equal rights, and the establishment of equal and impartial justice to all men."[88]

In addition to this sympathetic reference to Blacks voting early in Ohio history, Morris had consistently supported civil rights for Blacks and attacked the racial basis of slavery. At the 1842 Liberty Party Convention when he announced his intention to decline the vice presidential nomination, Morris said, "a person held to service in another state escaping into [Ohio] . . . has every right that any other person has."[89] In 1839 he had told the Senate: "It is color, not rights and justice, that is to continue slavery forever in our country. It is prejudice against color which is the strong ground of slavery. . . . slavery has no just foundation in color; it rests exclusively upon usurpation, tyranny, oppressive fraud and force."[90] He argued for jury trials for fugitive slaves, bitterly attacked a judge who had denied a marriage license to a Black couple, sought the repeal of the laws that barred Black children from attending public schools, and urged that Blacks be allowed to testify in cases against whites. Writing in 1840, he had said, "this denial of the right [to testify against whites] to the colored race is a flagrant injustice."[91]

Bailey's charges become even more open to suspicion when the rest of his letter is examined. The earlier reports of William Birney, who refused to take sides in the Cincinnati factional quarrels, clearly contradicted Bailey's declaration that Morris "is my friend." According to one of the editor's biographers, Bailey had "for years harbored serious doubts in regard to Morris' ideas and personal character."[92] Although the editor claimed to have disapproved of Morris's nomination from the beginning, on May 26, 1841, in an editorial on the new candidates, he had told his readers: "We need not say that we shall sustain this nomination. This our friends know from our past course. We are glad that the movement is made at this early period."[93] A month later, Bailey (as a member of the Business Committee) drafted a resolution declaring that the state convention "sustain the nomination for the Presidency and Vice Presidency recently made by the National Nominating Convention." The resolution "was adopted by a large majority."[94]

Bailey's allusion to Morris's general reputation among those outside the Liberty Party, although potentially politically damaging to Morris,[95] is particularly puzzling. Birney had lived in Ohio, his son still resided in Cincinnati, and Birney had been acquainted with Morris for several years. It is highly unlikely that Birney would be unaware of Morris's reputation or character.[96] Bailey never clarified (beyond the complaint about Blacks voting) what caused Morris to be not of good report,[97] but there are at least two possibilities.

Bailey may have had Morris's religious views in mind. Morris's father and one of his sons were ministers, but Morris was not "a religious man" nor a member of a church nor a "professer" of religion, although "he regretted . . . that he had lived so long without religion."[98] This long-standing position was well known and something Morris freely acknowledged publicly. Indeed, it was used by political opponents of the Liberty Party during the 1844 campaign.[99] Most of the Liberty Party leaders in Cincinnati were prominent leaders in established churches, and many antislavery voters (not to mention evangelical abolitionists) acted from religious motivation. Bailey may have believed Morris's lack of church membership prevented these voters from supporting the Liberty ticket.[100]

Another possibility was Morris's relationship to his son-in-law's business. When he was denied reelection to the Senate, Morris sold his home in Clermont County and moved with his wife and daughters to Elk Lick

Mill near Cincinnati.[101] The property, owned by his son-in-law, had a sawmill, gristmill, and distillery on the grounds. The business may have been operated as a partnership between Morris, his son-in-law, and others, but Morris's relationship to the distillery is somewhat murky. At his death, Morris held three mortgages on the property. He may have simply been a creditor and not a partner. Nevertheless, he lived on the property after returning from the Senate. During the 1844 campaign, Liberty Party opponents charged that Morris operated a distillery. In responding to the charge, Morris chose not to deny the allegations directly but rather said that he had "not drunk, sold, bought or distilled a single drop of intoxicating liquor" for at least twenty years.[102] Even if true, his family's association with Elk Lick Mill could hardly have been reassuring to the large number of temperance supporters Bailey would have liked to attract to the Liberty Party. Nevertheless, Morris had lived at Elk Hill for several years, and Birney could hardly have been unaware of Morris's arrangement.

The assertion that Morris injured the Liberty cause wherever he was "personally known" also contradicts much contemporary evidence. If the members of the Liberty Party felt that he hurt their efforts, they certainly would not have continued, as they did, to invite Morris to speak at various meetings and conventions throughout the state.[103] The desire of several county organizations to have Morris renominated casts additional doubt on Bailey's statement that Morris hindered the cause where he was personally known.[104] Whatever Bailey's concerns about Morris's reputation, Birney apparently did not find them troubling. His response to Bailey's letter was limited to the civil rights issue.

Yet Bailey was not entirely wrong. Morris's presence did hinder, to a degree, the vision of Chase and Bailey for the expansion of the party in Ohio, but not because of his conservative views on Blacks' civil rights. Instead, the problem was "the independence with which [Morris] form[ed] his opinions and the boldness with which he utter[ed] them." In other words, the editor disliked Morris's refusal to follow Bailey's lead and the often strident manner in which Morris articulated his increasingly radical views.[105] Chase and Bailey were concerned with bringing the essentially moderate antislavery men in Ohio within the Liberty fold. When Morris did such things as demand equal rights for Blacks, encourage slaves to escape, or argue that Congress had the power to abolish slavery in the states, he severely hampered the efforts of Chase and Bailey to broaden the party's base. The desire to discredit Morris among Eastern party leaders, many of whom shared his constitutional views, along with Bailey's personal animosity, generated this attack on Morris as a conservative.

The stark contradictions between Bailey's accusations and the other evidence, coupled with his antagonistic relationship with Morris, makes the truth of Bailey's charges doubtful. So does Bailey's subsequent inaction. In replying to Bailey's letter, Birney urged Bailey to "at once have a conversation with Mr. M on the subject; get from his own mouth a deliberate avowal or disavowal of the sentiment; and if he still entertains, it, let it by all means be known in *The Philanthropist*."[106] Bailey never printed anything on the subject.

CHAPTER 10

The Power to Abolish Slavery in Every State

Chase and Bailey had not yet given up on replacing Birney. On August 1, 1843, a few weeks before the national convention was to meet in Buffalo, the Hamilton County Liberty Party held their annual convention. The meeting's business committee, led by Chase and Bailey, reported several resolutions. In particular, "we respectfully but earnestly recommend to the National Liberty Convention, the nomination for the Presidency of William Jay, of New York, whose well known worth, extensive information, and practical statesmanship will command the respect of all parties and confidence of the whole people, while his devotion to the principles of the Declaration of Independence; and his services in the cause of Liberty, will ensure to him the support of every consistent opposer of Slavery."[1] The meeting also recognized "the elevated moral character and inflexible firmness" of Birney and commended Morris, "whose whole course, private and public" has "manifested inflexible adherence to the cause of liberty."[2]

When the Buffalo Convention convened later that month, more than three thousand persons, including Chase, Lewis, and King, met for two days under Rev. Charles Gadson Finney's revival tent in front of the courthouse. Recognizing, as Chase had,[3] that given Morris's declination of the vice presidential nomination, the convention would revisit the question of nominating both candidates, Birney asked that the convention consider the presidential nomination "as an open one." He asked only that "the persons in nomination be all unexceptional as abolitionists, and as persons of good moral character."[4] King was elected president of the convention with Lewis named a vice president. Chase was appointed to the committee to draft the platform.[5]

Despite the efforts of Chase and Bailey, the delegates unanimously renominated Birney and Morris and adopted as its platform a series of resolutions largely drafted by Chase that reflected "an antisouthernism that focused upon the economic impact of slavery upon the North." This approach had particular appeal to "less affluent artisans, merchants, and laborers."[6] The platform contained a "comprehensive expression of the [moderate antislavery] constitutional views" and reflected the "general agreement" of the party to each of these positions.[7]

Although the platform was silent on the question of slavery in the states, the impact of Morris's constitutional thought was evident throughout. "Rarely in American history has a political party's platform been so integrally shaped by constitutional thought."[8] The platform noted that the Fifth Amendment barred Congress from establishing slavery anywhere (paragraphs 11 and 12); demanded "the restoration of equality of rights" (paragraph 2); pledged to "carry out the principles of Equal Rights" (paragraph 4) as well as repeal of all Black Laws (paragraph 35); and recognized the Slave Power as controlling the national government, usurping the power of state governments and threatening the overthrow of popular freedom (paragraph 15). The party believed it was "indispensably necessary" that the "National Government be rescued from the grasp of the Slave Power" (paragraph 22).[9] Although these views were now widely accepted and frequently repeated by political antislavery proponents, Morris had been among the first (if not the first) to have articulated these positions. The "bold egalitarian statements" in the platform were "the uttermost Liberty salient toward radicalism the party ever achieved."[10]

Far from representing a concession to the moderates (as some historians have argued),[11] the renomination of Birney and Morris illustrated the failure of the moderate Ohio wing to control the national party. The *Emancipator* thought it "an omen of great good" that the delegates had "unanimously ratified the nominations" of Birney and Morris,[12] but the outcome discouraged Chase. He told Lewis Tappan that he supposed "the nomination . . . will be unacceptable to you as it doubtless is to many. . . . But nothing else could be done."[13]

Upon the return from Buffalo of the Cincinnati delegation, the leadership struggle within the Ohio party flared again. In the afterglow of the Ohio Liberty Party Convention in 1841, Morris had signed a letter (likely drafted by Chase) to Joshua Leavitt. The letter had argued: "It is almost universally conceded that the general government cannot act directly on slavery in the states. It seems to us that this concession should be frankly made, and that we disclaim all purpose of getting the political power of the country with a view to use it for the abolition of slavery in the states."[14] This view that only the states could regulate slavery in their borders, and that Congress lacked the power to abolish slavery in the states (the federal consensus) was widely shared and had been publicly articulated by Morris many times.[15] Moderates in the Liberty Party (and ultimately the Free-Soil and Republican Parties) believed that if slavery could not expand, it could not survive. Keeping slavery out of the territories, then, would ultimately lead to its abolition.[16]

Probably by the time of the December 1842 Ohio Liberty Party meeting, and certainly by early 1843, however, Morris had changed his mind and was ready to challenge Chase and Bailey on the power of Congress to abolish slavery in the states. The diligent William Birney informed his father:

> Little is said openly but a storm is brewing which may burst in fury before the winter months. Hon. T. Morris has grown quite out of temper with Dr. Bailey, Mr. Chase and Mr. Lewis. He thinks the Doctor doesn't do him justice and is entirely under the influence of the others named. He is now brought with difficulty to attend the meetings. He has made some advances to get me to back him in an onset on the doctrines of those gentlemen in relation to the distinction of the Liberty men and the abolitionists and the power of Congress over slavery in the states. But I have firmly resolved to have nothing to do with the matter one way or the other—to let them fight their own battles, if it should come to that. They have never co-operated with much cordiality and they have less now than ever.[17]

Morris's position on congressional power over slavery in the states had become public over the summer.

Morris had been forced to think through congressional power over slavery ever since Calhoun had challenged the power to abolish slavery in the District of Columbia. Although at the time he had accepted the federal consensus that Congress lacked power to reach slavery in the states, Morris did not believe that the Fifth Amendment barred action in the District of Columbia. As he had told the Senate, the Constitution did not recognize property in persons; therefore, the Fifth Amendment's prohibition against taking property did not apply to slaves. Moreover, if the Constitution protected slavery, as Calhoun argued, Congress not only lacked the power to prohibit slavery in the District of Columbia and the territories, but (by virtue of the Supremacy Clause) Ohio lacked the power to forbid slavery within its boundaries. For Morris, the Constitution compelled no such result; the entire thrust of the Constitution anticipated the abolition of slavery. Given the language of article I, section 8 of the Constitution ("Congress shall have Power to . . . exercise exclusive Legislation" for the District), there could be no doubt regarding congressional power to abolish slavery in the District of Columbia.[18]

Two years later, Calhoun offered his resolutions and demanded Senate approval. Although the Senate (over Morris's continued objection) accepted Calhoun's redefinition of federalism, it tempered his proposal on abolition in the District and the territories and adopted substitute resolutions drafted by Henry Clay. As adopted, the resolutions asserted that congressional power over slavery in the District would violate the understanding by which Virginia and Maryland had ceded the land to the United States. Absent consent of these states, abolition in the District was impermissible.[19]

Morris had denied that the wishes of Virginia or Maryland (or residents of the District) were constitutionally relevant at all. Because the Constitution had been adopted not as a compact between states but as an act of the people, Congress represented the people of all the states. The Constitution did not provide for residents of the District to elect any member of Congress. Instead, sovereignty over the District was vested by the Constitution in Congress as a whole. Thus in legislating for the District, Congress was acting neither for the residents nor the states but for the nation as a whole. The wishes of individual states imposed no constraint on congressional power. In 1838, Morris continued to believe, however, that abolition in the District was a question of expediency, not constitutional power.[20]

The debate on congressional power over slavery, however, was not limited to action for the District. In September 1837, Alvan Stewart announced that slavery in the states was unconstitutional as a result of the Fifth Amendment,[21] in a speech to the New York Anti-Slavery Society. Stewart's "speech marked the dramatic debut of radical antislavery constitutionalism."[22] At the 1838 annual meeting of the American Anti-Slavery Society he attempted to remove the language in the Society's Constitution acknowledging that slavery in the states was a matter to be determined by state law. Although Stewart's proposal received a majority of delegate votes, it fell short of the two-thirds needed to amend the Society's constitution.[23] Morris never accepted Stewart's understanding of the Fifth Amendment, but he did come to believe that Congress had the power to abolish slavery in the states.

Morris had always thought that it was the existence of slavery itself, not the extra seats in Congress and electoral votes resulting from the three-fifths clause, that gave the Slave Power its power. Chase's goal of divorcing government from slavery might halt its expansion and lead to its ultimate extinction but did not strike immediately at the source of the Slave Power. It would continue to threaten the nation while Chase was awaiting its demise. Only abolition of slavery in the states where it existed could accomplish the destruction of the Slave Power.[24] The Money Power had been destroyed when Jackson refused to recharter the Bank of the United States; the Slave Power would end when slavery was abolished. Aileen Kraditor mused that "it would perhaps be uncharitable to assume" the notion of the limits imposed by conceding the protection of slavery in the states "provided some political abolitionists with their motive for finding slavery unconstitutional."[25] Whatever may have motivated others, for Morris, finding a way to strike directly at the Slave Power was imperative.

Stewart's argument flew in the face of the federal consensus and suffered serious factual flaws. Abolition leaders criticized Stewart's position as "dangerous and seductive sophistry" resting on "a fundamental misreading of the U. S. Constitution."[26] In reporting the debate, the *Philanthropist* noted that after a thorough review of Stewart's argument, it had come to "a clear and firm conviction" that Stewart's position was "dangerous heresy," and that Stewart had "totally failed in making his case."[27] Morris, although agreeing that the Fifth Amendment did not bar Congress from abolishing slavery in the District of Columbia or territories, never accepted Stewart's view that the Fifth Amendment prohibited the states from adopting slavery. He did not believe slavery unconstitutional in the states. As William Birney's letter to his father made clear, Morris wanted to challenge Chase and Bailey on "the power of Congress over slavery in the states."[28] By 1843, Morris had decided that the federal consensus was wrong.

148   THE CREATION OF A CRUSADER

In 1836 Morris had argued that because the Constitution only recognized persons, Calhoun's view of the Fifth Amendment as depriving Congress of the power to abolish slavery in the District of Columbia and the territories was flawed. Although he believed Congress had been granted the power to legislate in all matters concerning the District, what constituted property was "entirely the creature of state laws."[29] As a result, Morris concluded that Congress lacked the power to establish slavery anywhere. Congress could not make persons property: "The United States can protect persons, but cannot make them property."[30] The Fifth Amendment prohibited any legislation establishing slavery. Since slavery existed only by virtue of positive law, slavery was unconstitutional "in all places over which Congress has exclusive power of legislation."[31] Rather than abolition being a question of expediency, slavery was unconstitutional in the District of Columbia. The status of slavery in the states, however, had still seemed to be beyond the reach of Congress.

Morris had been considering the prospect of congressional action against slavery in the states since his defeat for reelection.[32] By 1843, he had decided Congress possessed such a power. That summer, at the eighth annual meeting of the Ohio Anti-Slavery Society, Morris had been appointed to the Business Committee, in Chase's absence. He attempted to have the committee offer resolutions asserting congressional power to abolish slavery in the states where it already existed. Although the committee refused to support his resolutions, it agreed that Morris could present his ideas to the general meeting and speak in support of his resolutions. On Thursday evening he "occupied the attention of the Society with a bold argument upon the constitutional power of Congress to abolish slavery throughout the United States." This power, however, did not come from the Fifth Amendment or any other specific clause in the Constitution. Instead, Morris relied on the Preamble and concluded:

> That, the Congress of the United States have power, and it is their duty to carry into full and complete effect, the end and object for which the constitution was ordained and established. It is the duty of Congress, to "form a more perfect union" to "establish Justice in each State, to ensure domestic tranquility" throughout the country, to promote the general welfare; "and above all to" secure the blessings of Liberty to all our citizens and posterity; Congress therefore, have power by virtue of the Constitution of the United States, to abolish slavery in each and every State of the Union.[33]

He did not claim that slavery in the states was unconstitutional. Instead, Congress had the power to abolish slavery everywhere. Although he recognized that Congress had "the right to determine when and to what extent that power shall be exercised," Morris believed that it should act now: "Congress ought to abolish slavery at once throughout the country; for slavery is inimical to the Union of the States, destructive of justice, and a palpable denial of it to a large portion of our people. It disturbs our domestic tranquility and engenders strife and contention amongst us while it has reduced the colored race to absolute and unconditional bondage, while the slaveholders are endeavoring to subject the white laboring race of our country to a state of vassalage."[34] At the conclusion of Morris's speech, Leicester King briefly dissented and by agreement, Morris's resolutions were tabled with instruction for the *Philanthropist* to print them.[35]

The senator who had contended that Arkansas could do whatever it pleased as long as it had a republican form of government had been replaced by an abolitionist agitator who urged the federal government take immediate positive action to end slavery throughout the country. The leading authority on antislavery constitutionalism, William Wiecek, noted several years ago that "The Constitution was built on the principles of the Declaration of Independence and on the objectives outlined in its own preamble, but these were incompatible with the system of slavery ensconced in the document."[36] Morris had come to agree on both points. His solution was no longer to attempt to reconcile the irreconcilable. Instead, Congress could and should abolish slavery everywhere.

Morris's transformation and argument are remarkable. Throughout his career he had been deeply suspicious of the "centralizing" power of the federal government. He had gone to Washington determined to resist any attack on states' rights and was committed to limiting congressional power to the enumerated grants in the Constitution. Even in areas where Congress was granted power, Morris was concerned about its exercise. As a senator he had accused Congress of a "constant tendency . . . to extend the action of this Government into the orbit of State power," threatening "an end to the Sovereignty of the States."[37] Yet, he now believed that the Preamble was an affirmative grant of power to Congress to act on slavery,[38] not just in the District of Columbia or the territories but in the states where it already existed.

As a legal argument, Morris's approach was something of a tour de force. Stewart had combined the Fifth Amendment and natural law to argue that slavery was unconstitutional in the states. This approach ran directly contrary to the Supreme Court's holding in *Barron v. Baltimore* that the Bill of Rights did not apply to the states.[39] Morris's argument avoided this problem entirely. Instead of asserting that the Fifth Amendment was a grant of power or that slavery was unconstitutional in the states, he argued that Congress had the power to eliminate it. Until Congress acted, slavery in the states could continue.

This conclusion also resolved Morris's dilemma regarding the admission of new slave states. He had voted in favor of Arkansas's admission in 1836 and had reaffirmed that view in 1838. He thought that, although Congress could prohibit slavery in the territories, once the territory became a state, it could "instantly revise its constitution" to adopt slavery. Congress was powerless to prevent such an action because "the people have at all times a right to alter . . . their government."[40] Congressional power to abolish slavery in the states, however, eliminated this possibility and justified refusing to admit any new slave states.

His approach also avoided the Tenth Amendment as a constraint on congressional action. Because Morris found an explicit grant of power to Congress in the Preamble, the Tenth Amendment's reservation of unenumerated powers to the states was inapplicable. Moreover, while the Fifth Amendment did not prohibit the states from establishing slavery, neither did its prohibition on taking property without due process bar Congress from abolishing slavery. Morris's long-held position that under the Constitution, slaves were "persons," not "property," allowed him to avoid the Fifth Amendment's prohibition against taking without due process as well.[41] Finally, Morris's approach provided powerful justification for political antislavery: an abolitionist majority in Congress could emancipate all of the slaves.[42]

The Supreme Court has never held the Preamble to be an affirmative grant of power to the federal government. In relying on the Preamble as a grant of power to Congress to abolish slavery in the states, Morris was stretching the text. The Preamble was not part of article I (powers of Congress) nor did it contain any reference to congressional power like the Territories or District of Columbia clauses (article IV, §3; article I, §8). William Wiecek thought that in making similar arguments, "radical abolitionists produced a flawed and disingenuous constitutional program."[43] Morris's argument was certainly outside of traditional constitutional interpretation. Yet, his approach may not have been self-evidently flawed. Writing in 2015, Akhil Reed Amar, Sterling Professor of Law and Political Science at Yale University, laid out a "face value" interpretation of the Preamble that would empower Congress to strike down racial segregation in public schools. Although concluding that the words of the Preamble cannot be taken at "face value" when considering race or slavery, Amar's analysis differs only marginally from Morris's.[44]

In his commentary accompanying the report of the meeting, Bailey noted Morris's resolutions and speech. He was not persuaded by Morris's argument. "The truth," according to Bailey, was that "every fact in the history of the Constitution is against the Theory." As a result, neither Bailey nor "any considerable portion of the American people believed Congress had this power." Nevertheless, the meeting "listened with great respect to a man, who always thinks for himself and thinks vigorously."[45] Morris had a second opportunity two months later to again explain his views on Congress's constitutional power over slavery in the states.

As Chase and Bailey had attempted to move the Liberty Party away from its identification with abolitionism, a group of abolitionists, organized by Garrisonian lecturers, had founded the Ohio American Antislavery Society.[46] Although Garrison opposed political action and "characterized abolitionists who supported the Liberty Party as sinful backsliders," the "lines between the Garrisonians and the Liberty Party were still not well drawn in upstate New York or Ohio." Indeed, the largest Liberty vote totals in Ohio generally came from areas where the Garrisonians were strongest.[47] This new Ohio organization invited the Liberty leadership to attend its anniversary meeting on September 4, 1843. While Chase, King, and Lewis attended the national Liberty Party Convention in Buffalo, Morris participated in the proceedings of the Ohio Garrisonians' first state convention.[48]

Remarkably, Morris (the professional politician and Liberty Party nominee who had consistently argued that the Constitution was antislavery) was appointed to the convention's Business Committee, spoke on behalf of several resolutions, and was appointed to a committee encouraging Cincinnati merchants to maintain an inventory of goods made by free labor. Garrison generally "dismissed as naïve wordplay or deceptive political contrivance" any arguments that Congress could act on slavery directly.[49] Nevertheless, Morris chose this meeting of Garrison supporters (attended by several representatives from the East) to again urge "that Congress had the power to abolish slavery on the States, by the Constitution of the U. S. and that slavery exists nowhere by legal right." When an Eastern Garrisonian argued "that the Constitution was a pro-slavery instrument," Morris challenged his position and denied that the Constitution required the return of fugitive slaves or was otherwise pro-slavery.[50]

William Birney also outlined for his father the ideological positions of the Ohio Liberty Party leadership. In Hamilton County, where Chase, Lewis, and Bailey were most popular, Birney felt "Morris is in the minority, I should think, among the voters of our party here—not in the belief of the doctrines taught, but in the support of men." If an open split occurred, the younger Birney believed that "more would adhere to Chase or Lewis." He told his father that "all were pleased (except C and B) with his nomination and none with Morris."[51]

William Birney was probably correct in noting the acceptance of Morris's ideas by the Liberty rank and file.[52] Several weeks after his letter to his father, the state Liberty Party Convention (with Morris, Chase, and Lewis absent) unanimously adopted resolutions declaring that the Federal Fugitive Slave Law was unconstitutional, and that the Fifth Amendment made slavery unconstitutional in the District and the Territories. Indeed, the convention went further and declared that the Preamble, combined with the Fifth Amendment, made slavery unconstitutional in the states.[53] This resolution, drafted by Bailey, was a testament to the influence of Morris's constitutional theories and the closest the Ohio Liberty Party "ever came to countenancing direct federal authority over slavery in the states."[54]

There are at least two reasons, however, to doubt William Birney's assessment of Morris's local influence and popularity. First, the Cincinnati leadership repeatedly presented Morris as a leader in the local Liberty Party. For example, less than a month after Morris publicly announced his theory of congressional power over slavery in the states, they asked Morris to draft the call for the 1843 county Liberty Party Convention. In the call, Morris invited both party members and those opposed to the Liberty Party to attend. He told his readers that "the slave power has become omnipotent," and that "no person can enjoy that liberty promised and intended to be secured by the constitution while another is held in slavery." It was imperative "to abolish the wicked, the deplorable, and ruinous system of slavery in our country." The only way that "can be lawfully done . . . [was] through the ballot-box."[55] Morris's invitation was the antithesis of Chase and Bailey's effort to distinguish the Liberty Party from abolitionism.

At the convention held in August, the Hamilton County Liberty members nominated a full slate of candidates for state offices. The slate, which was proposed by the business committee led by Chase and Bailey, included Lewis for Congress and Morris for state senate.[56] In the five weeks prior to the election, the local party held twenty-two campaign events throughout the county featuring the candidates and party leaders. When the county returns were tallied, Morris had exceeded five hundred votes. Bailey claimed this vote "represented the true strength of the Liberty party" in Hamilton County.[57] Reporting on the outcome of the election, Bailey made no reference to Lewis whom Morris had out-polled by nearly 4 percent—certainly not an overwhelming difference, but hardly indicative of a strong preference for the Chase faction by Hamilton County Liberty Party voters.

Second, Chase's view of Morris's position with party members appears to have differed from William Birney's impression. Chase revealed his belief that Morris retained significant influence in his approach to a highly public fugitive slave case. In April 1842, John VanZandt had met nine fugitive slaves on a road north of Cincinnati. He had hidden them in his wagon, where they were subsequently discovered. After paying a reward to the men who had captured the fugitives, the owner sued VanZandt in federal court for damages. Well aware of Chase's earlier efforts on behalf of Birney, VanZandt asked Chase to defend him. To Chase, the case presented an opportunity "to remove the stigma of abolitionists from Ohio's Liberty Party and advance the claim that states' rights protected human liberty." Chase seized the opportunity, but in the midst of his campaign to remove Birney from the Liberty ticket, he also "decided to improve his standing with the Liberty party leadership by having Thomas Morris act as co-counsel."[58]

The case did not come on for trial for over a year. At the trial, held in Cincinnati before US Supreme Court Justice John McClean during the July 1843 term of court,[59] both men appeared on behalf of VanZandt. At the conclusion of the plaintiff's case, Morris moved to "overrule the evidence" (today a directed verdict) "on the ground that, admitting all the facts proved, they established no case of unlawful concealment, and no notice to the defendant that the alleged fugitives had escaped from Kentucky into Ohio." Chase recalled that both he and Morris argued the motion, but that he focused on the lack of notice issue. If Chase's memory was accurate, Morris likely argued that the Fugitive Slave Clause of the Constitution was "in derogation of natural liberty and of state rights," and that the Fugitive Slave "act of Congress under which the action was brought was repugnant to the national Constitution and to the ordinance of 1787, and therefore void."[60] An observer described the argument as "embracing the whole question of slavery, especially its relationship to the Constitution." He noted that Morris "advanced some of the boldest positions which he supported with ability." Chase closed (three hours) for the defense, which as "a specimen of forensic eloquence had seldom been equaled."[61]

The decision in *Prigg v. Pennsylvania*, 41 U. S. 536 (1842), affirming the constitutionality of the 1793 Fugitive Slave Act, made any challenge to the law under the US Constitution problematic. *Prigg*, however, was distinguishable on at least two grounds: (1) the issue in *Prigg* was the criminality of a peaceful recapture of an admitted fugitive as kidnapping under state law. In VanZandt, the issue was liability in damages under federal law for aiding fugitives; and (2) the Ordinance of 1787 (not applicable to Pennsylvania), combined with the local nature of slavery and the Tenth Amendment, could be argued to make the act unconstitutional as applied. The court denied the motion, and Chase and Morris called their own witnesses in an attempt to impeach the plaintiff's witnesses. The case was then submitted to the jury and Chase and Morris argued the "same legal positions as on the motion to overrule."[62] Despite Chase and Morris's efforts, the jury returned a verdict against VanZandt.

The campaign of 1843 dealt only with local offices and seats in the general assembly. Nevertheless, the Ohio Liberty Party mounted a campaign that roughly followed the lines of the effort in the preceding year. Conventions listened to Liberty orators and nominated local candidates. The combined vote for the party's nominees across all congressional districts in Ohio rose to 5,432.[63] As in the previous elections, the party failed to win a major race anywhere in the state. The Whig press, however, did blame several of their defeats on the desertions of Whigs to the Liberty Party.[64] On the eve of its second presidential campaign, the Liberty organization in Ohio was a growing but still largely insignificant force.

Eastern party members saw these results in Cincinnati as confirming Morris's influence. In mid-October Leavitt wrote a complimentary editorial in the *Emancipator* calling Morris "a statesman of the Jeffersonian school . . . [who] alone in the space of a quarter of a century has dared to speak with the voice of a free and honest man" in the Senate.[65] Two weeks later Leavitt took a deliberate slap at Chase and Bailey by ignoring their efforts while praising Morris's work: "*The Philanthropist* gives the returns from several of the Southern counties. Hamilton County, which last year gave 147 Liberty votes, this year gave 544. Here our candidate for Vice-President, Thomas Morris, has been diligently at' work."[66]

The internal struggle for state party leadership had existed for well over a year. Despite his contrary statements to Birney, Bailey had long been jealous of Morris and had expressed his "dislike" of Morris to Birney's son.[67] By the beginning of 1844, the relationship had deteriorated further. Bailey had still not published the Liberty ticket, causing Morris to consider again declining the vice presidential nomination.[68] Morris's fits of temper, particularly when he believed himself denied a position or recognition he deserved, were legendary. Age had not mellowed Morris: "Before leaving, I expressed to you the fear of an open rupture between Mr. Morris and Dr. Bailey. It occurred during my absence. Mr. M has discontinued his paper and denounced the editor. What will grow out of it does not yet appear. The doctor is much incensed and has privately threatened to expose some former shortcomings as a moral man of Mr. Morris."[69] The possible basis of Bailey's threat has puzzled historians. Birney's biographer reported that she had "found nothing in the records to indicate that there was any basis for Bailey's claims."[70] Bailey's most recent biographer speculated he was referring to Morris's opposition to Black suffrage.[71] William Birney's description of the matter as involving "former short comings as a moral man of Mr. Morris" and reflecting Bailey's "untimely zeal against a long past moral evil," however, make it unlikely that Bailey was referring to a recent dispute.

Although Bailey never articulated the basis for his assertions, he had likely learned of a criminal charge made against Morris more than three decades earlier. In May 1809, in the aftermath of the effort to impeach the Ohio Supreme Court justices, Morris had been accused of rape. He responded by charging the complainant with perjury. Both complaints were referred to the same Clermont County grand jury. After hearing evidence for both parties, the grand jury refused to return an indictment on either charge; only two jurors voted to indict Morris for rape, which was "twice the number that voted to charge Ireland with perjury." Morris then filed a civil action for slander against his accuser, but it does not appear that this slander claim was ever tried.[72]

All of these claims and counterclaims (as well as the grand jury's actions) were reported by the press at the time and, in all probability, Bailey had discovered them. Eastern Liberty Party leaders, however, may have already been aware of the charges and hesitated to nominate Morris in 1840, at least in part because of "an intimation in an Ohio paper . . . that a man lately high in national office, was charged with an aggravated crime."[73] Whatever may

156   THE CREATION OF A CRUSADER

have been the source or content of Bailey's threats, William Birney enlisted Chase's help to persuade Bailey to change his mind. Presumably, Chase's intervention was successful; Bailey did not follow through with his threat.[74]

In Ohio the Liberty Party campaign of 1844 began following the state convention in February. In addition to adopting resolutions built upon Morris's constitutional theories, the delegates renominated Leicester King for governor, concurred in the nominations of Birney and Morris, and urged increased local activity. The convention also finally appointed presidential electors to support Birney and Morris, and Bailey published the 1843 Buffalo nominations.[75] With the endorsement of the convention and Bailey's actions, Morris calmed down and decided not to decline the vice president nomination. By the end of March, "matters moved along more smoothly" in Cincinnati.[76]

The potential annexation of Texas had long been a concern of antislavery advocates. Antislavery efforts contributed to forcing the issue into the 1844 presidential contest. In early 1843, Lewis Tappan was approached by Stephen Andrews with a scheme to have Great Britain provide loans to purchase all slaves owned by Texans. The ultimate goal was the abolition of slavery in Texas and the prevention of the annexation of Texas by the United States. Tappan became enamored by the proposal and traveled to England to present it to British officials. The British demurred, although news of the proposal was made public and allowed the Tyler administration to present annexation as necessary to prevent Britain from controlling Texas.[77]

In April 1844, Tyler presented a treaty of annexation to the Senate, where it was referred to the Foreign Affairs Committee. Benjamin Tappan, Morris's old nemesis and Lewis Tappan's brother, was a member of the committee. Although the treaty and the committee's review were secret, Benjamin Tappan sent the treaty to his brother and asked that he have it published. After agonizing over the course he should pursue, Lewis gave it to the New York *Evening Post,* which published it. The uproar caused by the leak persuaded Van Buren to oppose annexation publicly. Tappan's breach of the Senate's rules helped propel James Polk to the nomination. It also allowed Tappan to make a $50,000 profit from speculation in Texas's bonds and earn the censure of the Senate.[78]

As the campaign began, then, the Ohio party had reason to be encouraged. The Tyler administration's move to annex Texas made the Slave Power salient to an increasing number of voters.[79] The Cincinnati Liberty leaders recognized the potential of this issue. In late March, the *Philanthro-*

pist editorialized that both parties were responsible and controlled by the Slave Power. The next day, a citywide meeting organized by local Whigs resolved to oppose annexation. Morris did not attend the meeting, but Chase, Lewis, Bailey, and other Liberty Party members did. After proposing several amendments to the resolutions, Chase moved to question potential presidential candidates about their position on Texas. Although approved by the meeting, the Whig leadership appointed only Liberty Party members to the committee to question candidates. Chase wrote Polk, seeking his position on Texas. Polk's response made clear his commitment to annexation.[80]

The release of Calhoun's Pakenham letter confirmed abolitionists' fears that annexation was part of the Slave Power's defense of slavery. The letter "explicitly cast the pending annexation treaty as . . . intended to . . . preserve slavery in Texas, and protect it in the existing slaveholding states."[81] Polk's nomination on a strong annexation platform, coupled with Clay's waffling on the issue, created an opportunity for the Liberty Party in Ohio. Annexation did not appear popular (both Democrat senators from Ohio had voted against the treaty). Among Democrats, the dumping of Van Buren for Polk caused many to "speak out indignantly against the domination of the slaveholding oligarchy."[82] To Ohio observers, Polk's nomination and Calhoun's machinations in support of annexation fit well within the Slave Power narrative.[83] Bailey and Chase believed large numbers would join the cause if the issue were presented as limiting the growth of the Slave Power.

By 1844, however, Morris, had accepted a radical antislavery interpretation of the Constitution. He still saw the Slave Power as an ominous threat but thought more than simply limiting its growth was necessary. He opposed annexation but believed Congress could and should abolish slavery in the States. Morris had moved from an antislavery politician to an abolitionist involved in politics.

Despite the Ohio convention's acceptance of Morris's constitutional theories, to Chase and Bailey, Morris's view of congressional power over slavery in the states promised to be the undoing of the Liberty Party. Morris's theory provided a compelling justification for political action, but also vindicated all the critics claiming the party was abolitionist. Limiting the party's goals to halting the expansion of slavery was more consistent with attracting support from nonabolitionists. The Cincinnati leaders continued to attempt to silence Morris. To reduce Morris's influence on the party and halt the spread of his radical doctrines, Chase and Bailey erected roadblocks against the ex-senator in Liberty meetings and the *Philanthropist:*

"As Mr. M [orris's] mode of action fell into disfavor with the party generally through the influence of Chase and Bailey, he himself urged it more strenuously and especially in meetings. He was met by Business Committees (of which the Dr. and Mr. C were always members) through whose hands all resolutions were to pass and he was prevented from discussion on topics deemed by him to be important. Some communications of his were not published with praise in the Philanthropist, while Mr. C's always were. Mr. C's efforts as a speaker were lauded, but Mr. M's passed unnoticed."[84] Although these tactics limited Morris's ability to publicize his views, they "wrought on the fiery mind of Mr. M[orris] until he became suspicious of everything from" Bailey and Chase.[85]

By the beginning of the organized campaign in June, most of the Ohio Liberty Party's differences appeared, at least on the surface, to have been overcome. Although he was sought after by Liberty organizers outside Ohio, Morris's age and health forced him to limit his efforts to Ohio.[86] He again participated in stumping the state, although not as extensively as in 1842. An increasing amount of the labor fell on Chase, King, Lewis, and William Birney.[87] With Texas as a central issue in the campaign, the third party at last had an issue that the rest of the electorate could understand.[88]

Both the Whigs and the Democrats were also aware of the potential for the Liberty Party to profit from the Texas controversy. After Van Buren's letter opposing annexation was published, the *Ohio Statesman,* echoing Morris's observation in opposing Calhoun's resolutions in 1838, opined that "the real object of annexation was the perpetuation and extension of slavery, and the political power of the slave states."[89] When Polk was nominated on a platform endorsing annexation, however, Ohio Democrats decided to downplay Texas for fear of driving Liberty Party supporters into the ranks of the Whigs. The Polk supporters simply hoped that enough Whig abolitionists would join the third party to give the election to the Democrats.[90]

But the Whigs, realizing that the Liberty Party's growth posed a threat to Clay's chances in Ohio, launched an assault of unprecedented vehemence. Thomas Ewing, a Whig candidate for the Senate, found the Liberty men "increasingly troublesome," while another Whig speaker called them "a gang of mercenary scamps whose only object is office."[91] The Ohio Whigs, however, did more than simply denounce the Liberty Party. In thoroughly antislavery districts they nominated antislavery Whigs who would support Clay. For example, the chair of the Ohio Whig Central Committee pressed for support for Joshua Giddings.[92] As the *Cleveland Herald* noted, "the nomination of [Joshua] Giddings would give the Whigs the abolition vote of the district without sacrifice, because Giddings was a Clay Whig."[93] When Giddings refused repeated overtures to join the Liberty Party and campaigned aggressively for Clay, "his effect on the Ohio Liberty Party vote was devastating."[94]

In addition, Clay's Raleigh letter seemed to say that he opposed the annexation of Texas. The use of this letter convinced many antislavery Whigs to stay with the party.[95] The other powerful weapon in the Whig arsenal was the obvious impossibility of a Liberty victory. They repeatedly told the Liberty men that the only way to keep Texas out of the Union was to vote the Whig ticket.[96]

Despite these attacks and arguments, the Liberty Party again increased its vote in the state elections. The final returns of the October gubernatorial election showed Tod (Democrat) 145,022; Bartley (Whig) 146,333; King (Liberty) 8,898.[97] The narrow margin of victory placed the outcome of November Ohio presidential balloting in doubt. The Whigs stepped up their attacks. Giddings led the assault on Birney, Morris, and the Liberty Party. Under his influence, the Ohio Liberty Party ranks began to waver, while the state Liberty Party Committee urged Western Reserve abolitionists, "For God and Duty Stand: Stand this once."[98]

In the closing days of the presidential canvass, the Whigs went beyond argument and abuse. In an attempt to save Clay, the party press published a forged letter purported to be from Birney to J. B. Garland in which Birney acknowledged being a Democrat.[99] The carefully timed release of the letter did not permit Birney to reply to the charges before the ballots were cast. Across the North, wavering Whigs returned to their party.[100] In Ohio the Liberty total declined by at least a thousand votes from its total in the state elections three weeks earlier, but William Birney believed the forgery had cost the party even more: "In the state the Rohrbach Garland letter lost us about 3,000 votes. From every quarter we heard news of certain accessions to our number and a large increase to our vote over the state election vote. But the Garland forgery appeared on the eve of the election, too late for us to get the contradiction before the people. Hundreds staid [sic] away from the polls and many voted for Clay."[101] Despite all of these adversities, the Liberty Party still managed to poll sixty-two thousand votes throughout the North. It took enough votes from Clay in New York to give the state and the election to Polk.[102] To Van Buren and his followers, however, the outcome in New York resulted from Silas Wright's candidacy for governor. Polk ran behind Wright by several thousand votes, which was attributed to the influence of the antislavery campaign. For these Democrats, it was time to move away from the South.[103]

The election of 1844 proved to be Thomas Morris's final campaign. On December 7, 1844, he suffered a massive stroke and died. Age and the strain of decades of stump speaking had taken their toll. He had given political antislavery an impetus in its formative years. Although his forceful expression of a radical position compromised his political effectiveness in his final years, he had retained a considerable influence within the antislavery movement. His consistent demand for principle had helped check the moderate drift of the antislavery organization. Far from being the conservative opponent of Black rights that some historians have portrayed, Morris had become a vocal proponent of Black rights and radical abolition.

Conclusion

In 1839 in the afterglow of Morris's dramatic reply to Henry Clay on the floor of the United States Senate, Joshua Leavitt confidently predicted that once slavery had been abolished, Morris would be more honored than Clay.[1] Whatever may be the current status of Clay's reputation, Leavitt missed the mark on Morris. Twentieth-century historians largely marginalized Morris. For nearly 150 years he languished in the footnotes of antislavery history. More recently, historians have acknowledged Morris's articulation of the Slave Power concept and his "martyrdom" by Ohio Jacksonians for his antislavery beliefs as significant events in the emergence of political antislavery.[2] They have generally continued, however, to overlook his substantial contributions to the development of antislavery constitutionalism.

The Slave Power's control of the federal government and Morris's fate at the hands of Jacksonians demonstrated both the limits of moral suasion and the futility of working with existing national parties and persuaded many abolitionists of the necessity of an independent political organization. While most abolitionists accepted the federal consensus and acknowledged the impossibility of taking action on slavery in the states where it already existed, the threat to civil liberty in the free states from Morris's Slave Power provided a compelling justification for entry into the political arena. Although Morris publicly described the evil of the Slave Power repeatedly beginning with the Incendiary Publications debate, his reply to Clay was crucial in generating widespread acceptance of the concept.

162 CONCLUSION

As William Birney recalled, the debate in the Senate acted as a "trumpet call" to political action.[3] The extensive publication of Morris's speech at this pivotal moment in the development of political antislavery ideology served to rivet the Slave Power in the political lexicon of the period.

The speech's effect was not so much to make immediate converts among nonabolitionists but to crystallize abolitionist support for an independent political effort. Events in the 1850s, however, such as the Kansas-Nebraska Act, the attack on Charles Sumner in the Senate, and the *Dred Scott* decision, seemed to confirm Morris's warnings of two decades earlier and convinced an increasing number of Northerners that an aggressive Slave Power was both a reality and a threat.[4] Morris's imagery provided a direct connection between the "master symbols" of two eras,[5] and was essential to the development of the sectionalism driving political antislavery in the 1850s. Indeed, "the image of the Slave Power was a necessary means for arousing the fears and galvanizing the will of the North to face a genuine moral and political challenge."[6] "Northern politics and thought were permeated by the Slave Power idea in the 1850's"; it "was the ideological glue of the Republican Party."[7]

The "founding of the American Anti-Slavery Society in 1833" with its demands for immediate abolition (particularly in the District of Columbia and the territories) "initiated more than two decades of extraordinary intellectual creativity among antislavery constitutionalists."[8] Morris was among antislavery's most creative and respected theorists of the decade following the American Anti-Slavery Society's creation. He had gone to the Senate committed "to think and act for [himself]." Over the next decade, Morris did just that.[9] He saw in the Slave Power's demands for special treatment for slaveholding elites the continuation of the same evil that the Money Power posed to individual rights and opportunities. His perception of the threat to liberty posed by the Slave Power drove him to think deeply about slavery's relationship to the Constitution and placed him at the forefront of antislavery constitutional thought. As James Oakes has noted, slavery's relationship to the Constitution was "the most important problem that antislavery faced" in the years leading up to the Civil War.[10]

As a result, before abolitionists "could begin to formulate a federal policy aimed at the destruction of slavery, they had to develop a constitutionally viable argument restricting the rights of property" in slaves.[11] Forced to confront this issue directly in 1836 because of Calhoun's objection to the Senate's reception of antislavery petitions, Morris articulated

CONCLUSION

what became the abolitionist answer: slaves were property under state statutes, but they were not property under the Constitution. This distinction between slaves as property under state law but as persons under the Constitution became the cornerstone of antislavery constitutionalism.[12] Within two years of Morris Incendiary Publications speech, "radical opponents of slavery were routinely dismissing the idea of a constitutional right to slaves."[13]

Morris also established the antislavery constitutional consequence of the "local" nature of slavery. The idea that slavery required positive law to exist had been around since Lord Mansfield decided *Somerset v. Stewart* (1772).[14] Absent some legislative act establishing slavery, freedom was the universal condition under the common law. Morris's 1836 response to Calhoun not only rejected the notion that the Constitution protected slave property created by state law but also argued that under the Constitution, only states—not Congress—could create this status. This theory of the absence of federal power to make persons property provided the constitutional support for political antislavery's proclamation of "freedom national."[15]

Morris's position as a United States senator, his rejection for reelection as a result of his antislavery views, and his ultimate expulsion from the Democrat Party gave him a national prominence and enhanced credibility within abolitionist ranks. National leaders repeatedly sought his attendance at national meetings and conventions. Abolitionists sought and published his views not only on the Slave Power but on the constitutional status of slavery. Building on his understanding of the impact of the absence of any recognition of property in persons in the constitutional text and the "local" nature of slavery, Morris's theories of the limited reach of the Fugitive Slave Clause, the antislavery character of the Constitution, and the constitutional prohibition on the establishment of slavery by Congress were given to the political antislavery effort early in its formative period. By the time of Morris's death, each of these ideas had become accepted antislavery dogma and core principles of antislavery constitutionalism. These tenets came to define political antislavery; each of them was incorporated into the Liberty Party platform in the 1844 election.[16]

The linchpin for all of Morris's constitutional thought was the absence of any explicit recognition of a right to property in man within the text of the Constitution. The status of slaves as constitutional persons, when combined with the egalitarian principles of the Declaration of Independence, which Morris believed infused the Constitution, meant not only that the

Slave Power's pro-slavery Constitution was a distortion, but that the document was inherently antislavery. Morris recognized that if Calhoun and Clay's pro-slavery interpretation was correct, "it is slavery, not liberty, that makes us one people."[17] For Morris, this was a "libel upon the Constitution," and "not the doctrine which the fathers of American Liberty held. It has only been promulgated by [this generation] of their degenerate sons."[18] For him, Calhoun's claim "that the Constitution of the United States countenances slavery" was as specious as a claim "that it countenances murder."[19] The pro-slavery Constitution was not the creation of the founders but the machination of the aristocratic Slave Power.

After Morris's death, his ideas were repeated with increasing frequency by antislavery political activists and became ingrained in the Free-Soil and Republican Parties' creeds. In large part the continued vitality of Morris's antislavery thought in the years preceding the Civil War was attributable to his Ohio Liberty Party rival Salmon Chase. He "would emerge as the Liberty Party's, and then the Republicans, most influential thinker about slavery and the Constitution," but his theories built "upon existing antislavery arguments." Indeed "most of his key points had already emerged in antislavery speeches and writings."[20] In particular, in developing his constitutional theory, Chase borrowed heavily from Morris.[21] Not only the threat of the Slave Power but the "local" nature of slavery, the constitutional limitations on congressional power to establish slavery in the District and the Territories, the logical consequences of Calhoun's view of the Fifth Amendment, the threat slavery posed to free labor, and the imperative for equal justice all found their way into Chase's speeches, resolutions, party platforms, and ultimately Republican Party orthodoxy.[22] It was a debt Chase freely acknowledged more than a decade after Morris's death.[23]

Although rejected by Chase and the moderates, Morris's identification of the Preamble as the essential text for determining congressional power over slavery in the states came to be accepted as part of radical antislavery constitutionalism.[24] "Political abolitionists" in particular came "to stress the [Constitution's] preamble."[25] For example, the year after Morris's death, William Goodell published *Views of American Constitutional Law,* which "embodied the principal ideas of the radical constitutionalists"[26] and accepted Morris's argument that the Preamble provided authority for Congress to act.[27] As Morris had argued, "if the Constitution was what its preamble claimed it to be . . . , the federal government had all the power it needed to abolish slavery in every locality."[28] Goodell's position at the

CONCLUSION

center of radical antislavery constitutional efforts until 1860 assured continued awareness of Morris's argument in antislavery circles.[29]

The influence of Morris's ideas around equality for Blacks is more difficult to assess. Abolitionists were opposed to Black Laws and discrimination based on race long before Morris expressed any concern. To the extent that Morris added to the argument, it was in his Jeffersonian demand that "equal and exact justice" be given to all persons and that this goal must be part of any political antislavery program. From the time of his effort at re-election to the Senate until his death, Morris never wavered in his demand that civil rights for Blacks be part of political antislavery. For Morris, civil rights for Blacks were necessary to defeat the Slave Power. Without his persistent demand for equal and exact justice, however, equal rights quickly became a distant murmur of a past Liberty Party. Within six months of Morris's death, the Southern and Western Liberty Convention (hosted by Chase and Bailey) met in Cincinnati and abandoned all calls for equal rights and "virtually repudiated" the Liberty Party's 1844 platform's "bold egalitarian statements."[30] But the ideal of equality lived on among radical politicians and even Morris's particular expression (equal and exact justice) survived and found its way into the discussion of the 1866 Civil Rights Act.[31]

Historians have long debated the extent of Morris's commitment to abolition. For example, at the conclusion of his brief review of Morris's antislavery actions in the Senate, John Neuenschwander thought "the question of whether Thomas Morris was ever a full-fledged abolitionist deserves consideration."[32] The Free-Soil and Republican nonabolitionists' acceptance of many of his ideas (for example, Slave Power and constitutional prohibition on slavery in the territories) demonstrates that Morris's articulation of these notions did not necessarily make him an abolitionist. Although the question of his status as an abolitionist has only marginal bearing on the impact of his ideas on political antislavery, the increasingly radical trajectory of Morris's thought may provide an answer.

He had arrived in the Senate as a supporter of colonization and in 1838 denied accepting "modern abolition" (that is, Garrisonianism). If Garrisonianism was the test for being an abolitionist, Morris failed. He believed the Constitution was antislavery, endorsed antislavery political action, and rejected nonresistance. All of these views were anathema to Garrison and his followers.[33] Although by 1838 both his political opponents and his antislavery friends called him an abolitionist, Morris at that point remained firmly committed to the federal consensus that Congress could not act on slavery in the states and was convinced that abolition in the District was discretionary (a matter of "expediency") with Congress. Because Congress could not act on slavery in the states, he believed it was pointless for Congress to refuse to admit new states that allowed slavery. These non-immediatist views were contrary to the position of most non-Garrisonian abolitionists at the time. At the end of his campaign for reelection to the Senate, then, many of Morris's views were outside both conventional and Garrisonian abolition.

Some historians have based their doubts not only on Morris's positions but his motivations. They correctly noted that Morris "was never filled with the deep religious indignation toward slavery, nor the empathy for Blacks that qualified so many of his friends as true abolitionists."[34] If religious motivation rather than principle defined abolition, Morris never met the standard. Yet he recognized the prejudice inherent in a system based on color. As he told the Senate, slavery rested entirely on "prejudice against color," not "right and justice . . . ; slavery had no just foundation in color; it rests exclusively upon usurpation, tyranny, oppressive fraud and force." In fact, "all ideas of right and wrong are compounded in the words: emancipate property. Emancipate a horse, or an ox, would not only be an unmeaning, but a ludicrous expression. To emancipate is to set free from slavery. To emancipate is to set free a man, not property."[35]

Although he often spoke in moral terms, Morris's opposition to slavery was always a political question. Morris never sought to save the slaveholder from the sin of slavery. Just as he had fought against monopolies, economic privilege, and the Money Power, Morris struggled against the elitist slaveholders who demanded special protection for their peculiar institution. The aristocratic Slave Power was a threat to civil liberty and to equal and exact justice for all. Because this power was derived solely from the existence of slavery, slavery had to be abolished. His antislavery Constitution was developed to allow the destruction of the Slave Power. In no other way could civil liberty be preserved and equal and exact justice for all be attained.

But if the belief (and advocacy) that immediate emancipation was possible and necessary defined abolitionism,[36] by the end of his life Morris was a thoroughgoing abolitionist. In the years following his 1838 campaign for reelection to the Senate, he articulated increasingly radical abolitionist views. He condemned colonization as simply an effort by slaveholders to eliminate free Blacks from the South. He repeatedly demanded equal and exact justice (civil rights) for all persons regardless of color. He concluded that slavery in the District of Columbia and the territories was not a matter of expediency but rather was unconstitutional. He rejected the federal consensus and argued that Congress had the power to abolish slavery throughout the country, including the states in which it existed, and had the duty to act immediately. Given this power, Congress should refuse to admit any new state that provided for slavery in its constitution. These views placed Morris among the most radical of abolitionists and far beyond most of his contemporary advocates of political antislavery.

In many respects, then, Chase's recollection that Morris "was ahead of his time,"[37] not just in terms of the Slave Power but in the antislavery interpretation of the Constitution, was certainly correct. Morris's ideas provided both the imperative for antislavery political action and the theoretical constitutional underpinnings for that action. His conclusion that Congress had the power to implement the Constitution's commitment to civil rights stretched the antislavery constitution to its limits. Not until two decades after his death and the adoption of the Civil Rights Act and the Fourteenth Amendment with its recognition of congressional power to enforce equal justice directly on persons within the states did political antislavery catch up with Morris.[38]

Notes

INTRODUCTION

1. Abraham Lincoln, "Address at Cooper Institute," New York City, Feb. 27, 1860, in Roy P. Basler, ed., *The Collected Works of Abraham Lincoln* (New Brunswick: Rutgers Univ. Press, 1958), 3:522–50.

2. Thomas Morris, "Speech on Incendiary Publications," Apr. 13, 1836, in Cong. Globe, 24th Cong., 1st Sess., appendix, 283–84 (1836).

3. Jonathan H. Earle, *Jacksonian Antislavery and the Politics of Free Soil, 1824–1854* (Chapel Hill: Univ. of North Carolina Press, 2004), 37.

4. Sean Wilentz, *Rise of American Democracy: Jefferson to Lincoln* (New York: W. W. Norton, 2005), 477.

5. Text of Report in Benjamin Franklin Morris, ed., *The Life of Thomas Morris: Pioneer and Long a Legislator of Ohio, and U.S. Senator from 1833 to 1839* (Cincinnati: Moore, Wilstach, Keys & Overend, 1856), 53–57.

6. Vernon L. Volpe, *Forlorn Hope of Freedom: The Liberty Party in the Old Northwest, 1838–1848* (Kent, OH: Kent State Univ. Press, 1990), 8–15; Gerald Sorin, *Abolitionism: A New Perspective* (Westport, CT: Praeger Publishers, 1972), 44–52.

7. James B. Swing, "Thomas Morris," *Ohio Archeological and Historical Quarterly* 10 (1902): 352. At the time of Morris's death, even his eulogist acknowledged that Morris "was not a religious man in the church sense of the term." W. H. Brisbane, *An Eulogium on the Life and Character of the Late Thomas Morris* (Cincinnati: L'Horridieu, 1845), 10–11.

8. Wilentz, *Rise of American Democracy*, 477.

9. Earle, *Jacksonian Antislavery*, 43.

10. Manisha Sinha, *The Slave's Cause: A History of Abolition* (London: Yale Univ. Press, 2016), 461.

NOTES TO PAGES 3–5   169

11. Sean Wilentz, *No Property in Man: Slavery and Antislavery at the Nation's Founding* (Cambridge, MA: Harvard Univ. Press, 2018), x.

12. Eric Foner, *Politics and Ideology in the Age of the Civil War* (New York: Oxford Univ. Press, 1980), 40.

13. "Debate in the Senate on Mr. Calhoun's Resolutions," Jan. 6, 1838, *Philanthropist*, Jan. 30, 1838.

14. Morris, "Speech on Incendiary Publications."

15. Morris, "Speech on Incendiary Publications."

16. Thomas Morris to "Dear Sir," Nov. 24, 1841, *Philanthropist*, Dec. 8, 1841.

17. Thomas Morris, Address "To the Democratic Portion of the People of Ohio," *Philanthropist*, Aug. 11, 1841.

18. Thomas Morris to Alexander Campbell, Nov. 13, 1837, *Philanthropist*, Dec. 26, 1837.

19. William M. Wiecek, *The Sources of Antislavery Constitutionalism in America, 1760–1848* (New York: Cornell Univ. Press, 1977), 208.

20. James Oakes, *The Crooked Path to Abolition: Abraham Lincoln and the Antislavery Constitution* (New York: W. W. Norton, 2021), 2–5, 23; see also William E. Gienapp, "The Republican Party and the Slave Power," in *New Perspectives on Race and Slavery in America: Essays in Honor of Kenneth M. Stampp,* ed. Robert H. Abzug and Stephen E. Maizlish (Lexington: Univ. Press of Kentucky, 1986), 74; Aileen S. Kraditor, *Means and Ends in American Abolitionism: Garrison and His Critics on Strategy and Tactics, 1834–1850* (New York: Pantheon Books, 1969), 189 (summarized the 1848 Free-Soil platform on slavery's constitutionality).

21. Oakes, *The Crooked Path,* 54–93.

22. David Brion Davis, *The Slave Power Conspiracy and the Paranoid Style* (Baton Rouge: Louisiana State Univ. Press, 1970); Avery O. Craven, *The Coming of the Civil War: A Stimulating and Profound Analysis of the Factors Which Brought a Nation into War with Itself* (Chicago: Univ. of Chicago Press, 1957), 241–72.

23. John A. Neuenschwander, "Senator Thomas Morris: Antagonist of the South, 1836–1839," *Cincinnati Historical Society Bulletin* 32 (Fall 1974): 123. This lack of attention to Morris is glaring, particularly in light of the substantial amount of recent scholarship on early antislavery advocates. In introducing his study of the Liberty Party, Reinhard Johnson noted "an increasing amount of scholarship on major figures in the party" and cataloged nearly thirty studies done in the past several years, yet no study of Morris has been undertaken. Reinhard D. Johnson, *The Liberty Party: Antislavery Third-Party Politics in the United States* (Baton Rouge: Louisiana State Univ. Press, 2009), 1n4.

24. See, for example, Eric Foner, *Free Soil, Free Labor, Free Men: The Ideology of the Republican Party before the Civil War* (New York: Oxford Univ. Press, 1970), 90–91; Wilentz, *The Rise of American Democracy,* 477; Earle, *Jacksonian Antislavery,* 8.

25. For example, Eric Foner, while convinced of Morris's importance, never discussed his constitutional theories, many of which were relied upon extensively by Salmon Chase (*Free Soil, Free Labor, Free Men,* 73–102). Jonathan Earle, who produced the most extended modern discussion of Morris, limited his impact: "Morris's contribution to political antislavery was twofold. . . . [T]he idea of the Slave Power . . . [and]

the story of [his] political excommunication" (*Jacksonian Antislavery*, 47). No mention of Morris's constitutional theories is made.

26. For example, neither Daniel Walker Howe, in *What Hath God Wrought; The Transformation of America, 1815–1848* (New York: Oxford Univ. Press, 2007), nor Wiecek, in *The Sources of Antislavery Constitutionalism*, discuss Morris at all.

27. Writing in 1857, in the *Life of Morris*, Morris's son quoted from several letters and Morris's diary for the period of Morris's Senate term. There are almost no references to similar material created after 1839.

28. The abolitionist colleague in whose papers we would most have expected to find, particularly for the period 1836–39 both references to and correspondence with Morris, was Gamaliel Bailey. Unfortunately, Bailey's papers have disappeared. Stanley Harrold, *Gamaliel Bailey and Antislavery Union* (Kent, OH: Kent State Univ. Press, 1986), xiv–xv.

29. In preparing this study, of necessity I have relied on Morris's published speeches and letters, as well as references to Morris's views and actions in the writings of his contemporaries. That his contemporaries consistently described Morris as an independent thinker who publicly expressed his views regardless of the consequences has given me confidence that his public statements reflect his private opinion. While Morris was a creative, often original commentator on slavery, he was not given to nuanced expressions.

30. William Birney to Birney, Feb. 26, 1844, in *Letters of James Gillespie Birney, 1831–1857*, ed. Dwight L. Dumond (New York: D. Appleton Century, 1938), 794–95.

31. The antislavery press did publish thousands of copies of Morris's 1839 "Reply to Clay" in pamphlet form and distributed them for years. The widespread availability of this speech may have contributed to historians' focus on the Slave Power as Morris's contribution.

32. Francis P. Weisenburger, *The Passing of the Frontier 1825–1850: The History of the State of Ohio* (Columbus: Ohio State Archaeological and Historical Society, 1941), 3:326; Dwight L. Dumond, *Antislavery: The Crusade for Freedom in America* (Ann Arbor: Univ. of Michigan Press, 1961), 92.

33. Theodore C. Smith, *The Liberty and Free Soil Parties in the Northwest* (New York: Longmans, Green, 1897), 85–86.

34. William Birney to Birney, Feb. 26, 1844, in Dumond, *Letters of James Gillespie Birney*, 794–95.

35. Sinha, *The Slave's Cause*, 254. Morris's colleagues in the leadership of the Ohio Liberty Party were particularly young. When Morris first challenged Calhoun, Gamaliel Bailey was twenty-nine, Salmon Chase was twenty-eight, Samuel Lewis was thirty-seven, and William Birney was seventeen. Even James Birney was only forty-four (Johnson, *The Liberty Party 1840–1848*, 324, 326–27, 331, 357).

36. Smith, *Liberty and Free Soil Parties*, 86.

37. Quoted in Morris, *Life of Thomas Morris*, xi.

NOTES TO PAGES 8–9

I. AVOIDING ANYTHING LIKE AGITATION

1. Diary of the Weather at Fort Washington, MD, Jan. 7, 1836, National Oceanic and Atmospheric Administration, National Climatic Data Center, Asheville, NC.

2. Cong. Globe, 24th Cong., 1st Sess., 69 (1836).

3. Cong. Globe, 24th Cong., 1st Sess., 69–70 and 77–78 (1836). The intervening day, however, had seen the introduction in the House of the first resolution regarding the gag rule. Cong. Globe, 24th Cong., 1st Sess., 75–76 (1836). See also David Waldstreicher and Matthew Mason, eds., *John Quincy Adams and the Politics of Slavery: Selections from the Diary* (New York: Oxford Univ. Press, 2017), 178–83. For Morris's seat next to Calhoun's desk, see Morris to Eldest Son, Nov. 30, 1833, in *The Life of Thomas Morris: Pioneer and Long a Legislator of Ohio, and U.S. Senator from 1833 to 1839*, ed. Benjamin Franklin Morris (Cincinnati: Moore, Wilstach, Keys & Overend, 1856), 345–46.

4. J. L. Rockey and R. J. Bancroft, *The History of Clermont County, Ohio* (Philadelphia: Louis H. Everts Press, 1880), 136; James B. Swing, "Thomas Morris," *Ohio Archeological and Historical Quarterly* 10 (1902): 352. Smith was active in territorial politics and was elected Ohio's first United States senator after statehood. His political career ended with censure by the Senate for his involvement with Aaron Burr.

5. William T. Utter, *The Frontier State, 1803–1825* (Columbus: Ohio State Archaeological and Historical Society, 1942), 32; Andrew R. L. Cayton, *The Frontier Republic: Ideology and Politics in the Ohio Country, 1780–1825* (Kent, OH: Kent State Univ. Press, 1989), 95–104.

6. Donald F. Melhorn Jr., *Lest We Be Marshalled: Judicial Powers and Politics in Ohio, 1806–1812* (Akron, OH: Univ. of Akron Press, 2003), 94–118. For the impeachment of Justice Chase, see Richard E. Ellis, *The Jeffersonian Crisis: Courts and Politics in the Young Republic* (New York: Oxford Univ. Press, 1971), 76–107.

7. Four decades after Morris's death, Henry Howe summarized Morris's career in the general assembly: "He opposed chartered monopolies, class legislation, and traffic in spiritous liquors. . . . He was a warm friend of the common schools, labored earnestly for the extinction of the law of imprisonment for debt, and advocated making all officials elective. In 1828 he introduced a bill to allow juries before justices of the peace, and one the next year that judges should not charge juries on matters of fact. . . . In 1828 he endeavored to obtain a law taxing all chartered institutions and . . . he alone of all public men opposed the canal system . . . and prophesied that in twenty years Ohio would be covered with a network of railroads and canals superseded." Henry Howe, *Historical Collections of Ohio* (Columbus: Henry Howe & Son, 1888), 415.

8. Richard P. McCormick, *The Second American Party System: Party Formation in the Jacksonian Era* (Chapel Hill: Univ. of North Carolina Press, 1966), 258–61; see also Jeffrey P. Brown, "The Political Culture of Early Ohio," in *The Pursuit of Public Power: Political Culture in Ohio, 1787–1861*, ed. Jeffrey P. Brown and Andrew R. L. Cayton (Kent, OH: Kent State Univ. Press, 1994), 6–10; Cayton, *The Frontier Republic*, 96.

9. Donald J. Ratcliffe, *The Politics of Long Division: The Birth of the Second Party System in Ohio, 1818–1828* (Columbus: Ohio State Univ. Press, 2002), 20.

10. Daniel Feller, "Benjamin Tappan: The Making of a Democrat," in *The Pursuit of Public Power: Political Culture in Ohio, 1787–1861*, ed. Jeffrey P. Brown and Andrew R. L. Cayton (Kent, OH: Kent State Univ. Press, 1994), 73, quoting Charles Hammond to John C. Wright, Dec. 15, 1822.

11. Harry R. Stevens, *The Early Jackson Party in Ohio* (Durham, NC: Duke Univ. Press, 1957), 45; *Ohio State Journal*, Dec. 12, 1832. Earlier in his career, Morris may have acted to protect his political position in Clermont County. It was long rumored that he had contrived to split Clermont County (creating Brown County in 1818) "to gratify a spite against people at the old county seat." Byron Williams, *History of Clermont and Brown Counties, Ohio: From the Earliest Historical Times Down to the Present* (Milford: Hobart, 1913), 1:386.

12. *Ohio State Journal*, Dec. 5 and 21, 1832.

13. Jonathan H. Earle, *Jacksonian Antislavery and the Politics of Free Soil, 1824–1854* (Chapel Hill: Univ. of North Carolina Press, 2004), 40–41.

14. Robert V. Remini, *Henry Clay: Statesman for the Union* (New York: W. W. Norton, 1991), 446.

15. David S. Reynolds, *Waking Giant: America in the Age of Jackson* (New York: Harper Collins, 2008), 98.

16. Quotes in Morris, *Life of Thomas Morris*, 61–62; see also Earle, *Jacksonian Antislavery*, 41.

17. John McClean to Morris, Jan. 23, 1833, in Morris, *Life of Thomas Morris*, 52–53.

18. Text of report. Morris, *Life of Thomas Morris*, 49–51.

19. Morris to Jonathan D. Morris, Jan. 1, 1834, and Jan. 20, 1834, in Morris, *Life of Thomas Morris*, 350–51, 354–55.

20. Morris to Jonathan D. Morris, Nov. 30, 1833, Dec. 22, 1833, and Dec. 24, 1833, in Morris, *Life of Thomas Morris*, 345–46, 348–50. This view was shared by the Jacksonian leadership in the Senate. See Wright to Azariah Flagg, Dec. 11, 1833, quoted in Remini, *Henry Clay*, 446.

21. Michel Chevalier, *Society, Manners, and Politics in the United States: Letter on North America* (Garden City, NY: Anchor Books, 1961), 144–55.

22. Morris to Jonathan D. Morris, Dec. 24, 1833, in Morris, *Life of Thomas Morris*, 349–50. Nullification attacked the Constitution by destroying the Union. The Bank, besides having a special charter, created unconstitutional paper money. The Constitution only granted the right to "coin" money.

23. He presented petitions and memorials from Ohio citizens and the general assembly. On occasion, he also aided party parliamentary maneuvering. See Cong. Globe, 23rd Cong., 1st Sess., 100, 152, 216, 293, 385, 469 (1833–34).

24. Morris to Jonathan D. Morris, Dec. 24, 1833, in Morris, *Life of Thomas Morris*, 349–50.

25. *Western Hemisphere*, July 2, 1834; see also *Western Hemisphere*, June 11 and 25, 1834.

26. Thirty-one Central Ohio Democrats to Morris, Nov. 8, 1834, in *Western Hemisphere*, Nov. 26, 1834. Report of dinner, as well as Morris's response to the invitation, in *Western Hemisphere*, Nov. 26, 1834.

NOTES TO PAGES 12–13 173

27. Tappan may have been the initial source for this plan. He coveted the Senate seat and was well aware of Morris's frustration at being denied the spot on the Ohio Supreme Court early in his career (Melhorn, *Lest We Be Marshalled*, 125–34).

28. "Sen. Thomas Morris: Former Senator for Ohio," GovTrack.us, https://www.govtrack.us/congress/members/thomas_morris/407957.

29. Moses Dawson to Benjamin Tappan, Nov. 14, 1835, in Feller, "Benjamin Tappan," 79; Samuel Medary to Benjamin Tappan, Nov. 21, 1835, in Feller, "Benjamin Tappan," 79; Benjamin Tappan to Benjamin Tappan Jr., Dec. 22, 1835, in Feller, "Benjamin Tappan," 79. Thomas Hamer, who had become a bitter enemy of Morris, was actively involved in this effort to replace him. See chapter 3 notes 20–24 and accompanying text.

30. Cong. Globe, 24th Cong., 1st Sess., 223–24, 265, 274, 336, 440 (1836); Cong. Globe, 24th Cong., 1st Sess., appendix, 152–55 (1836).

31. Leonard L. Richards, *Gentlemen of Property and Standing: Anti-Abolition Mobs in Jacksonian America* (New York: Oxford Univ. Press, 1970), 16. Although the Missouri controversy more than a decade earlier had thrust slavery into the center of national politics, with the compromise surrounding Missouri's admission to the Union, the national frenzy over slavery had subsided and been replaced by tariffs, banks, and nullification. The incendiary publication and petition campaigns brought slavery back to national politics. Donald J. Ratcliffe, "The Decline of Antislavery Politics, 1815–1845," in *Contesting Slavery: The Politics of Bondage and Freedom in the New American Nation,* ed. John Craig Hammond and Matthew Mason (Charlottesville: Univ. of Virginia Press, 2011), 267–89.

32. Sydney Nathans, *Daniel Webster & Jacksonian Democracy* (Baltimore: Johns Hopkins Univ. Press, 1973), 94–95; William G. Shade, "The Most Delicate and Exciting Topics: Martin Van Buren, Slavery, and the Election of 1836," *Journal of the Early Republic* 18, no. 3 (1998): 460.

33. Richards, *Gentlemen of Property and Standing*, 16.

34. Richards, *Gentlemen of Property and Standing*, 93.

35. Bertram Wyatt-Brown, *Lewis Tappan and the Evangelical War Against Slavery* (Cleveland: Press of Case Western Reserve, 1969), 142–46.

36. William W. Freehling, *The Road to Disunion, Secessionists at Bay, 1776–1854* (New York: Oxford Univ. Press, 1990), 1:291.

37. Robert V. Remini, *Andrew Jackson and the Course of American Democracy, 1833–1845* (New York: HarperCollins, 1984), 258–59.

38. Jackson to Amos Kendall, Aug. 9, 1835, in John Spencer Bassett, ed., *Correspondence of Andrew Jackson* (Washington, DC: Carnegie Institution of Washington, 1931), 5:360–61.

39. Clement Eaton, "Censorship of the Southern Mails," *American Historical Review* 48 (Jan. 1943): 267, 291–95; Lacy K. Ford, *Deliver Us from Evil: The Slavery Question in the Old South* (New York: Oxford Univ. Press, 2009), 483–96; Remini, *Andrew Jackson and the Course of American Democracy,* 259–61. Jackson may have had a personal stake in the controversy. The riot in Washington, DC, was rumored to have involved the possession of antislavery tracts by one of Jackson's servants (Remini, *Andrew Jackson and the Course of American Democracy,* 268–70).

174   NOTES TO PAGES 13–14

40. Ford, *Deliver Us from Evil*, 482.

41. Richards, *Gentlemen of Property and Standing*, 9–10, quoting *New York Herald*, Sept. 1, 1835.

42. Entry for Aug. 11, 1835, in Alan Nevins, ed., *The Diary of John Quincy Adams, 1794–1845* (New York: Charles Scribner's Sons, 1951), 462. Indeed, Adams seemed to have agreed with Jackson that "the abolitionists . . . are making every possible exertion to kindle the flame of insurrection among the slaves." Entry for August 14, 1835, in Nevins, *The Diary of John Quincy Adams*, 463. The initial struggle over the gag rule in the House did not change his mind. Russel B. Nye, *Fettered Freedom: Civil Liberties and the Slavery Controversy 1830–1860* (Lansing: Michigan State Univ. Press, 1963), 47–48. Despite claims to the contrary—see Avery O. Craven, *The Coming of the Civil War: A Stimulating and Profound Analysis of the Factors Which Brought a Nation into War with Itself* (Chicago: Univ. of Chicago Press, 1957), 176–77—Adams was far from a "thorough-going abolitionist."

43. James C. Curtis, "In the Shadow of Old Hickory: The Political Travail of Martin Van Buren," *Journal of the Early Republic* 1, no. 3 (1981): 254–56; Reynolds, *Waking Giant*, 308–9.

44. Remini, *Andrew Jackson and the Course of American Democracy*, 252–57. This view of Calhoun's intent to use abolition against Van Buren was widespread among Van Buren's supporters and continued for years. Eric Foner, *Free Soil, Free Labor, Free Men: The Ideology of the Republican Party before the Civil War* (New York: Oxford Univ. Press, 1970), 151.

45. Prior to the nominating meeting in May 1835, Van Buren felt compelled to proclaim his commitment to protecting slavery to numerous Southern correspondents. James Campbell Curtis, *The Fox at Bay: Martin Van Buren and the Presidency, 1837–1841* (Lexington: Univ. Press of Kentucky, 1970), 46–47; Shade, "Most Delicate and Exciting Topics," 465; William J. Cooper, *The South and the Politics of Slavery, 1828–1856* (Baton Rouge: Louisiana State Univ. Press, 1978), 74–92.

46. Andrew Jackson, Seventh Annual Message, Dec. 7, 1835, in *A Compilation of Messages and Papers of the Presidents*, ed. James D. Richardson (New York: Bureau of National Literature, 1897), 3:1394.

47. Jackson, Seventh Annual Message, 1395. Jasckson's efforts (and ultimate complicity) in "the refusal of the Post Office to deliver abolitionist mail to the South may well represent the largest peacetime violation of civil liberty in U.S. history." Daniel Walker Howe, *What Hath God Wrought; The Transformation of America, 1815–1848* (New York: Oxford Univ. Press, 2007), 430.

48. Don E. Fehrenbacher, *The Slaveholding Republic: An Account of the United States Government's Relations to Slavery* (New York: Oxford Univ. Press, 2001), 263–66; Glover Moore, *The Missouri Controversy, 1819–1821* (Lexington: Univ. of Kentucky Press, 1953).

49. Glyndon G. Van Deusen, *The Jacksonian Era 1828–1848* (New York: Harper & Row, 1963), 108; Eaton, "Censorship of the Southern Mails," 272–73.

50. M. Henkle to American Colonization Society, Columbus, OH, Jan. 4, 1837, quoted in E. L. Fox, *The American Colonization Society, 1817–1840* (Baltimore: Johns Hopkins Univ. Press, 1919), 81–82; see generally P. J. Staudenraus, *The African Colonization Movement, 1816–1865* (New York: Columbia Univ. Press, 1961), 138–40.

NOTES TO PAGES 14–16

51. Herman V. Ames, *State Documents on Federal Relations: The States and United States* (Philadelphia: Department of History of the Univ. of Pennsylvania, 1906), 203–4. Although the Resolves triggered strong negative reactions from Southern legislatures, the approach recommended by the general assembly was echoed by former president James Monroe in the Virginia Constitutional Convention of 1829. Eva Sheppard Wolf, *Race and Liberty in the New Nation: Emancipation in Virginia from the Revolution to Nat Turner's Rebellion* (Baton Rouge: Louisiana State Univ. Press, 2006), 191; Eric Burin, *Slavery and the Peculiar Solution: A History of the American Colonization Society* (Gainesville: Univ. Press of Florida, 2005), 18. These resolutions contributed to Calhoun's apprehension of congressional action on slavery and, perhaps, made him particularly suspicious of Ohio's objectives. See Matthew Mason, *Slavery and Politics in the Early American Republic* (Chapel Hill: Univ. of North Carolina Press, 2006), 236–37.

52. William M. Wiecek, *The Sources of Antislavery Constitutionalism in America, 1760–1848* (New York: Cornell Univ. Press, 1977), 108. Morris would later claim to have opposed the 1807 Act "on the ground of its injustice and ineffectiveness." Morris, "To the Democratic Portion of the People of Ohio," *Philanthropist*, Aug. 11, 1841. He does not appear to have sought the Act's repeal any time before 1836.

53. Kate Masur, *Until Justice Be Done: America's First Civil Rights Movement from Reconstruction* (New York: W. W. Norton, 2021), 87–89; Stephen Middleton, *The Black Laws: Race and the Legal Process in Early Ohio* (Athens: Ohio Univ. Press, 2005), 80.

54. Text of the report in Morris, *Life of Thomas Morris*, 53–57. Describing slavery as a moral evil or sin was simply a standard phrase of Ohio colonizationists. Francis P. Weisenburger, *The Passing of the Frontier 1825–1850: The History of the State of Ohio* (Columbus: Ohio State Archaeological and Historical Society, 1941), 3:373. Indeed, even George McDuffie, during an earlier congressional debate regarding slavery in the District of Columbia, had called slavery a "deplorable evil" (Fehrenbacher, *Slaveholding Republic*, 69).

55. Wiecek, *Antislavery Constitutionalism*, 15–16.

56. James Oakes, *Freedom National: The Destruction of Slavery in the United States, 1861–1865* (New York: W. W. Norton, 2013), 3. Although acknowledging the belief that Congress could not act on slavery in the states was widely held, Mark Graber (relying on the Necessary and Proper Clause) argues that "the constitutional text provides little support for subsequent claims that Congress had no power to emancipate the slave." Mark Graber, *Dred Scott and The Problem of Constitutional Evil* (New York: Cambridge Univ. Press, 2006), 95.

57. Text of report in Morris, *Life of Thomas Morris*, 55. For the context of Morris's report, see Masaur, *Until Justice Be Done*, 87. The expectation that slavery would end of its own accord had been widespread at the time of the adoption of the Constitution. Garber, *Constitutional Evil*, 106–9. The belief continued in the years following ratification as "the growing numbers of free blacks in the Upper South convinced many that the institution of slavery was indeed dying." Gorden Wood, *Power and Liberty: Constitutionalism in the American Revolution* (New York: Oxford Univ. Press, 2021), 117.

58. Morris, *Life of Thomas Morris*, 55.

59. *The Sixteenth Annual Report of American Society for Colonizing the Free People of Color of the United States* (Washington, DC: James C. Dunn, 1833), vii–viii.

176   NOTES TO PAGES 16–19

60. *Emancipator*, Dec. 2, 1834.

61. Weisenburger, *Passing of the Frontier*, 369–71.

62. *Ohio State Journal*, Oct. 30, 1835, and Dec. 4, 1835.

63. Wyatt-Brown, *Lewis Tappan*, 163.

64. On December 16, 1835, a huge fire destroyed much of New York City, including the Tappans' business. Although they reopened quickly, the loss from the fire combined with the Panic of 1837 to bankrupt the firm. Wyatt-Brown, *Lewis Tappan*, 162–74.

65. Fehrenbacher, *Slaveholding Republic*, 66–72.

66. Sean Wilentz, *No Property in Man: Slavery and Antislavery at the Nation's Founding* (Cambridge, MA: Harvard Univ. Press, 2018), 154–64; Richard S. Newman, *The Transformation of American Abolitionism: Fighting Slavery in the Early Republic* (Chapel Hill: Univ. of North Carolina Press, 2002), 50–58.

67. Freehling, *Road to Disunion*, 1:343; Samuel Flagg Bemis, *John Quincy Adams and the Union* (New York: Knopf, 1956), 331–32.

68. Freehling, *Road to Disunion*, 1:310. See also Eaton, "Southern Mails," 273–74, for an argument that the incendiary publications issue lacked support in the North (not simply Southern opposition) so as to cause the antislavery activists to change strategies to a petition campaign.

69. Michael Kent Curtis, "The Curious History of Attempts to Suppress Anti-Slavery Speech, Press, and Petition in 1835–37," *Northwestern University Law Review* 89 (1995): 785, 800; Newman, *Transformation of American Abolitionism*, 52–59, 141–49. In earlier years the petition effort had been generally sporadic and unorganized. See *Emancipator*, Aug. 12, 1834, and Mar. 10, 1835.

70. *Emancipator*, Apr. 14, 1835.

71. Cong. Globe, 24th Cong., 1st Sess., 69, 77 (1836).

72. Although the *Congressional Globe* reports Calhoun present and active on the day Ewing offered his petitions, Calhoun claimed to have been absent from the Senate when Ewing had presented his petitions. See Cong. Globe, 24th Cong., 1st Sess., 69 and 81 (1836).

73. William Lee Miller, *Arguing about Slavery* (New York: Knopf, 1996), 31–35.

74. John M. McFaul, "Expediency vs. Morality: Jacksonian Politics and Slavery," *The Journal of American History* 62 (June 1975): 32n23. In 1835–36 the *Washington Globe* seems to have viewed the petition issue in a different light from incendiary publications. See Remini, *Andrew Jackson and the Course of American Democracy*, 270–72. Calhoun, however, intended to use both issues to attack the administration and to create a Southern party.

75. *Washington Globe*, May 18, 1835.

76. Shade, "Most Delicate and Exciting Topics," 475–77; *Washington Globe*, Dec. 31, 1835, and Jan. 1, 1836.

77. Calhoun's delay until after Hammond's moves in the House has led some historians to speculate about the origin of the gag-rule idea. While Calhoun returned to Washington in December 1835 focused on the incendiary publications controversy, he was quick to seize on the petition issue as well. The lag between the House action and Calhoun's Senate effort resulted from the absence of any efforts to introduce pe-

NOTES TO PAGES 19–21 177

titions in that chamber until January rather than any hesitancy on Calhoun's part. Robert Elder, *Calhoun: American Heretic* (New York: Basic Books, 2021), 314–15.

78. Cong. Globe, 24th Cong., 1st Sess., 77 (1836). Not until a month after the vote to reject the request of the petition did Calhoun identify what language offended him in Morris's petitions. Cong. Globe, 24th Cong., 1st Sess., 291 (1836). The petitions had referred to slavery as a sin and accused slaveholders of "trafficking in human flesh." To Calhoun, "any moral condemnation of slavery . . . would be taken to have the tone of insult and slander and libel" (Miller, *Arguing about Slavery*, 130; Ford, *Deliver Us from Evil*, 506–7).

79. Cong. Globe, 24th Cong., 1st Sess., 77 (1836). This argument, at its core, is a substantive due process claim (Freehling, *Road to Disunion*, 322–23). The notion was subsequently adopted by Chief Justice Taney in *Dred Scott v. Sandford*, 60 U.S. 393 (1857). The Missouri territorial delegate and a Virginia congressman had anticipated this argument during the Missouri controversy (Wiecek, *Antislavery Constitutionalism*, 116).

80. Cong. Globe, 24th Cong., 1st Sess., 77 (1836). See also report of the debate in *Philanthropist*, Jan. 22, 1836. Even antiabolition mobs in Cincinnati had agreed Congress could legislate for the District. See report of Cincinnati antiabolition meeting in the *Washington Globe*, Feb. 4, 1836. These antiabolition resolutions were ultimately presented to the Senate by Morris's Whig colleague from Ohio. See Cong. Globe, 24th Cong., 1st Sess., 236 (1836).

81. Cong. Globe, 24th Cong., 1st Sess., 77 (1836).

82. Cong. Globe, 24th Cong., 1st Sess., 77 (1836).

83. Morris had waited to present his petitions until after he had seen the Senate's response to the petitions presented by Senator Ewing. Calhoun's highly charged reaction was not anticipated. Cong. Globe, 24th Cong., 1st Sess., 121 (1836); cf. Earle, *Jacksonian Antislavery*, 42.

84. Buchanan presented his petitions on January 11. Cong. Globe, 24th Cong., 1st Sess., 85 (1836).

85. Cong. Globe, 24th Cong., 1st Sess., 121 (1836). Petition campaigns for a particular cause were not unusual. For instance, the supporters and opponents of the Bank had petitioned extensively. See Morris to Jonathan D. Morris, Jan. 20 and Mar. 12, 1834, in Morris, *Life of Thomas Morris*, 354–56.

86. The description is from Louis Filler, *The Crusade against Slavery, 1830–1860* (New York: Harper and Brothers, 1960), 102.

87. Cong. Globe, 24th Cong., 1st Sess., 274 (1836). Morris may have simply lacked confidence to challenge the other members in extemporaneous debate. During the exchange from which the quotes in the text are taken, Morris was criticized for using prepared remarks.

88. Cong. Globe, 24th Cong., 1st Sess., 221 (1836).

89. Cong. Globe, 24th Cong., 1st Sess., 229 (1836). This "became the standard Senate practice" (Nye, *Fettered Freedom*, 55), which one recent commentator described as "an esoteric procedural mechanism" that "ironically proved more effective" than the gag rule adopted in the House of Representatives. Corey M. Brooks, *Liberty Power: Antislavery Third Parties and the Transformation of American Politics* (Chicago: Univ. of Chicago Press, 2016), 20, 240.

178   NOTES TO PAGES 22–25

2. THEY ARE ATTEMPTING TO OVERWHELM US

1. Address to the People of the United States, in Joel H. Silbey, "The Election of 1836," in *The History of American Presidential Elections 1789–1968*, ed. Arthur M. Schlesinger Jr. (New York: Chelsea House Publishers, 1971), 1:623.

2. Van Buren to Junius Amis in *Washington Globe*, Mar. 11, 1836; James Campbell Curtis, *The Fox at Bay: Martin Van Buren and the Presidency, 1837–1841* (Lexington: Univ. Press of Kentucky, 1970), 48. As a result of these efforts, during the campaign, Southern Jacksonians claimed that "next to Andrew Jackson, Martin Van Buren is the most powerful enemy of the abolitionists." *Federal Union*, Oct. 3, 1836, quoted in Joel H. Silbey, "'There Are Other Questions Beside That of Slavery Merely': The Democratic Party and Antislavery Politics," in *Crusaders and Compromisers*, ed. Alan M. Kraut (Westport: Greenwood Press, 1983), 148.

3. Morris to "Eldest Son," Dec. 24, 1833, in Benjamin Franklin Morris, ed., *The Life of Thomas Morris: Pioneer and Long a Legislator of Ohio, and U.S. Senator from 1833 to 1839* (Cincinnati: Moore, Wilstach, Keys & Overend, 1856), 349.

4. *Emancipator*, Mar.-Apr., 1836; Cong. Globe, 24th Cong., 1st Sess. 298, 328 (1836).

5. Ohio Anti-Slavery Society, *Report of the Second Anniversary of the Ohio Anti-Slavery Society* (Apr. 1837): 42–43.

6. William Lee Miller, *Arguing about Slavery* (New York: Knopf, 1996), 210–12. The objections to the admission of Arkansas generally restated the arguments made against the admission of Missouri fifteen years earlier. William M. Wiecek, *The Sources of Antislavery Constitutionalism in America, 1760–1848* (New York: Cornell Univ. Press, 1977), 111–22.

7. Cong. Globe, 24th Cong., 1st Sess. 270 (1836).

8. Theodore C. Smith, *The Liberty and Free Soil Parties in the Northwest* (New York: Longmans, Green, 1897), 24.

9. Cong. Globe, 24th Cong., 1st Sess. 279 (1836). During the Missouri controversy fifteen years earlier, several Northern Jeffersonians had read the guarantee of a republican form of government clause with the Declaration of Independence to conclude that Congress could prohibit slavery in new states. Sean Wilentz, *Rise of American Democracy: Jefferson to Lincoln* (New York: W. W. Norton, 2005), 222–31. Morris never accepted this view. Indeed, Morris's application of the federal consensus to the admission of the new states implies he would have voted to admit Missouri without any prohibition on future slavery in the Louisiana Purchase. See also Thomas Hart Benton, *Thirty Years' View* (New York: D. Appleton, 1856), 1:629–31.

10. Cong. Globe, 24th Cong., 1st Sess. 279 (1836). For the earlier debate over slavery (and the argument that Congress lacked the power to ban slavery in the territories) in the organizing of the Arkansas Territory, see Sean Wilentz, *No Property in Man: Slavery and Antislavery at the Nation's Founding* (Cambridge, MA: Harvard Univ. Press, 2018), 188–95; Stephen E. Maizlish, *The Triumph of Sectionalism: The Transformation of Ohio Politics, 1844–1856* (Kent, OH: Kent State Univ. Press, 1983), 6.

11. Maizlish, *Triumph of Sectionalism*, 6; *Washington Globe*, Apr. 5, 1836. Morris was much more concerned about the admission of Michigan, which was admitted at the

same time. For background on the dispute regarding the Ohio-Michigan border, see Francis P. Weisenburger, *Passing of the Frontier 1825–1850: The History of the State of Ohio* (Columbus: Ohio State Archaeological and Historical Society, 1941), 297–309.

12. William J. Cooper, *The South and the Politics of Slavery, 1828–1856* (Baton Rouge: Louisiana State Univ. Press, 1978), 182–83.

13. Cong. Globe, 24th Cong., 1st Sess. 331–32 (1836).

14. Cong. Globe, 24th Cong., 1st Sess. 393–97 (1836). Whether influenced by Jackson or not, Morris's change of heart was in accord with the president's view. Glyndon G. Van Deusen, *The Jacksonian Era 1828–1848* (New York: Harper & Row, 1963), 109–10.

15. Weisenburger, *Passing of the Frontier*, 373.

16. *Niles Weekly Register*, Dec. 26, 1835.

17. Clement Eaton, "Censorship of the Southern Mails," *American Historical Review* 48 (Jan. 1943): 270–72; Louis Filler, *The Crusade against Slavery, 1830–1860* (New York: Harper and Brothers, 1960), 97–98; Alice Felt Tyler, *Freedom's Ferment: Phases of American Social History to 1860* (Minneapolis: Univ. of Minnesota Press, 1944), 508; Lacy K. Ford, *Deliver Us from Evil: The Slavery Question in the Old South* (New York: Oxford Univ. Press, 2009), 496–98; Robert Elder, *Calhoun: American Heretic* (New York: Basic Books, 2021), 330–31.

18. Cong. Globe, 24th Cong., 1st Sess. 36 (1835).

19. For Calhoun's rejection of Jackson's proposal, see William W. Freehling, *Road to Disunion, Secessionists at Bay, 1776–1854* (New York: Oxford Univ. Press, 1990), 1:309–10. Jackson's initial proposal was motivated at least in part by a desire to reassure Southerners that they could trust Van Buren. Paul Goodman, *Of One Blood: Abolitionism and the Origins of Racial Equality* (Berkeley: Univ. of California Press, 1998), 170–71. Once Jackson understood Calhoun's effort to use it against Van Buren, he opposed the bill. Jackson's opposition provoked Calhoun's ire. Cong. Globe, 24th Cong., 1st Sess., 352–53 (1836). Ultimately Congress rejected both the Jackson and Calhoun position and passed a bill that "upheld the government's traditional commitment to the inviolability of the mails." Wilentz, *Rise of American Democracy*, 411; Robert V. Remini, *Andrew Jackson and the Course of American Democracy, 1833–1845* (New York: HarperCollins, 1984), 261–63.

20. Benton, *Thirty Years' View*, 584; Cong. Globe, 24th Cong., 1st Sess. 150–51 (1836).

21. Benton, *Thirty Years' View*, 584–85; Cong. Globe, 24th Cong., 1st Sess., 164–65 (1836).

22. Benton, *Thirty Years' View*, 585. Over the course of the prior year, Southern legislatures had adopted resolutions demanding that the Northern states enact laws regulating the publication and mailing of antislavery materials. The free-state legislatures, however, had refused to comply. Russel B. Nye, *Fettered Freedom: Civil Liberties and the Slavery Controversy 1830–1860* (Lansing: Michigan State Univ. Press, 1963), 138–44. Receipt of the Southern requests is what triggered Governor Lucas's comments to the Ohio General Assembly in support of free speech.

23. Benton, *Thirty Years' View*, 585.

24. Cong. Globe, 24th Cong., 1st Sess. 291 (1836).

180 NOTES TO PAGES 27–30

25. Cong. Globe, 24th Cong., 1st Sess. 291 (1836).

26. Cong. Globe, 24th Cong., 1st Sess. 291 (1836). The *Congressional Globe* chose not to publish Calhoun's threat of interposition (Wiecek, *Antislavery Constitutionalism,* 176n15).

27. Inexpediency was the preferred Northern Democratic explanation for opposing emancipation in the District (Ford, *Deliver Us from Evil,* 502). Morris was expressing the consensus Jacksonian view, but directly contrary to the abolitionist position. See *Emancipator,* Oct. 21, 1834, quoting the *New-York Evangelist.* Morris also suggested relocating the nation's capital out of the District of Columbia as a means of ending antislavery petitions. Joshua Giddings would make a similar proposal three years later. Cong. Globe, 25th Cong., 3rd Sess., 181 (1838–39).

28. Cong. Globe, 24th Cong., 1st Sess., appendix, 283–84 (1836).

29. Cong. Globe. 24th Cong., 1st Sess. 274 (1836).

30. Cong. Globe, 24th Cong., 1st Sess., appendix, 283–84 (1836).

31. Wiecek, *Antislavery Constitutionalism,* 62–63; David Waldstreicher, *Slavery's Constitution: From Revolution to Ratification* (New York: Hill and Wang, 2009), 3–9. Some historians add the Tenth Amendment to the list of constitutional provisions protecting slavery. While the amendment added some support to the federal consensus, it did not play the role some suggest. For example, James Brewer Stewart believes it "gave slave holders ample constitutional support for adding new slave states." James Brewer Stewart, *Abolitionist Politics and the Coming of the Civil War* (Amherst: Univ. of Massachusetts Press, 2008), 9. The admission of new states, like power over the District and the territories, were express powers of Congress and thus outside the scope of the Tenth Amendment. To the extent the Tenth Amendment played a role in the debate, it simply confirmed the federal consensus (Congress had no express power to emancipate slaves in the states) and protected the emancipation of slaves by the free states (Congress had no express power to prohibit emancipation by the states). James Oakes, *The Crooked Path to Abolition: Abraham Lincoln and the Antislavery Constitution* (New York: W. W. Norton, 2021), 19–21. Morris, on the other hand, believed the Tenth Amendment made the Fugitive Slave Act unconstitutional and protected emancipation in the free states.

32. Waldstreicher, *Slavery's Constitution,* 101.

33. Noah Feldman, *The Broken Constitution: Lincoln, Slavery and the Refounding of America* (New York: Farrar, Strauss & Corex, 2021), 7.

34. Nikole Hannah-Jones, *"Democracy" in the 1619 Project* (New York: One World, 2021), 19. For a "random list" of works taking a similar position, see Wilentz, *No Property in Man,* 271–72n1. Cf. Mark Graber, *Dred Scott and the Problem of Constitutional Evil* (New York: Cambridge Univ. Press, 2006), 101. Acknowledging that the founders wrote the Fugitive Slave Clause "to avoid any implication that human bondage was legal," Graber argues that rather than any specific provision of the Constitution guaranteeing slavery, the structure of the Constitution made slavery a political (not constitutional) issue to be resolved by agreement between elites in the North and South.

35. Wilentz, *No Property in Man,* 4.

36. James Oakes, *Freedom National: The Destruction of Slavery in the United States, 1861–1865* (New York W. W. Norton, 2013), 6.

NOTES TO PAGES 30–31

37. Wilentz, *No Property in Man*, 99.

38. On the difficulty of determining original intent in the drafting and ratification of the Constitution, see Jack W. Rakove, *Original Meanings: Politics and Ideas in the Making of the Constitution* (New York: Alfred A. Knopf, 1996).

39. Compare Article I §9, clause 3 ("no bill of attainder or expost facto law shall be passed"). Several Southern antifederalists, most prominently Patrick Henry, commented on this omission during the ratification process (Waldstreicher, *Slavery's Constitution*, 143–45), although Rakove speculates that Henry's concerns may have been more "a mark, perhaps of political desperation" than genuine concern (*Original Meanings*, 124). Moreover, the Constitution contained no limitation on states' actions to abolish slavery within their own borders. Whatever the accommodation of slavery the founders included in the Constitution applied only to the federal government. States were free to abolish (or establish) slavery as they chose.

40. Tellingly during the Missouri Crisis Calhoun had acknowledged Congress's power to prohibit slavery in the territories (Wiecek, *Antislavery Constitutionalism*, 115).

41. Cong. Globe, 24th Cong., 1st Sess., 77 (1936). This argument against receiving antislavery petitions as seeking unconstitutional legislation had been made since the Second Congress (Wilentz, *No Property in Man*, 155–57).

42. Wilentz, *No Property in Man*, 193–98. This argument from the Fugitive Slave Clause had appeared at least as early as the debate over organization of the Louisiana Purchase Territory (Wilentz, *No Property in Man*, 179).

43. See, for example, Stewart, *Abolitionist Politics*, 9.

44. Don E. Fehrenbacher, *The Dred Scott Case: Its Significance in American Law & Politics* (New York: Oxford Univ. Press, 1978), 24–25.

45. Morris to Eldest Son, Nov. 30, 1833, in Morris, *Life of Thomas Morris*, 345–56.

46. Oakes, *The Crooked Path*, 31.

47. Remini, *Andrew Jackson*, 14. Morris had won election to the Senate in large part because of his inveterate opposition to two of Calhoun's creations: nullification and the Bank of the United States. Jonathan H. Earle, *Jacksonian Antislavery and the Politics of Free Soil, 1824–1854* (Chapel Hill: Univ. of North Carolina Press, 2004), 41.

48. For Calhoun's actions during Morris's first two years in the Senate, see Elder, *Calhoun*, 294–300; Wilentz, *Rise of American Democracy*, 397–98: "The banks supporters might have expected Calhoun to defend the BUS, which had largely been his creation. But for Calhoun, though he would praise the bank . . . attacking Jackson and sustaining his own states-rights doctrine took precedence."

49. *Sturges v. Crowningshield*, 17 U.S. (4 Wheat.) 122, at 202–3 (1819). Noah Feldman has recently argued that this focus on the text "approach did not so much ignore the idea that the Constitution should be interpreted according to its history and origins as suggest that the framers' literal words mattered more than the fact that the Constitution in practice preserved slavery" (*The Broken Constitution*, 65–66). Yet, as Chief Justice Marshall made clear, the words of the text were the primary means to interpret the Constitution. Indeed, through at least the mid-nineteenth century, "courts and commentators frequently asserted that the plain meaning [the approach Morris was taking] of the text was the surest guide to the intent of the adopters." Paul Brest,

182   NOTES TO PAGES 32–34

"The Misconceived Quest for the Original Understanding," *Boston University Law Review* 60 (1980): 204, 215–16.

50. Cong. Globe, 24th Cong. 1st Sess., 274 (1836).

51. Cong. Globe, 24th Cong., 1st Sess., 77 (1836).

52. Cong. Globe, 24th Cong., 1st Sess. appendix, 283–84 (1836).

53. Wilentz, *No Property in Man,* 5. The understanding that states alone determined what qualified as property, however, did not lead inexorably to an antislavery conclusion. Two weeks earlier Morris had justified his vote to admit Arkansas because the federal government had "not right to . . . prescribe what shall or shall not be considered property in the different states." Cong. Globe, 24th Sess. 279 (1831). Indeed, proslavery advocates would ultimately agree that Congress could not define what was property; only states could do that. But, claimed that "whatever [State] Constitutions and laws validly determined to be property, the Federal Government [must] recognize to be property." *Dred Scott,* 555 (Campbell concurring).

54. Cong. Globe, 24th Cong., 1st Sess., appendix, 283–84 (1836). For the history of the drafting of the Fugitive Slave Clause, see Wiecek, *Antislavery Constitutionalism,* 78–80. Vermont Congressman Charles Rich had made a similar argument during the Missouri Crisis as a basis for opposing admission of a slave state (Wilentz, *No Property in Man,* 198–203). As his vote to admit Arkansas reveals, Morris was either unaware or unpersuaded of the applicability of this argument of the admission of states.

55. The quote refers to Taney's adoption of Calhoun's argument (Wilentz, *No Property in Man,* 243, 245). Morris would have found it equally applicable to Calhoun's argument in 1836. The Calhoun-Taney interpretation was based "largely on the Fifth Amendment's protection of the right to property" (Feldman, *Broken Constitution,* 124). Indeed, Calhoun's 1836 agreement was "a notable anticipation of Taney's Dred Scott opinion (Fehrenbacher, *The Dred Scott Case,* 122).

56. Feldman, *Broken Constitution,* 124. In the aftermath of Taney's *Dred Scott* acceptance of Calhoun's construction of the Fifth Amendment, this understanding became commonplace among political antislavery advocates. Wilentz, *No Property in Man,* 246–47; Richard H Sewell. *Ballots for Freedom: Antislavery Politics in the United States, 1837–1860.* New York: Oxford Univ. Press, 1976), 299–304. Indeed, Lincoln would acknowledge that it was the fear of "a powerful plot to make slavery universal and perpetual" that motivated him to run for Senate in 1858. Roy P. Basler, ed., *The Collected Works of Abraham Lincoln* (New Brunswick: Rutgers Univ. Press, 1958), 548–50.

57. Cong. Globe, 24th Cong., 1st Sess., appendix, 282–84 (1836). Cory Brooks argues that Morris learned "his Anti-Slave Power political argument from moralistic associates." Corey M. Brooks, *Liberty Power: Antislavery Third Parties and the Transformation of American Politics* (Chicago: Univ. of Chicago Press, 2016), 26. Morris's argument was not moral but constitutional. His position was a response to Calhoun's effort to protect slaveholding elites by attacking civil liberties.

58. Cong. Globe, 24th Cong., 1st Sess., appendix, 282–84 (1836). Calhoun's most recent biographer argues that Calhoun made his disunion statements in an effort to maintain the Union. Nevertheless, he acknowledges that "the line between warning and threat was a thin one." Elder, *Calhoun,* 358–60. Whatever may have been Calhoun's intent, Morris understood it as a threat.

NOTES TO PAGES 34–36

59. Earle, *Jacksonian Antislavery*, 44.

60. Oakes, *Crooked Path*, 67.

61. Cong. Globe, 24th Cong., 1st Sess., appendix, 283–84 (1836); *Philanthropist*, June 17, 1836.

62. For Republican views of slavery's relationship to the Constitution on the eve of the Civil War, see Oakes, *Freedom National*, 33–34, 47–48.

63. Leonard L. Richards, *The Slave Power: The Free North and Southern Domination, 1780–1860* (Baton Rouge: Louisiana State Univ. Press, 2000). Richards acknowledged Morris's role in the development of the Slave Power concept, but traces it to his reply to Henry Clay in 1839. This view overlooks Morris's 1836 response to Calhoun and much of Morris's correspondence and Senate speeches in 1837 and 1838. Identifying the Slave Power as a threat to civil liberty and having designs on extending slavery into the free states had its origins in Morris's Incendiary Publication Speech.

64. William Jay, *A View of the Action of the Federal Government, in Behalf of Slavery* (New York: J. S. Taylor, 1839).

65. Jackson appointed five justices between 1835 and 1837—all Southerners. Harold M. Hyman and William M. Wiecek, *Equal Justice under Law: Constitutional Development 1835–1875* (New York: Harper & Row, 1982), 62. Morris voted to confirm all of them.

66. Earle, *Jacksonian Antislavery*, 43.

67. Smith, *Liberty and Free Soil Parties*, 24; see also Earle, *Jacksonian Antislavery*, 38.

68. Morris, *Life of Morris*, 15.

69. See, for example, Weisenburger, *Passing of the Frontier*, 362; Stephen Middleton, *The Black Laws: Race and the Legal Process in Early Ohio* (Athens: Ohio Univ. Press, 2005), 120–21.

70. John M. McFaul, "Expediency vs. Morality: Jacksonian Politics and Slavery," *Journal of American History* 62 (June 1975): 35.

71. Cong. Globe, 24th Cong., 1st Sess., 291 (1836).

72. *Washington Globe*, Mar. 12, 1836; Benton, *Thirty Years' View*, 611–21; Freehling, *Road to Disunion*, 326–27.

73. Remini, *Andrew Jackson*, 272.

74. Wilentz, *Rise of American Democracy*, 409–10.

75. Eric Foner, *Free Soil, Free Labor, Free Men: The Ideology of the Republican Party before the Civil War* (New York: Oxford Univ. Press, 1970), 90. For example, on the other major issue (Clay's plan to distribute the federal surplus) confronting the Senate during the spring of 1836, Morris was a consistent supporter of the president. He cogently argued for tariff reduction and against distribution by "perceptively" arguing that Clay's plan would further inflation. Carl Lane, *A Nation Wholly Free: The Elimination of the National Debt in the Age of Jackson* (Yardly: Westholme Publishing, 2014), 185. Jonathan Earle, however, believes "Morris returned to Ohio a changed man . . . who had shed his role as a dutiful supporter of the administration" (*Jacksonian Antislavery*, 44). Although the attack on the Slave Power was outside Jacksonian orthodoxy, Morris's votes on Arkansas, Texas, Calhoun's incendiary publications bill, and Taney's appointment to the Supreme Court were all consistent with the Democratic position. His current and future support of the Jacksonian financial program and the expungement of Jackson's censure were clearly within the party's mainstream. In

184   NOTES TO PAGES 37–40

other words, Morris remained a consistent supporter of the party, except on the issue of abolitionists' actions, throughout his Senate career.

76. See *Washington Globe*, Feb. 5, Feb. 17, Apr. 14, 1836. The large overlap in the Senate of Southern members opposed to the expunging resolutions surrounding Jackson's removal of the bank deposits and the petition debate made this an easy connection to make. See, for example, *Washington Globe*, April 18, 1836.

77. Remini, *Andrew Jackson*, 271.

3. KEEPER OF THE JEFFERSONIAN CONSCIENCE

1. Arthur Schlesinger Jr., *The Age of Jackson* (Boston: Little, Brown, 1945), 18–29.

2. Nancy Isenberg and Andrew Burstein, *The Problem of Democracy: The Presidents Adams Confront the Cult of Personality* (New York: Viking, 2019), 406.

3. Sean Wilentz, *Rise of American Democracy: Jefferson to Lincoln* (New York: W. W. Norton, 2005), 442–44.

4. Calhoun, who supported the bill, believed Jackson failed to veto this bill out of fear that he would split the party going into the fall election. Robert Elder, *Calhoun: American Heretic* (New York: Basic Books, 2021), 331–32.

5. *Niles Weekly Register*, July 16, 1836. Van Buren to Sherrod Williams, Aug. 8, 1836, in *Niles Weekly Register*, Sept. 10, 1836.

6. David S. Reynolds, *Waking Giant: America in the Age of Jackson* (New York: HarperCollins, 2008), 309–11.

7. Cong. Globe, 24th Cong., 1st Sess., appendix, 284 (1836).

8. Reynolds, *Waking Giant*, 110–11.

9. Wilentz, *Rise of American Democracy*, 477.

10. Bertram Wyatt-Brown, *Lewis Tappan and the Evangelical War against Slavery* (Cleveland: Press of Case Western Reserve, 1969), 161. Moving across the Ohio River did not eliminate the threat of physical harm. Mobs were a common reaction to abolitionists in Ohio. Several threats had been previously made to Birney. See Robert Price, "Ohio Anti-Slavery Convention," *Ohio State Archaeological and Historical Society Quarterly* 45 (1936): 185; Francis P. Weisenburger, *Passing of the Frontier 1825–1850: The History of the State of Ohio* (Columbus: Ohio State Archaeological and Historical Society, 1941), 372–74; *Ohio State Journal*, Oct. 30, and Dec. 4, 1835.

11. Leonard L. Richards, *Gentlemen of Property and Standing: Anti-Abolition Mobs in Jacksonian America* (New York: Oxford Univ. Press, 1970), 92–100.

12. Ohio Anti-Slavery Society, *Report of the First Anniversary of the Ohio Anti-Slavery Society* (Apr. 1836): 13; Price, "The Ohio Anti-Slavery Convention of 1836," 186; Paul R. Grim, "The Rev. John Rankin, Early Abolitionist," *Ohio State Archaeological and Historical Society Quarterly* 46 (1937): 231–32.

13. Rankin to Elizur Wright, Sept. 6, 1836, *Emancipator*, Sept. 29, 1836; Ann Hagedorn, *Beyond the River: The Untold Stories of the Heroes of the Underground Railroad* (New York: Simon & Schuster, 2002), 188–89. Joliffe went on to have a distinguished

NOTES TO PAGES 41–42

career representing fugitive slaves. He ultimately "succeeded Chase as the attorney general for fugitive slaves upon Chase's election to the U.S. Senate." Stephen Middleton, *The Black Laws: Race and the Legal Process in Early Ohio* (Athens: Ohio Univ. Press, 2005), 199; Jeffrey P. Brown, "Political Culture of Early Ohio," in *The Pursuit of Public Power: Political Culture in Ohio, 1787–1861*, ed. Jeffrey P. Brown and Andrew R. L. Cayton (Kent, OH: Kent State Univ. Press, 1994), 13.

14. Ohio Anti-Slavery Society, *Report of the First Anniversary*, 10–11; Hagendorn, *Beyond the River*, 86–87; Donald F. Melhorn Jr., *Lest We Be Marshalled: Judicial Powers and Politics in Ohio, 1806–1812* (Akron, OH: Univ. of Akron Press, 2003), 99–118. Campbell would ultimately join Morris as an early member of the Ohio Liberty Party. Reinhard D. Johnson, *Liberty Party: Antislavery Third-Party Politics in the United States* (Baton Rouge: Louisiana State Univ. Press, 2009), 330.

15. Wilentz, *Rise of American Democracy*, 409.

16. Julie A. Mujic, "A Border Community's Unfulfilled Appeals: The Rise and Fall of the 1840s Anti-Abolitionist Movement in Cincinnati," *Ohio Valley History* (Summer 2007): 53, 58.

17. Betty Fladeland, *James Gillespie Birney: From Slaveholder to Abolitionist* (New York: Cornell Univ. Press, 1955); *Philanthropist*, July 29, 1836. Mujic, "A Border Community," 58. Burnett is included on the list of prominent men Richards identified as part of the Cincinnati mob. Richards, *Gentlemen of Property and Standing*, appendix A, 173.

18. Byron Williams, *History of Clermont and Brown Counties, Ohio: From the Earliest Historical Times Down to the Present* (Milford: Hobart, 1913), 313–14.

19. William T. Utter, *Frontier State, 1803–1825* (Columbus: Ohio State Archaeological and Historical Society, 1942), 26, 50, 278; Weisenburger, *Passing of the Frontier*, 284.

20. Williams, *History of Clermont and Brown Counties*, 416–17.

21. Harry R. Stevens, *The Early Jackson Party in Ohio* (Durham: Duke Univ. Press, 1957), 99–100; J. L. Rockey and R. J. Bancroft, *History of Clermont County, Ohio* (Philadelphia: Louis H. Everts Press, 1880), 265; *State v. Hess* 5 Ohio Reports Hammond 1 (1831).

22. *Ohio State Journal*, Sept. 15, 1832. Although both were Jacksonians, Hamer differed diametrically from Morris on support for internal improvements and the Bank of the United States. Donald J. Ratcliffe, "The Crisis of Commercialization: National Political Alignments and the Market Revolution, 1819–1844," in *The Market Revolution in America: Social, Political, and Religious Expressions, 1800–1860*, ed. Melvyn Stokes and Stephen Conway (Charlottesville: Univ. Press of Virginia, 1996), 194–95.

23. Nelson Wiley Evans and Emmons B. Strivers, *A History of Adams County, Ohio: From Its Earliest Settlement to the Present Time, Including Character Sketches of the Prominent Persons Identified with the First Century of the Country's Growth* (West Union: E. B. Strivers, 1900), 306; *Ohio State Journal*, Dec. 12, 1832.

24. Weisenburger, *Passing of the Frontier*, 241, 326, 374; Melhorn, *Lest We Be Marshalled*, 98. Weisenburger suggests that the enmity did not arise until after the antislavery petitions, but Morris's distaste preceded the petition campaign and likely played a role in his refusal to resign and accept an appointment to the Ohio Supreme Court

186 NOTES TO PAGES 42–45

in the fall of 1835. John Ashworth, *Slavery, Capitalism, and Politics in the Antebellum Republic*, vol. 1, *Commerce and Compromise, 1820–1850* (Cambridge: Cambridge Univ. Press, 1995), 381.

25. Fladeland, *James Gillespie Birney*, 125–48.

26. *Philanthropist*, Jan. 22, 1836.

27. Birney to Elizur Wright, Sept. 26, 1836, *Emancipator*, Oct. 20, 1836.

28. Birney to Lewis Tappan, Sept. 26, 1836, in Dwight L. Dumond, ed., *Letters of James Gillespie Birney, 1831–1857* (New York: D. Appleton Century, 1938), 358–60.

29. *Philanthropist*, Nov. 25, 1836, and Aug. 11, 1841.

30. Theodore C. Smith, *Liberty and Free Soil Parties in the Northwest* (New York: Longmans, Green, 1897), 24. This overestimate of Birney's influence on Morris continues today. For example, Corey Brooks speculated that it seemed "probable that Morris learned more of his anti-Slave Power political argument from moralistic associates like Birney than from fellow Democrats." Corey M. Brooks, *Liberty Power: Antislavery Third Parties and the Transformation of American Politics* (Chicago: Univ. of Chicago Press, 2016), 26. This conclusion not only ignores the fact that Morris had delineated his Slave Power theory before meeting Birney but assumes Morris "learned" the argument from someone else. The explosion of references to the Slave Power among antislavery activists (which Brooks effectively chronicles) following Morris's speech on incendiary publications is strong evidence that the antislavery movement was learning from Morris.

31. More likely, Morris's views reinforced Birney's position on petitions and incendiary publications. See, for example, *Cincinnati Gazette*'s report of Morris's January 7, 1836, defense of the right of petition and Birney's defense of that right, both published in the *Philanthropist*, January 22, 1836.

32. Betty Fladeland, "James G. Birney's Anti-Slavery Activities in Cincinnati, 1835–1837," *Bulletin of the Historical and Philosophical Society of Ohio* 9 (Oct. 1951): 251–53. Morris thought slavery "immoral," but not in the sense that abolitionists used the term. He did not believe he had a duty to redeem slaveholders.

33. Fladeland, "Birney's Anti-Slavery Activities," 251–53.

34. Writing more than fifty years later, Birney's son recalled that Morris (along with several other prominent Cincinnatians) had visited Birney at his home during 1836. William Birney, *James G. Birney and His Times: The Genesis of the Republican Party* (New York: Bergman Publishers, 1890), 206. Nothing is known about the substance of these additional meetings. Given Birney's description of his September meeting with Morris, however, these visits to the Birney home must have occurred (if at all) after the first meeting in Clermont County.

35. Report of the meeting of November 23, 1836, in the *Philanthropist*, December 9, 1836. Although no reason was given for Morris's decision not to join, the Society's constitution required members to believe that "slave-holding is a heinous sin against God" and that it was "the duty . . . of all concerned [to] require its immediate abandonment." Morris's view that abolition in the District was "inexpedient" may have caused him to decline to join.

36. Rankin to Elizur Wright, Feb. 27, 1837, in *Emancipator*, Mar. 16, 1837.

NOTES TO PAGES 45–48 187

37. Birney's son later claimed that Birney had appointed Morris as a "local lecturer without pay" during 1836. Birney, *James G. Birney and His Times*, 258. Given Birney not meeting Morris until September, Morris's involvement in Van Buren's 1836 presidential campaign in Ohio, his return to Washington in early December, Morris's refusal to join the county antislavery society, and Rankin's description of Morris's speech, it is unlikely that Morris became an antislavery lecturer in 1836. The son's "memory" (on which this report was admittedly based) was probably inaccurate.

38. Cong. Globe, 24th Cong., 2nd Sess., 170 (1836–37). Robert V. Remini, *Andrew Jackson and the Course of American Democracy, 1833–1845* (New York: HarperCollins, 1984), 3:409–11; Wilentz, *Rise of American Democracy*, 444.

39. Cong. Globe, 24th Cong., 2nd Sess., 99 (1836–37). Senator Benton later recalled that following the vote to expunge the censure, President Jackson gave a "grand dinner" in honor of the "expungers." Thomas Hart Benton, *Thirty Years' View* (New York: D. Appleton, 1856), 727–31; Remini, *Andrew Jackson*, 3:378–81. Presumably Morris attended.

40. Benton, *Thirty Years' View*, 729–31.

41. Cong. Globe, 24th Cong., 2nd Sess., 99–100 (1836–37).

42. Cong. Globe, 24th Cong., 2nd Sess., 114 (1836–37); *Niles Weekly Register*, Jan. 28, 1837.

43. Cong. Globe, 24th Cong., 2nd Sess., 114 (1836–37).

44. The Ohio Anti-Slavery Society opposed recognition of Texas "until slavery shall be abolished" and petitioned Congress to that end. The petitions, however, were presented by Morris's Whig colleague. Cong. Globe, 24th Cong., 2nd Sess., 191 (1836–37).

45. Donald Cole, *Martin Van Buren and the American Political System* (Princeton: Princeton Univ. Press, 1984), 44–45.

46. Cong. Globe, 24th Cong., 2nd Sess., 21, 214 (1836–37). The 1837 Ohio Antislavery Society meeting (chaired by Birney) appeared to recognize Morris's divergence on Texas when it only acknowledged his support on the petition campaign. Ohio Anti-Slavery Society, *Report of the Second Anniversary*, 13.

47. See, for example, Resolutions of the Georgia and Vermont legislatures in *Niles Weekly Register*, December 3, 1836.

48. The presentation of petitions from Tennessee triggered an immediate response from Calhoun and Felix Grundy (a senator from Tennessee). Both demanded to know the source of the petition. Morris blithely claimed he no longer had the envelope that had contained the petition so that he did not know. Cong. Globe, 24th Cong., 2nd Sess., 158–59 (1836–37).

49. Cong. Globe, 24th Cong., 2nd Sess., 158–59 (1836–37); Van Buren may have suggested this approach in 1836. Wilentz, *Rise of American Democracy*, 451–52; see also Leonard L. Richards, *The Slave Power: The Free North and Southern Domination, 1780–1860* (Baton Rouge: Louisiana State Univ. Press, 2000), 131–32.

50. Cong. Globe, 24th Cong., 2nd Sess., 158–59 (1836–37).

51. Elder, *Calhoun*, 337–40; William Lee Miller, *Arguing about Slavery* (New York: Knopf, 1996), 107; Cong. Globe, 24th Cong., 1st Sess., 80, 236 (1835–36).

52. Cong. Globe, 24th Cong., 1st Sess., 83 (1835–36). This view of slavery as evil, however, was neither new nor limited to the abolitionists. The 1832 graduates of the

188 NOTES TO PAGES 48–51

University of North Carolina were told that slavery was "the worst evil that affects the southern states." Avery O. Craven, *Coming of the Civil War: A Stimulating and Profound Analysis of the Factors Which Brought a Nation into War with Itself* (Chicago: Univ. of Chicago Press, 1957), 153–54. As late as the spring of 1833, the *Washington Globe* concluded that "in principle, slavery has no advocates North or South of the Potomac." Quoted in John M. McFaul, "Expediency vs. Morality: Jacksonian Politics and Slavery," *Journal of American History* 62 (June 1975): 28.

53. Speech on Abolition Petitions, Mar. 9, 1836, in Robert Lee Meriwether, William Edwin Hemphill, and Clyde Norman Wilson, eds., *The Papers of John C. Calhoun* (Columbia: Univ. of South Carolina Press, 1959), 13:262–65; Ford, *Deliver Us from Evil*, 506–7.

54. Miller, *Arguing about Slavery*, 132–33; Ford, *Deliver Us from Evil*, 526–27.

55. Cong. Globe, 24th Cong., 2nd Sess., 159 (1836–37). Although this was not the first time this sentiment had been expressed (see Larry E. Tise, *Proslavery: A History of the Defense of Slavery in America, 1701–1840* [Athens: Univ. of Georgia Press, 1987], 101–3), "in its force, clarity and content, Calhoun's argument marked a significant departure in the political debate over slavery." He had created "an aggressive political ideology designed to counter the abolitionist campaign" (Elder, *Calhoun*, 336–40). Calhoun's stature in the Senate and the widespread publication of the Senate's debate made his claim the best known.

56. Wolf, *Race and Liberty*, 231; Annals of Cong., 9th Cong., 2nd Sess., 237–38 (1806–07). The Missouri controversy also generated positive defenses of slavery. See, for example, Speech of William Smith (South Carolina) in Annals of Cong., 16th Cong., 1st Sess., 259–74 (1819–20).

57. Cong. Globe, 24th Cong., 2nd Sess., 159 (1836–37). Tabling the motion to receive the petition remained the practice in the Senate until 1850. Daniel Walker Howe, *What Hath God Wrought: The Transformation of America, 1815–1848* (New York: Oxford Univ. Press, 2007), 513.

58. Howe, *What Hath God Wrought*, 160, 163, 166, 184, 216.

59. James D. Richardson, ed., *A Compilation of Messages and Papers of the Presidents* (New York: Bureau of National Literature, 1897), 4:1535.

60. Smith, *Liberty and Free Soil Parties*, 24.

61. Ohio Anti-Slavery Society, *Report of the Second Anniversary*, 13.

62. Stanton to Birney, June 26, 1837, in Dumond, *Letters of James Gillespie Birney*, 388–89.

4. THE ABSOLUTE CREED OF THE ABOLITIONISTS

1. This discussion of the Matilda case follows John Niven, *Salmon P. Chase: A Biography* (New York: Oxford Univ. Press, 1995), 50. The attack on the *Philanthropist* first brought Salmon Chase into antislavery prominence when the mob also threatened his sister. In the following weeks, Chase led an effort to condemn violence. He ultimately brought suit on behalf of Birney to recover damages for the property destroyed by the mob. Frederick J. Blue, *Salmon P. Chase: A Life in Politics* (Kent, OH: Kent State Univ. Press, 1987), 28–31.

NOTES TO PAGES 51–53

2. Jonathan H. Earle, *Jacksonian Antislavery and the Politics of Free Soil, 1824–1854* (Chapel Hill: Univ. of North Carolina Press, 2004), 240n57; James Oakes, *Freedom National: The Destruction of Slavery in the United States, 1861–1865* (New York: W. W. Norton, 2013), 16–17. Birney, in the words of Jacobus tenBroek, was a "quartermaster of ideas in the movement rather than an original producer of them." Jacobus tenBroek, *Equal under the Law: The Antislavery Origins of the Fourteenth Amendment* (London: Collier Books, 1969), 296. Much of the material he provided Chase was drawn from Morris. As Birney reported to Elizer Wright, he had followed Morris's Senate actions closely. Birney to Elizer Wright, Sept. 26, 1836, in Dwight L, Dumond, ed., *Letters of James Gillespie Birney, 1831–1857* (New York: D. Appleton Century, 1938), 358–60.

3. Earle, *Jacksonian Antislavery*, 240n57; Niven, *Salmon Chase*, 54.

4. *Philanthropist*, Feb. 24, 1837.

5. Salmon P. Chase, *Speech of Salmon P. Chase in the Case of the Colored Woman, Matilda: Who Was Brought before the Court of Common Pleas of Hamilton County, Ohio, by Writ of Habeas Corpus, March 11, 1837* (Cincinnati: Pugh & Dodd, 1837).

6. The timing, subject, and source of the petition, as well as the extent and quality of Morris's response to the committee, suggest Morris's involvement. The petition came from the Clermont County antislavery group almost immediately after Morris had attended their organizational meeting in November 1836, at which he made several "valuable suggestions" (*Philanthropist*, Dec. 9, 1836). The focus of the petition on the absence of juries for fugitive slaves was a particular concern for Morris. Early in his career, Morris had urged juries even in cases tried before a justice of the peace. He believed everyone, including purported fugitive slaves, were entitled to the protection of a jury trial. See Benjamin Franklin Morris, ed., *Life of Thomas Morris: Pioneer and Long a Legislator of Ohio, and U.S. Senator from 1833 to 1839* (Cincinnati: Moore, Wilstach, Keys & Overend, 1856), 38. Finally, Morris's desire to draw the author of the Committee's report into "a controversy" (that is, public debate) indicates Morris had hoped to use the petition to challenge the Ohio Fugitive Slave Law.

7. Report of Ohio Senate Judiciary Committee, Jan. 10, 1837, in *Philanthropist*, Feb. 24, 1837.

8. Morris to Sir, Mar. 30, 1837, in Morris, *Life of Thomas Morris*, 248.

9. Morris to Sir, Mar. 30, 1837, in Morris, *Life of Thomas Morris*, 248–51. The clause was "located elsewhere than among powers delegated to Congress." Its location and language meant that whether "the clause . . . even authorized congressional implementation is open to question." Don E. Fehrenbach, *The Dred Scott Case: Its Significance in American Law & Politics* (New York: Oxford Univ. Press, 1978), 40. Morris consistently argued that it did not. For the background on the adoption for the 1793 Fugitive Slave Act, see Sean Wilentz, *No Property in Man: Slavery and Antislavery at the Nation's Founding* (Cambridge, MA: Harvard Univ. Press, 2018), 164–66. Morris based his conclusion that the Constitution anticipated the abolition of slavery on (1) the adoption of the Northwest Ordinance while the convention met and its ratification by Congress; (2) the acts of the Northern states to abolish slavery; and (3) the provision (article 1, section 9) empowering Congress to abolish the slave trade.

10. Morris to Sir, Mar. 30, 1837, in Morris, *Life of Thomas Morris*, 250.

11. Morris to Sir, Mar. 30, 1837, in Morris, *Life of Thomas Morris*, 253.

12. Morris to Sir, Mar. 30, 1837, in Morris, *Life of Thomas Morris*, 247. This desire to engage in public debate on issues beyond the right to petition set Morris apart from most of his fellow antislavery advocates in Congress. For example, at the same time Morris was writing his letter, John Quincy Adams was confiding to his diary that "upon this subject of anti-slavery my principles and my position make it necessary to be more circumspect. . . . [He had] already committed indiscretions of which all the political parties avail themselves to proscribe me in the public opinion. . . . The exposure through which I passed at the late Session of Congress was greater than I could have imagined. It would do me well to consider my ways before I put myself in the way of being cast into it again." Entry for Apr. 19, 1837, in David Waldstreicher and Matthew Mason, eds., *John Quincy Adams and the Politics of Slavery: Selections from the Diary* (New York: Oxford Univ. Press, 2017), 201–2.

13. James Campbell Curtis, *The Fox at Bay: Martin Van Buren and the Presidency, 1837–1841* (Lexington: Univ. Press of Kentucky, 1970), 66–67. Morris had followed Jackson's lead and opposed the bill. Cong. Globe, 24th Cong., 1st Sess., 336 (1835–36).

14. "Special Session Message," Sept. 4, 1837, in *A Compilation of Messages and Papers of the Presidents*, ed. James D. Richardson (New York: Bureau of National Literature, 1897), 4:1541–63.

15. Donald Cole, *Martin Van Buren and the American Political System* (Princeton: Princeton Univ. Press, 1984), 301–7; Curtis, *The Fox at Bay*, 86–110.

16. Cole, *Martin Van Buren*, 276–77; Curtis, *The Fox at Bay*, 68–85.

17. Cong. Globe, 25th Cong., 1st Sess. 73–74 (1837).

18. Curtis, *The Fox at Bay*, 104–5. In voting against a bill to authorize payments for federal lands in notes from specie-paying banks, Morris had made his views of state banks (and a possible federal fiscal agent) clear: "I would at once give my vote to create such a fiscal agent for the use of this Government, rather than adopt a whole litter of state banks for that purpose." Cong. Globe, 25th Cong., 2nd Sess., appendix, 161 (1837–38).

19. Cong. Globe, 25th Cong., 1st Sess., 100 (1837). Weisenburger, apparently relying on a report in the *Ohio State Journal*, says Morris did not vote on the bill. Francis P. Weisenburger, *Passing of the Frontier 1825–1850: The History of the State of Ohio* (Columbus: Ohio State Archaeological and Historical Society, 1941), 342. This confusion may be the result of the timing of the final vote. After supporting the administration on Rives and Prentiss's attempts to amend the bill, Morris did not remain to vote to advance the bill to its third reading. When the bill was brought forward the next day for final approval, Morris voted in favor. See also Morris to Mr. Medary, June 6, 1838, *Daily Ohio Statesman*, June 15, 1838, defending his vote in favor of the Independent Treasury.

20. Cong. Globe, 25th Cong. 1st Sess., 22, 49, 94 (1837).

21. Stanley Harrold, *Border War: Fighting over Slavery before the Civil War* (Chapel Hill: North Carolina Univ. Press, 2010), 58; Ann Hagedorn, *Beyond the River: The Untold Stories of the Heroes of the Underground Railroad* (New York: Simon & Schuster, 2002), 123–28.

22. *Ohio State Journal*, Nov. 7, 1837.

23. Morris to Alexander Campbell, Nov. 13, 1837, *Philanthropist*, Dec. 26, 1837.

NOTES TO PAGES 55–57

24. Morris to Alexander Campbell, Nov. 13, 1837, *Philanthropist*, Dec. 26, 1837. Morris still felt the same way five years later when Kentuckians again abducted a Black resident of Clermont County and his family. This time Morris thought that "between nations such an act might be considered a good cause of war." He wondered when Ohio would "wake up to our rights" and put an end to "the negro hunting tribe [that] break open our dwellings and steal our people" (Harrold, *Border War*, 61).

25. Morris to Alexander Campbell, Nov. 13, 1837, *Philanthropist*, Dec. 26, 1837. These rights included, at a minimum, the right to a jury trial in fugitive slave cases. Perhaps more frightening for the slave owners, Morris also thought that Mrs. Johnson had the right to use deadly force to defend herself from the Kentucky slave catchers. Benjamin Wade would make a similar claim two years later in the Ohio General Assembly (Harrold, *Border War*, 86–87).

26. Not until after the *Dred Scott* decision in 1857 would the Ohio General Assembly explicitly recognize free Blacks residing in Ohio as citizens. Eric Foner, *The Fiery Trial: Abraham Lincoln and American Slavery* (New York, W. W. Norton, 2010), 94.

27. Morris to Alexander Campbell, Nov. 13, 1837, *Philanthropist*, Dec. 26, 1837. Although arguing that "the likelihood of any such holding was surely remote," Feldman cites Lincoln as making a similar assertion about the consequences of this interpretation of the Fifth Amendment. Noah Feldman, *The Broken Constitution: Lincoln, Slavery and the Refounding of America* (New York: Farrar, Strauss & Corex, 2021), 115. Other legal historians, however, find Lincoln (and Morris) fears justified. Hyman and Wiecek, *Equal Justice under the Law*, 195: "Taney never had an opportunity so to rule, but Lincoln's fears were not groundless or demagogic."

28. Hyman and Wiecek, *Equal Justice under the Law*, 195.

29. *Philanthropist*, Nov. 14, 1837.

30. William M. Wiecek, *The Sources of Antislavery Constitutionalism in America, 1760–1848* (New York: Cornell Univ. Press, 1977), 188. Text of Calhoun's resolutions as offered can be found in Cong. Globe, 25th Cong., 2nd Sess. 55 (1837–38) and in Wiecek, *Antislavery Constitutionalism*, appendix 2, 291–93.

31. William J. Cooper, *The South and the Politics of Slavery, 1828–1856* (Baton Rouge: Louisiana State Univ. Press, 1978), 103; Robert Elder, *Calhoun: American Heretic* (New York: Basic Books, 2021), 347–52.

32. Lacy K. Ford, *Deliver Us from Evil: The Slavery Question in the Old South* (New York: Oxford Univ. Press, 2009), 524; Elder, *Calhoun*, 353–54.

33. Ford, *Deliver Us from Evil*, 524; Elder, *Calhoun*, 353–54.

34. Cong. Globe, 25th Cong., 2nd Sess., 73 (1837–38).

35. Senator Niles to Gideon Wells, Jan. 6 and 11, 1838, quoted in Curtis, *The Fox at Bay*, 118–19; Thomas Hart Benton, *Thirty Years' View* (New York: D. Appleton, 1856), 137–38; John Ashworth, *Slavery, Capitalism, and Politics in the Antebellum Republic*, vol. 1, *Commerce and Compromise, 1820–1850* (Cambridge: Cambridge Univ. Press, 1995), 137–38; William J. Cooper, *The South and the Politics of Slavery, 1828–1856* (Baton Rouge: Louisiana State Univ. Press, 1978), 105, 112.

36. Wilentz, *No Property in Man*, 220; Wiecek, *Antislavery Constitutionalism*, 187. Although Chief Justice Taney would largely adopt Calhoun's understanding of the

192   NOTES TO PAGES 57–61

Fugitive Slave Clause in combination with the Fifth Amendment, Calhoun seems to have concluded that whatever protection of slavery the Constitution contained was insufficient. Jamelle Bouie, *"Politics" in the 1619 Project* (New York: One World, 2021), 199–202. The experience of the prior session had persuaded Calhoun that "reliance on constitutional law repeatedly proved to be politically inadequate." Mark Graber, *Dred Scott and the Problem of Constitutional Evil* (New York: Cambridge Univ. Press, 2006), 138. If the Constitution was pro-slavery, it was not pro-slavery enough.

37. Cong. Globe, 25th Cong., 2nd Sess., 55 and 133–34 (1837–38). Fehrenbacher, *Dred Scott*, 123.

38. Cong. Globe, 25th Cong., 2nd Sess., 55 and 133–34 (1837–38).

39. Cong. Globe, 25th Cong., 2nd Sess., 55 and 133–34 (1837–38).

40. Wiecek, *Antislavery Constitutionalism*, 187; Sean Wilentz, *American Democracy: Jefferson to Lincoln* (New York: W. W. Norton, 2005), 476.

41. After Morris left the Senate, Calhoun would again claim that the Fugitive Slave Clause recognized a right to property in slaves. See Cong Globe, 26th Cong., 2nd Sess., 188, 191 (1840). Even later, in a speech on the Oregon Territory, Calhoun would cite the three-fifths clause as evidence that the Constitution guaranteed the right to own slaves. Cong. Globe, 30th Cong., 1st Sess., appendix, 868–73 (1848). After his exchange with Morris, however, Calhoun was reticent to locate a right to slave property in any particular provision of the Constitution (Wilentz, *No Property in Man*, 233–34).

42. Cooper, *The Politics of Slavery*, 112, 122; Elder, *Calhoun*, 354.

43. Entry for Jan. 3, 1838, in Morris, *Life of Thomas Morris*, 105–6.

44. Resolutions of Mr. Morris, *Philanthropist*, Jan. 9, 1838.

45. Resolutions of Mr. Morris, *Philanthropist*, Jan. 9, 1838.

46. Cong. Globe, 25th Cong., 2nd Sess., 67 (1837–38). Although he had originally asked for separate votes on his substitute, Morris agreed to vote on Calhoun's proposals. Cong. Globe, 25th Cong., 2nd Sess., 67 (1837–38), 73. The full text of all of Morris's resolutions was published in *Philanthropist*, Jan. 9, 1838.

47. Thomas Hart Benton, *Abridgement of the Debates of Congress, from 1799 to 1856* (New York: D. Appleton, 1859), 13:568 note.

48. Cong. Globe, 25th Cong., 2nd Sess., 73 (1837–38).

49. Cong. Globe, 25th Cong., 2nd Sess., 73 (1837–38). The debate spanned several days with Morris speaking throughout. The *Congressional Globe* reported only bits of his speeches. In the fall, the *Philanthropist* requested that Morris provide a complete version of his remarks throughout the debate. These compiled remarks were published in their entirety in *Philanthropist*, Oct. 2, 1838.

50. *Philanthropist*, Oct. 2, 1838.

51. *Philanthropist*, Oct. 2, 1838.

52. Elder, *Calhoun*, 357.

53. Cong. Globe, 25th Cong., 2nd Sess., appendix, 25–26 (1837–38).

54. Cong. Globe, 25th Cong., 2nd Sess., 74 (1837–38).

55. I am following Professor Miller's analysis (*Arguing about Slavery*, 131–34)—based on Robert Lee Meriwether, William Edwin Hemphill, and Clyde Norman Wilson, eds., *The Papers of John C. Calhoun* (Columbia: Univ. of South Carolina Press, 1959),

NOTES TO PAGES 61–63   193

13:389–91)—of Calhoun's exchange with Rives. The *Congressional Globe* merely reported that "the debate further continued" without reporting the substance of the exchange between Calhoun and Rives. Cong. Globe, 24th Cong., 2nd Sess., 160 (1836–37). See also Elder, *Calhoun,* 337–38.

56. Miller, *Arguing about Slavery,* 133.

57. Miller, *Arguing about Slavery,* 133; Elder, *Calhoun,* 329–30.

58. Report of debate in *Philanthropist,* Jan. 9, 1838.

59. Cong. Globe, 25th Cong., 2nd Sess., 55 (1837–38).

60. Cong. Globe, 25th Cong., 2nd Sess., 73 (1837–38).

61. Cong. Globe, 25th Cong., 2nd Sess., 73 (1837–38). Morris did not identify the sources of Southern power (the three-fifths clause, equal representation in the Senate, or the disproportionate representation in the Democratic Caucus; see Richards, *The Slave Power*). Instead, he focused on the manifestation of the power in the demands made and the individual (Calhoun) making the demands.

62. Rankin to Elizur Wright, Feb. 27, 1837, *Emancipator,* Mar. 16, 1837.

63. Elder, *Calhoun,* 357. Cong. Globe, 25th Cong., 2nd Sess., 73–99 (1837–38). They passed with substantial majorities, although the *Ohio State Journal* reported that several senators enjoyed seeing Calhoun directly challenged. See *Ohio State Journal,* Jan. 3, 1838.

64. Cong. Globe, 25th Cong., 2nd Sess., 26 (1837–38). Personally, Morris may have been feeling particularly alone. During this session, for the only time during his Senate career, he was staying in a private residence in Washington. During all other sessions, he had stayed in a boardinghouse with other senators and congressmen. Perry M. Goldman and James S. Young, eds., *The United States Congressional Directories, 1789–1840* (New York: Columbia Univ. Press, 1973), 268–80, 293, 305, 318, 344.

65. Cong. Globe, 25th Cong., 2nd Sess., appendix, 26 (1837–38).

66. Cong. Globe, 25th Cong., 2nd Sess., appendix, 26 (1837–38), 32.

67. *Philanthropist,* Oct. 9, 1838.

68. *Philanthropist,* Oct. 9, 1838.

69. *Philanthropist,* Oct. 9, 1838.

70. *Emancipator,* Feb. 1, 1838.

71. Donald J. Ratcliffe, "The Crisis of Commercialization: National Political Alignments and the Market Revolution, 1819–1844," in *The Market Revolution in America: Social, Political, and Religious Expressions 1800–1860,* ed. Melvyn Stokes and Stephen Conway (Charlottesville: Univ. Press of Virginia, 1996), 185.

72. "First Annual Message," Dec. 5, 1837, in *A Compilation of Messages and Papers of the Presidents,* ed. James D. Richardson, 4:1590–1612.

73. Cong. Globe, 25th Cong., 2nd Sess., appendix, 203–9 (1837–38). Morris may have felt it necessary to explain his disregard for the general assembly's instructions. Two years earlier he had severely criticized then Senator Ewing for failing to follow the Ohio legislature's directions to vote in favor of expunging the censure of President Jackson. Cong. Globe, 24th Cong., 1st Sess., 274 (1836).

74. Curtis, *The Fox at Bay,* 122–26; Cong. Globe, 25th Cong., 2nd Sess., 250–51 (1837–38).

75. Cong. Globe, 25th Cong., 2nd Sess., 259 (1837–38).

194   NOTES TO PAGES 64–67

76. Cong. Globe, 24th Cong., 2nd Sess., 214 (1836–37); Curtis, *The Fox at Bay*, 152–56.

77. Cong. Globe, 25th Cong., 2nd Sess., 76 (1837–38). The timing of Senator Preston's resolution may have contributed to Morris's view that Calhoun's resolutions were also directed at Texas. See note 49 supra.

78. *Slave Trade Acts*, 3rd Cong., 1st Sess., Chapter XI (1794); *Slave Trade Acts*, 6th Cong., 1st Sess., Chapter LI (1800).

79. Daniel Walker Howe, *What Hath God Wrought: The Transformation of America, 1815–1848* (New York: Oxford Univ. Press, 2007), 671.

80. Cong. Globe, 25th Cong., 2nd Sess., 246 (1837–38). In selecting the Judiciary Committee for referral of the resolution, Morris was insuring at least a minority report back to the full Senate. Morris was a member of the committee (Goldman and Young, *United States Congressional Directories*, 340). Morris's defeat for reelection and the annexation of Texas seven years later prevented this approach from being pursued further.

81. Cong. Globe, 25th Cong., 2nd Sess., 247 (1837–38); *Philanthropist*, Apr. 3, 1838.

82. *Emancipator*, Oct. 4, 1838. Morris's willingness to present petitions signed by women earned the praise of the 1838 Antislavery Convention of America Women meeting in Philadelphia. Manisha Sinha, *The Slave's Cause: A History of Abolition* (London: Yale Univ. Press, 2016), 283.

83. After his death, the story circulated that while in Washington, Morris had seen some wagons loaded with slave children who were to be sold. Supposedly the scene so unnerved him that he was unable to attend the Senate that day and it motivated his antislavery actions. Byron Williams, *History of Clermont and Brown Counties, Ohio: From the Earliest Historical Times Down to the Present* (Milford: Hobart, 1913), 399. The story may have been apocryphal. It is not contained in his son's overwhelmingly laudatory biography. Or it may have been taken from Morris's 1839 Reply to Clay. During that speech, Morris told of seeing empty wagons and being informed in the evening by his Washington landlady that they were to be filled with slaves (including children) to be sold further south. Although the information "unnerved and unfitted him" for thought on any other subject, he did not claim the information motivated his actions in the Senate. Not until Calhoun's Constitution-based attack on the press, speech, and petitions did Morris say anything in the Senate about slavery.

84. Cong. Globe, 25th Cong., 3rd Sess., appendix, 169 (1838–39).

5. I ASK NO FORGIVENESS

1. At the time, Morris was "the leading hard money Jacksonian" in the Senate. Sean Wilentz, *Rise of American Democracy: Jefferson to Lincoln* (New York: W. W. Norton, 2005), 477.

2. Robert Elder, *Calhoun: American Heretic* (New York: Basic Books, 2021), 349.

3. *Ohio State Journal*, Oct. 20, 1837.

4. *Ohio State Journal*, June 6, 1838.

5. *Cincinnati Daily Gazette*, Sept. 11, 1838. Morris may have been singled out because his seat was up for election. Senator Allen, the other Democratic senator from Ohio, also spoke in support of Democratic candidates throughout Ohio. Francis P.

NOTES TO PAGES 67–70

Weisenburger, *Passing of the Frontier 1825–1850: The History of the State of Ohio* (Columbus: Ohio State Archaeological and Historical Society, 1941), 348–49.

6. Morris to Messrs. A. McCully and Others, June 22, 1838, *Ohio Statesman,* July 17, 1838.

7. Morris to Medary, June 6, 1838, *Ohio Statesman,* June 15, 1838.

8. Some historians have claimed that the Whig resolutions "were passed denouncing his antislavery views." See, for example, John A. Neuenschwander, "Senator Thomas Morris: Antagonist of the South, 1836–1839," *Cincinnati Historical Society Bulletin* 32 (Fall 1974): 133. The resolutions, however, attacked both Ohio senators for failure to follow the general assembly's instructions to oppose the Independent Treasury. No mention was made of Morris's antislavery actions. In a lengthy response to Morris's letter, the state Whig party organ, the *Ohio State Journal,* again focused almost exclusively on Morris's support for Jacksonian economic policy (*Ohio State Journal,* June 20, 1838). Some other Whig papers, however, complained that Morris's letter "abounds in the Abolition cant of the day" and portrayed Morris as "boasting . . . of his votes in favor of abolition doctrines" (*Circleville Herald,* n.d., *Ohio State Journal,* July 25, 1838).

9. Morris to Medary, June 6, 1838, *Ohio Statesman,* June 15, 1838.

10. Morris to Sir, Mar. 30, 1837, in Benjamin Franklin Morris, *Life of Morris: Pioneer and Long a Legislator of Ohio, and U.S. Senator from 1833 to 1839* (Cincinnati: Moore, Wilstach, Keys & Overend, 1856), 248.

11. Morris to Alexander Campbell, Nov. 13, 1837, *Philanthropist,* Dec. 26, 1837.

12. *Philanthropist,* Oct. 2, 1838.

13. Morris to Medary, June 6, 1838, *Ohio Statesman,* June 15, 1838.

14. Ohio Constitution of 1802, article VIII, section 1. For a review of the Ohio courts' application of the bill of rights to Black residents, see Jonathan L. Entin, "An Ohio Dilemma: Race Equal Protection and the Unfulfilled Promise of a State Bill of Rights," *Cleveland State. Law Review* 51 (2004): 395.

15. Morris to Messers A. McColly and others, June 22, 1838, *Ohio Statesman,* July 17, 1838.

16. *National Intelligencer,* Mar. 4, 1801.

17. Morris to Joseph M. Truman and Others, May 11, 1838, *Philanthropist,* June 26, 1838.

18. Morris to Joseph M. Truman and Others, May 11, 1838, *Philanthropist,* June 26, 1838.

19. Morris to Joseph M. Truman and Others, May 11, 1838, *Philanthropist,* June 26, 1838.

20. Morris to Joseph M. Truman and Others, May 11, 1838, *Philanthropist,* June 26, 1838.

21. Morris to Joseph M. Truman and Others, May 11, 1838, *Philanthropist,* June 26, 1838.

22. Kate Masur, *Until Justice Be Done: America's First Civil Rights Movement from Reconstruction* (New York: W. W. Norton, 2021), 85, 96, 107–9. Although the *Ohio Statesman* in 1838 printed Morris's demand for "equal and exact justice for all" and his effort to tie the Whigs to the Slave Power, in the state elections the following year, Medary rejected both claims. Instead, the *Statesman* portrayed the abolitionists and Whigs as united and claimed that Blacks "can never become equal citizens with us," and that "patriotism . . . requires us to protect the State from the introduction of this class of beings" (*Daily Ohio Statesman,* Sept. 17, 1839).

23. Masur, *Until Justice Be Done,* 107.

196   NOTES TO PAGES 70–73

24. *Philanthropist,* July 24, 1838.

25. Report in *Philanthropist,* Jan. 30, 1838; Weisenburger, *Passing of the Frontier,* 433; William Lee Miller, *Arguing about Slavery* (New York: Knopf, 1996), 287. Although the resolutions were supported by both parties, the Whigs controlled both the general assembly and the governor's office. As a result, the resolutions were not sent to Morris.

26. Paul Goodman, *Of One Blood: Abolitionism and the Origins of Racial Equality* (Berkeley: Univ. of California Press, 1998), 124–25. The year 1838 was the "peak" of membership in the American Anti-Slavery Society nationally. There were three hundred thousand members in two thousand local organizations across the North (Wilentz, *Rise of American Democracy,* 403).

27. Ohio Anti-Slavery Society, *Report of the Third Anniversary of the Ohio Anti-Slavery Society* (May 1838): 5–7.

28. *Philanthropist,* Oct. 2, 1838. Morris compounded the risk by also publishing his critique of Senator Allen's effort to reaffirm the right to petition (*Philanthropist,* Oct. 9, 1839). Attacking Calhoun might have been excusable, but denigrating the efforts of a fellow Ohio Jacksonian senator was beyond the pale.

29. *Ohio Statesman,* Oct. 2, 1838; *Ohio State Journal,* Sept. 25, 1838. A year earlier, Vance had intervened in the Eliza Johnson case, which had caused Morris to write to Alexander Campbell. Vance, however, chose not to aid Mahan. See Stephen Middleton, *The Black Laws: Race and the Legal Process in Early Ohio* (Athens: Ohio Univ. Press, 2005), 96–98, 122. See also Ann Hagedorn, *Beyond the River: The Untold Stories of the Heroes of the Underground Railroad* (New York: Simon & Schuster, 2002), 153–65.

30. *Cincinnati Republican,* Oct. 25, 1838, *Philanthropist,* Nov. 20, 1838. Far from manufacturing the story, the *Philanthropist* reported that Morris had advised Mahan's supporters that the governor had no choice. The language of the Democratic Press reports, however, echo Morris's June 6, 1838, letter to Medary. Indeed, the *Ohio Statesman* essentially acknowledged that Morris was the source for its coverage of the affair (*Ohio Statesman,* Oct. 6, 1838).

31. Vernon L. Volpe, *Forlorn Hope of Freedom: The Liberty Party in the Old Northwest, 1838–1848* (Kent, OH: Kent State Univ. Press, 1990), 25–26; *Philanthropist,* Oct. 23, 1838. The *Philanthropist* had urged abolitionists to vote only for antislavery supporters for at least a year (*Philanthropist,* June 23, 1837).

32. Volpe, *Forlorn Hope of Freedom,* 26; Ohio Anti-Slavery Society, *Report of the Second Anniversary* (Apr. 1827): 13–14; Ohio Anti-Slavery Society, *Report of the Third Anniversary* (May 1838), 5–7. For a list of the recommended questions to be addressed to candidates, see *Philanthropist,* Aug. 21, 1838.

33. *Philanthropist,* Mar. 13 and Aug. 7, 1838; Volpe, *Forlorn Hope of Freedom,* 26–27.

34. Volpe, *Forlorn Hope of Freedom,* 26–28.

35. *Emancipator,* Nov. 1, 1838. For Whig support of Morris, see *Emancipator,* Oct. 23 and 30, 1838; *Emancipator,* Nov. 1, 1838, quotes several New York papers as attributing the Whig defeat in Ohio to Morris. An analysis of county returns, however, suggests that not only was split-ticket voting rare, Whig turnout in 1838 was consistent with historic patterns. Vernon L. Volpe, "The Ohio Election of 1838: A Study in the Historical Method?," *Ohio History Journal* 95 (1986): 92–96.

NOTES TO PAGES 73–76   197

36. Volpe, "The Ohio Election of 1838." If this estimate was correct, every Ohio abolitionist voted for the Democrats—an unlikely event. See Caleb Atwater, *A History of the State of Ohio: Natural and Civil* (Cincinnati: Glezen & Shepard, 1838), 324.

37. *Philanthropist*, Nov. 6, 1838.

38. *Ohio State Journal*, Oct. 23, 1838.

39. Volpe, *Forlorn Hope of Freedom*, 26–28. At least one Van Buren biographer ascribed the result in Ohio to the improving financial conditions, although he believed that the president's "financial and slavery policies" led to the Whig success in New York. Cole, *Martin Van Buren*, 339; Volpe, "The Ohio Election of 1838," 99.

40. *Cincinnati Republican*, Oct. 25, 1838, *Philanthropist*, Nov. 20, 1838. "It was a notorious fact that a large majority of the abolitionists of this State voted the Loco-foco ticket." The belief persisted among abolitionists for years. See, for example, Bailey to Gerrit Smith, July 21, 1840, quoted in Joel Goldfarb, "The Life of Gamaliel Bailey, Prior to the Founding of the National Era: The Orientation of a Practical Abolitionist" (PhD diss., Univ. of California, 1958).

41. Cong. Globe, 25th Cong., 1st Sess., appendix, 25 (1837).

42. Andrew Jackson, Farewell Message, Mar. 4, 1837, in James D. Richardson, ed., *A Compilation of Messages and Papers of the Presidents* (New York: Bureau of National Literature, 1897), 4:1517; Robert V. Remini, *Andrew Jackson and the Course of American Democracy, 1833–1845* (New York: HarperCollins, 1984), 3:425; *Cincinnati Advertiser*, Mar. 27, 1837.

43. *Ohio Statesman*, Oct. 30, 1838.

44. Perry Goldman and James Sterling Young, eds., *The United States Congressional Directories, 1789–1840* (New York: Columbia Univ. Press, 1973), 274, 287–89, 300–302, 313–15, 325–26, 339–40, 352–54.

45. See, for example, Cong. Globe, 25th Cong., 2nd Sess., 74, 81, 84 (1837–38).

46. Glyndon G. Van Deusen, *The Jacksonian Era 1828–1848* (New York: Harper & Row, 1963), 115.

47. Van Buren "Inaugural Address," in *A Compilation of Messages and Papers of the Presidents*, ed. James D. Richardson (New York: Bureau of National Literature, 1897), 4:1535.

48. *Emancipator*, Dec. 29, 1838. See also *Philanthropist*, Dec. 25, 1838, for Buchanan's views on opposing abolitionism.

49. *Philanthropist*, Nov. 27, 1838. See also *Philanthropist*, Dec. 25, 1838.

50. Several reports of Southern newspapers demanding Morris's defeat appeared in the antislavery press. For example, see *Philanthropist*, Dec. 11, 1838. Morris also recognized this campaign for his defeat. See Morris to Dear Sir, Jan. 15, 1839, *Philanthropist*, Feb. 5, 1839.

51. *Philanthropist*, Dec. 11, 1838.

52. *Cincinnati Daily Gazette*, Nov. 26 and 30, 1838; *Emancipator*, Dec. 29, 1838.

53. *Emancipator*, Dec. 29, 1838.

54. *Emancipator*, Dec. 29, 1838.

55. By the 1830s, the Declaration of Independence had become a "sacred text" that described not only the justification for revolt against England but also the qualities that

198   NOTES TO PAGES 76–77

are inherent in good government. See Pauline Marier, *American Scripture: Making the Declaration of Independence* (New York: Alfred A. Knopf, 1997). Most of the reform movements of the early nineteenth century claimed the Declaration's proclamation of equality as justifying their efforts. See Alexander Tsesis, *For Liberty and Equality: The Life and Times of the Declaration of Independence* (New York: Oxford Univ. Press, 2013), chap. 6 and 7. Morris would apply the Declaration to amplify the Constitution, but he more often used the language of the Ohio Bill of Rights (taken from the Declaration), which was legally enforceable and "equal and exact justice" taken from Jefferson's First Inaugural, which he understood to justify political action, to support his positions.

56. *Emancipator*, Dec. 29, 1838. Twenty years later, while debating Douglas, Lincoln would take a similar position on the admissibility of additional slave states. Noah Feldman, *The Broken Constitution: Lincoln, Slavery and the Refounding of America* (New York: Farrar, Strauss & Corex, 2021), 118.

57. Feldman, *The Broken Constitution*. This answer asserting the discretionary nature of congressional action on slavery in the District was contrary to the abolitionist position. In 1838 Theodore Dwight Weld had published "The Power of Congress over the District of Columbia" (in Jacobus tenBroek, *Equal under Law: The Antislavery Origins of the Fourteenth Amendment* [London: Collier Books, 1969], appendix A) but concluded that Congress had a duty to act immediately. Indeed, Wiecek argued that "the influence of Weld's tract derived from his argument that Congress had not only the power, but the duty to abolish slavery in the District." William M. Wieck, *The Sources of Antislavery Constitutionalism in America, 1760–1848* (New York: Cornell Univ. Press, 1977), 190.

58. *Emancipator*, Dec. 29, 1838.

59. The antislavery press, however, identified him as the "only manly advocate of immediate abolition in the Senate." *Pennsylvania Freemen*, reprinted in *Philanthropist*, May 1, 1838.

60. *Pennsylvania Freemen*, reprinted in *Philanthropist*, May 1, 1838. "The most salient feature of the racial ideology of the Republican Party was its insistence that, when it came to the natural rights of life, liberty, and property . . . Whites and Blacks were fundamentally equal." James Oakes, *The Crooked Path to Abolition: Abraham Lincoln and the Antislavery Constitution* (New York: W. W. Norton, 2021), 107.

Stanley Harrold thought Morris "misrepresented himself in a futile effort to convince the Ohio legislature to reelect him to the U.S. Senate." Stanley Harrold, *Border War: Fighting over Slavery before the Civil War* (Chapel Hill: Univ. of North Carolina Press, 2010). Criticism appears to be the result of Harrold's misreading of Morris's statements regarding Black rights. Harrold quotes Morris as telling the general assembly that "the Negro has no claim in our country to the enjoyment of equal, social or political privileges with the white race." Stanley Harrold, *American Abolitionism: Its Direct Political Impact from Colonial Times into Reconstruction*. A Nation Divided: Studies in the Civil War Era (Charlottesville: Univ. of Virginia Press, 2019). By placing a comma between "equal" and "social," Harrold reads Morris as distinguishing three types of rights: civil, social, and political. The text of the letter, however, has no commas (Morris to Gentleman, Dec. 11, 1838, *Philanthropist*, Jan. 22, 1839). Rather, Morris specifically said that Blacks "ought to be protected in and enjoy their natural rights." Given his public statements during the campaign regarding "equal and exact justice," any effort to deny supporting

NOTES TO PAGES 77–78

Black civil rights would have been pointless. Morris's response to the committee was consistent with his position at least since 1837. Morris to Alexander Campbell, Nov. 13, 1837, *Philanthropist*, Dec. 26, 1837.

61. *Emancipator* did not object to Morris's views on Black rights. This emphasis on civil rights had long been the favored approach of abolitionists working in Ohio. Kate Masur, *Until Justice Be Done: America's First Civil Rights Movement from Reconstruction* (New York: W. W. Norton, 2021), 92. The *Emancipator*, however, expressed great surprise "at the views which [Morris took] respecting the obligations and responsibilities of Congress" in regard to slavery in the District. The editor did not view abolition as any more "dangerous or injurious" than other legislation. In short, expediency should be no issue to an abolitionist (*Emancipator*, Dec. 29, 1838).

62. *Ohio Statesman*, Dec. 21, 26, and 31, 1838. Tappan's brothers' antislavery activities appeared to give the Democrats a way of rejecting Morris while reassuring abolitionists. See William Birney, *James G. Birney and His Times: The Genesis of the Republican Party* (New York: Bergman Publishers, 1890), 341. Tappan's hard-money views (and commitment to not offer antislavery petitions) may have been of more importance than his brothers' antislavery prominence. His two most significant rivals, Thomas Hamer and Robert Lytle, were both firmly aligned with Ohio banking interests.

63. Weisenburger, *Passing of the Frontier*, 378–79; James Roger Sharp, *The Jacksonians Versus the Banks: Politics in the States after the Panic of 1837* (New York: Columbia Univ. Press, 1970), 123–59; Volpe, *Forlorn Hope of Freedom*, 28; Donald Ratcliffe, ed., "The Autobiography of Benjamin Tappan," *Ohio History Journal* 85 (Spring 1976): 145–46; Daniel Feller, "A Brother in Arms: Benjamin Tappan and the Antislavery Democracy," *Journal of American History* 88 (June 2001): 48–54.

64. Feller, "Benjamin Tappan," 77.

65. Elijah Haywood to Benjamin Tappan, Nov. 4, 1833, in Benjamin Tappan, *Benjamin Tappan Papers* (Library of Congress): https://www.loc.gov/item/mm76042309/; Morris to Benjamin Tappan, May 31 and July 10, 1833, in Tappen, *Benjamin Tappan Papers*. Hamer had been a former law partner of Morris and had defeated him for a congressional seat in the 1832 elections. Morris never forgave him. See Medary to Benjamin Tappan, Nov. 21, 1835, in Tappen, *Benjamin Tappan Papers*.

66. *Ohio State Journal*, Dec. 24, 1838; Tod to Benjamin Tappan, Oct. 28, 1838, in Tappan, *Benjamin Tappan Papers*; Brough to Benjamin Tappan, Nov. 8, 1838, in Tappan, *Benjamin Tappan Papers*.

67. Joel H. Silbey, "'There Are Other Questions Beside That of Slavery Merely': The Democratic Party and Antislavery Politics," in *Crusaders and Compromisers*, ed. Alan M. Kraut (Westport, CT: Greenwood Press, 1983), 156.

68. Morris to Gentlemen, Dec. 11, 1838, *Philanthropist*, Jan. 22, 1839. In distinguishing civil "(or natural) rights from "political and social" rights, Morris's view was well within the well-established antislavery position (Masur, *Until Justice Be Done*, 92) and continued to be so through the 1850s. Eric Foner, *Free Soil, Free Labor, Free Men: The Ideology of the Republican Party before the Civil War* (New York: Oxford Univ. Press, 1970), 290–91.

69. At least one historian characterized Morris's position as "extreme and unequivocal" (Weisenburger, *Passing of the Frontier*, 379). Nevertheless, in 1838 Morris still

200   NOTES TO PAGES 79–80

differed with most abolitionists on the admission of states that established slavery in their constitution and on the duty of Congress to act immediately to abolish slavery in the District.

70. Stephen E. Maizlish, *The Triumph of Sectionalism: The Transformation of Ohio Politics, 1844–1856* (Kent, OH: Kent State Univ. Press, 1983), 6–7. For the range of contemporary views on who was an abolitionist, see Larry Gara, "Who Was an Abolitionist," in *The Antislavery Vanguard: New Essays on the Abolitionists,* ed. Martin Duberman (Princeton: Princeton Univ. Press, 1965), 32.

71. See, for example, David Tod to Benjamin Tappan, Oct. 28, 1838, in Tappan, *Benjamin Tappan Papers;* G. M. Cook to Benjamin Tappan, Oct. 30, 1838, in Tappan, *Benjamin Tappan Papers;* Joseph H. Zarwell to Benjamin Tappan, Nov. 3, 1838, in Tappan, *Benjamin Tappan Papers;* Jonathan Taylor to Benjamin Tappan, Nov. 3, 1838, in Tappan, *Benjamin Tappan Papers.* Professor Earle thought "Morris was thrown over for his response" to the committee's question regarding abolition. Jonathan H. Earle, *Jacksonian Antislavery and the Politics of Free Soil, 1824–1854* (Chapel Hill: Univ. of North Carolina Press, 2004), 238. Tappan had been campaigning for this seat, however, for months and had already lined up his support before the inquiries were sent.

72. William Trevitt to Benjamin Tappan, July 12, 1840, in Tappan, *Benjamin Tappan Papers.*

73. *Philanthropist,* Jan. 29, 1839; Volpe, *Forlorn Hope of Freedom,* 28. Tappan honored his commitment to the Ohio Democratic caucus. In his first speech in the Senate, he refused to present abolitionist petitions. Cong. Globe, 26th Cong., 1st Sess., 160–61 (1839–40); *Philanthropist,* Feb. 18, 1840.

74. Benjamin Tappan to Dear Brother, Jan. 4, 1839, in Tappan, *Benjamin Tappan Papers;* Benjamin Tappan to Dear Brother, Feb. 3, 1839, in Tappan, *Benjamin Tappan Papers.*

75. Lewis Tappan to Benjamin Tappan, Dec. 28, 1838, in Tappan, *Benjamin Tappan Papers.*

76. *Ohio State Journal,* Dec. 21, 1838; *Cincinnati Daily Gazette,* Dec. 27, 1838.

77. Dowty Utter to Benjamin Tappan, Feb. 9, 1840, in *Benjamin Tappan Papers.*

78. Morris to Messrs. Medary and Brothers, Dec. 26, 1838, *Philanthropist,* Jan. 22, 1839. This understanding of Tappan's opposition to slavery may have also contributed to Morris's willingness to campaign on his antislavery record. Recognizing Tappan as his primary rival for the Senate seat, Morris may well have assumed the party would not choose between them on their antislavery views. Morris could not have anticipated Tappan's willingness to commit to refusing to submit abolition petitions.

79. *Clermont Courier,* Nov. 24, 1838.

80. *Washington Globe,* Dec. 28, 1838. Remarkably, this defense of Morris in the *Washington Globe* came a week after he lost his bid for reelection. Even more remarkably, it was the same letter the *Emancipator* found to be "generally correct" (Dec. 29, 1838).

81. See *Ohio Statesman,* Jan. 8, 1840. For example, Morris's Ohio senatorial colleague, William Allen, frequently presented antislavery petitions and added a rider to Calhoun's resolutions asserting the importance of the right of petition and free speech without incurring the wrath of Ohio Democrats. He did not, however, defend abolitionists nor attack the Slave Power (Weisenberger, *Passing of the Frontier,* 376).

82. Alan M. Kraut, "Partisanship and Principles: The Liberty Party in Antebellum

Culture," in *Crusaders and Compromisers: Essays of the Relationship of the Antislavery Struggle to the Antebellum Party System* (Westport: Greenwood Press, 1983), 77. "Tolerating agitation over slavery would destroy the nation's political fabric.—and both parties knew it" (Wilentz, *Rise of American Democracy*, 451).

83. Maizlish, *Triumph of Sectionalism*, 6.

84. John M. McFaul, "Expediency vs. Morality: Jacksonian Politics and Slavery," *Journal of American History* 62 (June 1975): 27, 39; see also Gerald S. Henig, "The Jacksonian Attitude toward Abolitionism in the 1830s," *Tennessee Historical Quarterly* 28 (1969): 42. The party leadership in particular was concerned "about the danger of slavery disputes to current politics, ultimately, to the union" (Silbey, "There Are Other Questions," 157).

85. Silbey, "There Are Other Questions," 166. "For Jackson and his follows, slavery was a dangerous political issue—one to be avoided." Richard Ellis, "The Market Revolution and the transformation of American Politics, 1801–1837," in *The Market Revolution in America: Social, Political, and Religious Expressions, 1800–1860*, ed. Melvyn Stokes and Stephen Conway (Charlottesville: Univ. of Virginia, 1996), 171.

86. Theodore C. Smith, *Liberty and Free Soil Parties in the Northwest* (New York: Longmans, Green, 1897), 25.

87. Morris to Samuel Medary, Dec. 26, 1838, in Morris, *Life of Thomas Morris*, 195–203.

88. Some Cincinnati Democrats had held a Jackson Day (January 8) meeting, which adopted resolutions commenting favorably upon Morris's course as senator. After expressing "sincere thanks for the approbation of [his] democratic fellow citizens," Morris said that he had sought to earn their approval "by constant, unwavering adherence to democratic principles." Morris to Dear Sir, Jan. 15, 1839, *Philanthropist*, Feb. 5, 1839.

89. *Alabama Beacon* (n.d.) quoted in *Philanthropist*, Nov. 6, 1838; see also, for example, *Ohio State Journal*, Nov. 25, 1838.

90. Morris to Dear Sir, Jan. 15, 1839, *Philanthropist*, Feb. 5, 1839.

91. Morris to Dear Sir, Jan. 15, 1839, *Philanthropist*, Feb. 5, 1839. This view of the general assembly yielding to Southern demands to reject Morris was common among Ohio abolitionists (*Philanthropist*, Dec. 11, 1838).

92. Middleton, *The Black Laws*, 50–52, 173–75; Weisenburger, *Passing of the Frontier*, 380–81.

93. Morris to Dear Sir, Jan. 15, 1839, *Philanthropist*, Feb. 15, 1839.

94. Morris to Jonathan D. Morris, Jan. 20, 1834, in Morris, *Life of Thomas Morris*, 354–55.

6. THE BEACON FIRES OF LIBERTY

1. Kate Masur, *Until Justice Be Done: America's First Civil Rights Movement from Reconstruction* (New York: W. W. Norton, 2021), 111–12.

2. [Morris] to Dear Sir, Jan. 5, 1839, *Philanthropist*, Jan. 29, 1839. The printed extract is unsigned but identified as sent to the editor from a "Member of Congress." The language is clearly Morris; no other politician from Ohio used this terminology in 1839.

202   NOTES TO PAGES 84–87

3. Jonathan H. Earle, *Jacksonian Antislavery and the Politics of Free Soil, 1824–1854* (Chapel Hill: Univ. of North Carolina Press, 2004), 46.

4. Cong. Globe, 25th Cong., 3rd Sess., 104 (1838–39).

5. [Morris] to Dear Sir, Jan. 5, 1839, *Philanthropist*, Jan. 29, 1839.

6. [Morris] to Dear Sir, Jan. 14, 1839, *Philanthropist*, Jan. 29, 1839. This letter is also unsigned but bears the unmistakable marks of Morris. Bailey identified it as "coming from a friend of the leading measures of the present administration." In January 1839, this could only refer to Morris.

7. Cong. Globe, 25th Cong., 3rd Sess., appendix, 168 (1839).

8. [Morris] to Dear Sir, Jan. 14, 1839, *Philanthropist*, Jan. 29, 1839.

9. [Morris] to Dear Sir, Jan. 14, 1839, *Philanthropist*, Jan. 29, 1839.

10. Cong. Globe, 25th Cong., 3rd Sess., 164–65 (1838–39); Text of Resolutions in the *Philanthropist*, Feb. 19, 1839.

11. *Journal of Commerce* (n.d.), *Emancipator*, Feb. 14, 1839. Morris's resolution also asked the committee to consider whether moving the nation's capital to Cincinnati would be expedient and end the controversy over slavery in the District of Columbia.

12. Cong. Globe, 25th Cong., 3rd Sess., 164–65 (1838–39).

13. *Ohio State Journal*, Oct. 23, 1838.

14. Clay to Francis Brooker, Nov. 8, 1838, cited in John A. Neuenschwander, "Senator Thomas Morris: Antagonist of the South, 1836–1839," *Cincinnati Historical Society Bulletin* 32 (Fall 1974): 134.

15. Richard H. Sewell, *Ballots for Freedom: Antislavery Politics in the United States, 1837–1860* (New York: Oxford Univ. Press, 1976), 47–52; Thomas G. Mitchell, *Antislavery Politics in Antebellum and Civil War America* (Westport, CT: Greenwood Publishing Group, 2007), 15.

16. Robert V. Remini, *Henry Clay: Statesman for the Union* (New York: W. W. Norton, 1991), 525–26; David Stephen Heidler and Jeanne T. Heidler, *Henry Clay: The Essential American* (New York: Random House, 2010), 34–36, 298–300; David S. Reynolds, *Waking Giant: America in the Age of Jackson* (New York: HarperCollins, 2008), 320; H. W. Brands, *Heirs of the Founders: The Epic Rivalry of Henry Clay, John Calhoun and Daniel Webster, the Second Generation of American Giants* (New York: Knopf Doubleday Publishing Group, 2018), 259–64, 297.

17. Clay may have drafted the petition against abolition in the District himself to provide a pretext to speak. Louis Filler, *Crusade against Slavery, 1830–1860* (New York: Harper and Brothers, 1960), 150.

18. Henry Clay to James G. Birney, Nov. 3, 1838, in Robert Seager II, ed., *The Papers of Henry Clay*, vol. 9, *The Whig Leader, January 1, 1837–December 31, 1843* (Lexington: Univ. Press of Kentucky, 1988), 244–45.

19. Cong. Globe, 25th Cong., 3rd Sess., appendix, 354–59 (1838–39).

20. Cong. Globe, 24th Cong., 1st Sess., 291 (1835–36).

21. Remini, *Henry Clay*, 526; Cong. Globe, 25th Cong., 3rd Sess., 167 (1838–39). One historian has described Clay's constitutional analysis "as making him almost . . . a Calhounite." William J. Cooper, *The South and the Politics of Slavery, 1828–1856* (Baton Rouge: Louisiana State Univ. Press, 1978), 123. For his part, Calhoun told his col-

leagues "of all the dangers to which we have ever been exposed this [abolition] has been the greatest. We may now consider it passed." Calhoun, *Remarks on Abolition*, Feb. 7, 1839, quoted in Robert Elder, *Calhoun: American Heretic* (New York: Basic Books, 2021), 372.

22. Cong. Globe, 25th Cong., 3rd Sess., appendix, 168 (1839).

23. Cong. Globe, 25th Cong., 3rd Sess., 169 (1838–39).

24. Cong. Globe, 25th Cong., 3rd Sess. 169 (1838–39).

25. *Emancipator,* Mar. 21, 1839. Morris had been considering the "tyranny" of the Slave Power for several weeks. In early January he had written A. A. Guthrie that "a power . . . whose character is marked by every act which may define a tyrant is unfit to exist among a free people." Morris to A. A. Guthrie, Jan. 9, 1839, *Philanthropist,* Feb. 26, 1839.

26. Cong. Globe, 25th Cong., 3rd Sess., 170 (1838–39).

27. *Emancipator,* May 8, 1844.

28. David Waldstreicher, *Slavery's Constitution: From Revolution to Ratification* (New York: Hill and Wang, 2009), 101, 114.

29. *Emancipator,* May 8, 1844.

30. Cong. Globe, 25th Cong., 3rd Sess., appendix, 167–75 (1838–39).

31. Cong. Globe, 25th Cong., 3rd Sess., appendix, 167–75 (1838–39).

32. James Oakes, *The Crooked Path to Abolition: Abraham Lincoln and the Antislavery Constitution* (New York: W. W. Norton, 2021), xxvii.

33. Cong. Globe, 25th Cong., 3rd Sess., appendix, 167–75 (1838–39).

34. Nikole Hannah-Jones, *"Democracy" in the 1619 Project* (New York: One World, 2021), 19.

35. Cong. Globe, 25th Cong., 3rd Sess., appendix, 167–75 (1838–39).

36. Cong. Globe, 25th Cong., 3rd Sess., appendix, 167–75 (1838–39).

37. Cong. Globe, 25th Cong., 3rd Sess., appendix, 167–75 (1838–39).

38. Cong. Globe, 25th Cong., 3rd Sess., appendix, 167–75 (1838–39).

39. Cong. Globe, 25th Cong., 3rd Sess., appendix, 167–75 (1838–39).

40. Cong. Globe, 25th Cong., 3rd Sess., appendix, 167–75 (1838–39).

41. Cong. Globe, 25th Cong., 3rd Sess., appendix, 167–75 (1838–39).

42. Cong. Globe, 25th Cong., 3rd Sess., appendix, 167–75 (1838–39).

43. Cong. Globe, 25th Cong., 3rd Sess., appendix, 167–75 (1838–39).

44. Cong. Globe, 25th Cong., 3rd Sess., appendix, 167–75 (1838–39).

45. Morris to "Dear Sir," Jan. 15, 1839, *Philanthropist,* Feb. 5, 1839.

46. *Emancipator,* Mar. 21, 1839; *Philanthropist,* Mar. 19 and Apr. 30, 1839; *Liberator,* Mar. 8, 1839.

47. H. B. Stanton to Birney, June 10, 1839, in Dumond, *Letters of James Gillespie Birney,* 489–91; *Antislavery Examiner,* part 3, no. 10 and 10A, May 4, 1839.

48. *Liberator,* Mar. 1, 1839.

49. *Philanthropist,* Apr. 16, 1839. Wiecek mistakenly says that the general assembly "vindictively refused to reelect Morris because he had criticized the pro-slavery views of Whig Henry Clay." William M. Wiecek, *The Sources of Antislavery Constitutionalism in America, 1760–1848* (New York: Cornell Univ. Press, 1977), 200. While the general assembly's action was vindictive, it occurred two months before Morris's reply to Clay.

50. Cong. Globe, 25th Cong., 3rd Sess., appendix, 167–75 (1838–39).

51. Cong. Globe, 25th Cong., 3rd Sess., appendix, 167–75 (1838–39).

52. Earle, *Jacksonian Antislavery*, 47.

53. Eric Foner, *Politics and Ideology in the Age of the Civil War* (New York: Oxford Univ. Press 1980), 41.

54. *Philanthropist*, Apr. 30, 1839.

55. *Emancipator*, Mar. 21, 1839.

56. *Philanthropist*, Apr. 16, 1839.

57. Theodore C. Smith, *The Liberty and Free Soil Parties in the Northwest* (New York: Longmans, Green, 1897), 26.

58. Russel B. Nye, *Fettered Freedom: Civil Liberties and the Slavery Controversy 1830–1860* (Lansing: Michigan State Univ. Press, 1963), 223–25.

59. Sean Wilentz, *Rise of American Democracy: Jefferson to Lincoln* (New York: W. W. Norton, 2005), 897n51.

60. Quoted in Benjamin Franklin Morris, ed., *The Life of Thomas Morris: Pioneer and Long a Legislator of Ohio, and U.S. Senator from 1833 to 1839* (Cincinnati: Moore, Wilstach, Keys & Overend, 1856), xi. Harrold claimed that Gamliel Bailey was "one of the earliest, if not the earliest, formulators of the Slave Power theory" and argued that Morris's speech was a year after Bailey had begun talking about the Slave Power. Stanley Harrold, *Gamaliel Bailey and Antislavery Union* (Kent, OH: Kent State Univ. Press 1986), 29. This contention ignores not only Chase's acknowledgment of the primacy of Morris's role but also Morris's speech on Incendiary Publications and his letter to Alexander Campbell regarding the Eliza Johnson kidnapping, both of which attacked the Slave Power and both of which were published in the *Philanthropist*. See *Philanthropist*, June 17, 1836, and Dec. 26, 1837.

61. William Birney, *James G. Birney and His Times: The Genesis of the Republican Party* (New York: Bergman Publishers, 1890), 345; also Margaret L. Plunkett, "A History of the Liberty Party, with Emphasis on Its Activities in the Northeastern States" (PhD diss., Cornell Univ., 1930), 68–69.

62. *Philanthropist*, Sept. 17, 1839. For the immediate development of the Slave Power idea after Morris's speech, see William Goodell, ed., *Anti-Slavery Lecturer*, New York State Anti-Slavery Society (Utica, NY: 1839); David Brion Davis, *The Fear of Conspiracy: Images of Un-American Subversion from the Revolution to the Present* (Ithaca, NY: Cornell Univ. Press, 1971), 109–11.

63. Birney, *James G. Birney and His Times*, 345–48. The reply to Clay was the trigger for many to decide that political action was necessary. For example, Myron Holley, who became a driving force behind the organization of the Liberty Party, did not "throw himself whole heartedly into antislavery politics" until after the February debate (Sewell, *Ballots for Freedom*, 55–56).

64. Nye, *Fettered Freedom*, 219.

65. Corey M. Brooks, *Liberty Power: Antislavery Third Parties and the Transformation of American Politics* (Chicago: Univ. of Chicago Press, 2016), 16, 26.

66. Earle, *Jacksonian Antislavery*, 38. For the use of symbols to define political reality, see Marvin Meyers, *The Jacksonian Persuasion: Politics and Belief* (Stanford, CA: Stanford Univ. Press, 1960), 9–15, 254.

NOTES TO PAGES 93–97 205

67. David Brion Davis, *The Slave Power Conspiracy and the Paranoid Style* (Baton Rouge: Louisiana State Univ. Press, 1970), 16; Eric Foner, *Free Soil, Free Labor, Free Men: The Ideology of the Republican Party before the Civil War* (New York: Oxford Univ. Press, 1970), 90–92.

68. Morris to "Dear Sir," Jan. 15, 1839, *Philanthropist*, Feb. 5, 1839.

7. A ROTTEN BRANCH TO BE LOPPED OFF

1. Leonard L. Richards, *The Slave Power: The Free North and Southern Domination, 1780–1860* (Baton Rouge: Louisiana State Univ. Press, 2000), 23.

2. *Philanthropist*, Apr. 16 and 23, 1839; American Anti-Slavery Society, *Sixth Annual Report of the Executive Committee of the American Anti-Slavery Society* (New York: William Dorr, May 1839).

3. [Morris] to Dear Sir, Jan. 5, 1839, *Philanthropist*, Jan. 29, 1839.

4. Morris to A. A. Guthrie, Jan. 9, 1839, *Philanthropist*, Feb. 26, 1839.

5. After losing his bid for reelection, Morris had sold his home in Bethel to Ulysses Grant's parents and moved to Cincinnati to practice law. Morris had been friends with the Grant family for several years. They had asked him to nominate Ulysses to West Point. Morris declined, telling the Grants that West Point nominations were handled by congressmen. Byron Williams, *History of Clermont and Brown Counties, Ohio: From the Earliest Historical Times Down to the Present* (Milford: Hobart, 1913), 439–40, 442.

6. *Philanthropist*, May 19, 1839.

7. *Philanthropist*, May 19, 1839. The meeting and Morris's views were given exposure to Eastern abolitionists two weeks later (*Emancipator*, May 30, 1839).

8. Morris to Dr. Bailey, n.d., in Benjamin Franklin Morris, ed., *The Life of Thomas Morris: Pioneer and Long a Legislator of Ohio, and U.S. Senator from 1833 to 1839* (Cincinnati: Moore, Wilstach, Keys & Overend, 1856), 239–40. Morris had held this position on the effect of the Tenth Amendment for some time. See Morris to Dear Sir, Mar. 30, 1837, in Morris, *Life of Thomas Morris*, 247.

9. *Prigg v. Pennsylvania*, 41 U.S. 536 (1842): 615–16. For a modern application of the limitation of Congress in compelling state officials to enforce federal laws, see *Printz v. United States* 521 U.S. 898 (1997).

10. *Emancipator*, May 30, 1839.

11. *Emancipator*, May 30, 1839.

12. Jonathan H. Earle, *Jacksonian Antislavery and the Politics of Free Soil, 1824–1854* (Chapel Hill: Univ. of North Carolina Press, 2004), 147.

13. On April 1, 1839, just as Morris's final Senate session was ending, a group of whites, led by a local constable, had attacked a freed slave. In response, several men, including John Mahan, had come to her aid and were subsequently charged. Morris initially led a team of three attorneys in defending Mahan. Ann Hagedorn, *Beyond the River: The Untold Stories of the Heroes of the Underground Railroad* (New York: Simon & Schuster, 2002), 185–89. Although Mahan was convicted, the Ohio Supreme Court ultimately reversed *Mahan v. State*, 10 Ohio St. 232 (1840). By then, however, Morris had left the defense team.

14. Birney to Lewis Tappan, Sept. 12, 1839, in Dwight L. Dumond, *Letters of James Gillespie Birney, 1831–1857* (New York: D. Appleton Century, 1938), 498–501.

15. *Emancipator*, Sept. 26, 1839; *Philanthropist*, Sept. 17, 1839.

16. In January 1839, the Democratic-controlled general assembly had passed a series of laws restricting the rights of Blacks alleged to be fugitive slaves (*Emancipator*, Feb. 7, 1839). See also Kate Masur, *Until Justice Be Done: America's First Civil Rights Movement from Reconstruction* (New York: W. W. Norton, 2021), 111–12.

17. *Daily Ohio Statesman*, Sept. 6, 10, and 17, 1839.

18. *Daily Ohio Statesman*, Nov. 8, 1839.

19. Morris to G. W. Ells, Jan. 30, 1840, *Philanthropist*, Aug. 11, 1840; Francis P. Weisenburger, *Passing of the Frontier 1825–1850: The History of the State of Ohio* (Columbus: Ohio State Archaeological and Historical Society, 1941), 353–54.

20. Morris to G. W. Ells, Jan. 30, 1840, *Philanthropist*, Aug. 11, 1840. Morris believed that the convention's actions had been orchestrated by George Flood, a state representative from Licking County. Flood had split with Morris in 1835 over support for state banks and worked with Thomas Hamer to support state officials, including Shannon, who favored banks. Flood was also strongly opposed to antislavery. He was the "progenitor" of the resolutions passed by the general assembly denying Blacks the right to petition and the strengthening of the Fugitive Slave law in 1839. Masur, *Until Justice Be Done*, 112; Wiesenburger, *Passing of the Frontier*, 308–10, 402–3. For Morris, Flood personified the alliance of the Money Power with the Slave Power in Ohio.

21. *Philanthropist*, Oct. 11, 1839; *Liberator*, Aug. 16, 1839. The Democrats had even done extremely well in the traditionally Whig areas of the Western Reserve—the most antislavery area of the state (Weisenburger, *Passing of the Frontier*, 352–53).

22. *Daily Ohio Statesman*, Jan. 4, 1840.

23. Weisenburger, *Passing of the Frontier*, 384.

24. *Daily Ohio Statesman*, Jan. 8, 1840.

25. *Daily Ohio Statesman*, Jan. 10, 1840. In the early 1840s, this position was orthodox throughout the party. See, for example, Cong. Globe, 27th Cong., 4rd Sess., appendix (Aug. 19, 1842). Slaveholders "have no other allies, to sustain their Constitutional rights, except the Democracy of the North" (James Buchanan).

26. *Western Telegraph*, n.d., *Philanthropist*, Jan. 28, 1840. G. W. Ells was Morris's only supporter at the convention. He was also thrown out of the party and followed Morris into the Liberty organization. Theodore C. Smith, *Liberty and Free Soil Parties in the Northwest* (New York: Longmans, Green, 1897), 60.

27. *Philanthropist*, Jan. 28, 1840.

28. Alice Felt Tyler, *Freedom's Ferment: Phases of American Social History to 1860* (Minneapolis: Univ. of Minnesota Press, 1944), 478

29. Richard H. Sewell, *Ballots for Freedom: Antislavery Politics in the United States, 1837–1860* (New York: Oxford Univ. Press, 1976), 18–20; Smith, *Liberty and Free Soil Parties*, 31; Gerald Sorin, *Abolitionism: A New Perspective* (Westport: Praeger Publishers, 1972), 79.

30. *Philanthropist*, Apr. 30, 1839. A clear example of the futility of the abolitionists operating within the two-party structure was the election of Thomas Buchanan as a

NOTES TO PAGES 100–103 207

state representative in 1838. In order to aid Morris, a man they favored, abolitionists had to support a man opposed to their goals.

31. Margaret L. Plunkett, "A History of the Liberty Party, with Emphasis on Its Activities in the Northeastern States" (PhD diss., Cornell Univ., 1930), 68.

32. *Emancipator*, Aug. 8, 1839.

33. *Emancipator*, June 13, 1839.

34. Birney to Tappan, July 4, 1839, in Dumond, *Letters of James Gillespie Birney*, 494–95; Morris to Denison, July 6, 1839, *Emancipator*, Aug. 15, 1839. Inexplicably, Fladeland asserted that "Morris owed his reelection to the Senate" to abolitionists, and he was expected to attend the Albany convention so they could take advantage of their effort. Betty Fladeland, *James Gillespie Birney: From Slaveholder to Abolitionist* (New York: Cornell Univ. Press, 1955), 170, 181.

35. Morris to Charles Denison, July 6, 1839, *Emancipator*, Aug. 15, 1839.

36. Text of letter, *Emancipator*, Aug. 9, 1839. Antislavery leaders thought the letter expressed "genuine democracy." Lewis Tappan to Benjamin Tappan, Aug. 26, 1839, in *Benjamin Tappan Papers* (Library of Congress).

37. Weisenburger, *Passing of the Frontier*, 354.

38. *Liberator*, Mar. 1, 1839.

39. *Liberator*, Aug. 16, 1839.

40. Aileen S. Kraditor, *Means and Ends in American Abolitionism: Garrison and His Critics on Strategy and Tactics, 1834–1850* (New York: Pantheon Books, 1969), 159.

41. Plunkett, "A History of the Liberty Party," 87; Myron Holley to Birney, Jan. 1, 1840, in Dumond, *Letters of James Gillespie Birney*, 518.

42. *Emancipator*, Aug. 8, 1839; Plunkett, "History of the Liberty Party," 72–77.

43. Birney to Lewis Tappan, Sept. 12, 1839, in Dumond, *Letters of James Gillespie Birney*, 499.

44. *Philanthropist*, Nov. 19, 1839; Reinhard O. Johnson, *The Liberty Party, 1840–1848: Antislavery Third-Party Politics in the United States* (Baton Rouge: Louisiana State Univ. Press, 2009), 14–15.

45. Ohio Anti-Slavery Society, *Report of the Third Anniversary of the Ohio Anti-Slavery Society* (May 1838): 6.

46. Stanley Harrold, *Gamaliel Bailey and Antislavery Union* (Kent, OH: Kent State Univ. Press, 1986), 20.

47. *Philanthropist*, Mar. 27, 1838, and Sept. 3, 1839. It was probably inexpedient because of Bailey's Whig leanings. See Bailey to Gerrit Smith, July 21, 1840, in Joel Goldfarb, "The Life of Gamaliel Bailey, Prior to the Founding of the National Era: The Orientation of a Practical Abolitionist" (PhD diss., Univ. of California, 1958), 201–2.

48. *Philanthropist*, Nov. 12, 1839.

49. *Philanthropist*, Nov. 12, 1839. For the view that the delegates simply deferred action until the Democrat and Whig nominees had been selected, see Sewell, *Ballots for Freedom*, 56–57.

50. Johnson, *The Liberty Party*, 14.

51. Johnson, *The Liberty Party*, 14; Plunkett, "History of the Liberty Party," 84–86. Both letters declining the nomination were published in the *Emancipator*, January 9, 1840.

208   NOTES TO PAGES 103–106

52. Fladeland, *James Gillespie Birney*, 182–83; Sewell, *Ballots for Freedom*, 62; Birney to Myron Holley, Nov. 16, 1839, in Plunkett, "A History of the Liberty Party," 87.

53. *Philanthropist*, Nov. 12, 1839; Sewell, *Ballots for Freedom*, 64.

54. *Philanthropist*, May 26, 1840; Sewell, *Ballots for Freedom*, 66–74.

55. Bailey to Birney, Apr. 18, 1840, in Dumond, *Letters of James Gillespie Birney*, 555–58. Bailey also claimed that Morris, "who is certainly good authority when he speaks well of an opponent," said that he and Corwin (the Whig candidate for Governor) agreed on the Black Laws and Fugitive Slave Laws.

56. Report and minutes, *Philanthropist*, June 16, 1840; see also Goldfarb, "Life of Gamaliel Bailey," 184–87.

57. *Philanthropist*, June 30, 1840, and July 14, 1840; William J. Cooper, *The Politics of Slavery, 1828–1856* (Baton Rouge: Louisiana State Univ. Press, 1978), 137–38.

58. *Philanthropist*, July 7, 1840. Despite Bailey's apparent conversation, many abolitionists continued to support Harrison as a means of preventing the reelection of Van Buren. John Rankin to Thomas E. Thomas, July 31, 1840, in Alfred A Thomas, ed., *Correspondence of Thomas Ebenezer Thomas. Mainly Relating to the Antislavery Conflict in Ohio, Especially in the Presbyterian Church* (Dayton, OH: Privately published by his son, 1909), 18–19.

59. Bertram Wyatt-Brown, *Lewis Tappan and the Evangelical War against Slavery* (Cleveland: Press of Case Western Reserve, 1969), 197–99.

60. *Philanthropist*, June 16, 1840; Johnson, *The Liberty Party*, 8–10.

61. *Philanthropist*, Sept. 8, 1840.

62. *Philanthropist*, Sept. 8, 1840.

63. William Birney to Birney, Sept. 9, 1840, in Dumond, *Letters of James Gillespie Birney*, 600.

64. Leavitt subsequently published his speech in the *Emancipator*, October 22, 1840. It circulated as a pamphlet for several years.

65. Leavitt to Birney, Oct. 1, 1840, in Dumond, *Letters of James Gillespie Birney*, 603–4.

66. Harrold, *Gamaliel Bailey*, 6–21; Bailey to Gerrit Smith, July 21, 1840, in Goldfarb, "Life of Gamaliel Bailey," 201–2.

67. *Philanthropist*, Sept. 8, 1840. By the time of the convention, Bailey also had agreed to help identify persons willing to serve as Birney electors in Ohio. Thomas E. Thomas to Jonathan W. Scott, July 11, 1840, in *Correspondence of Thomas Ebeneezer Thomas: Mainly Relating to the Anti-Slavery Conflict in Ohio*, ed. Alfred A. Thomas (Dayton, OH: Published by his son, 1909), 18–19.

68. *Philanthropist*, Sept. 8, 1841. Goldfarb thought Morris's failure to appreciate the potential consequences of his request "a political faux pas for which Bailey seems never to have forgiven him" (Goldfarb, "Life of Gamaliel Bailey," 209).

69. Goldfarb, "Life of Gamaliel Bailey," 208.

70. *Emancipator*, Oct. 1, 1840.

71. *Philanthropist*, Aug. 11, 1840.

72. Goldfarb, "Life of Gamaliel Bailey," 208–9; reports of both meetings in *Philanthropist*, June 9 and 16, and Sept. 8, 1840; See Daniel Gilmer to Bailey, Sept. 9, 1840, *Philanthropist*, Oct. 6, 1840, for the breakdown of votes supporting Birney's nomination.

NOTES TO PAGES 106–110

73. *Philanthropist*, Sept. 8, 1840.

74. Smith, *Liberty and Free Soil Parties*, 45.

75. *Ohio State Journal*, Sept. 22, 1840. Morris and Harrison had been political adversaries for nearly two decades. In 1822, Harrison (in a run for Congress) had attempted to use Morris to divide the opposition votes and thereby improve Harrison's chances of winning. Harry R. Stevens, *The Early Jackson Party in Ohio* (Durham: Duke Univ. Press, 1957), 42–46.

76. *Philanthropist*, Oct. 6, 1840.

77. *Philanthropist*, Oct. 6, 1840. Bailey's defense of Morris was reprinted in the *Emancipator*, December 31, 1840.

78. *Philanthropist*, Sept. 22, 1840. For the campaign activities of the Liberty Party, see *Philanthropist*, September 15 and 22, and October 6 and 13, 1840. Vernon L. Volpe, *Forlorn Hope of Freedom: The Liberty Party in the Old Northwest, 1838–1848* (Kent, OH: Kent State Univ. Press, 1990), 47. For devotion of antislavery Whigs to Harrison, see John Rankin to Thomas E. Thomas, July 31, 1840, in *Correspondence of Thomas E. Thomas*, 18–19.

79. Fladeland, *James Gillespie Birney*, 190–206.

80. Samuel Medary to Martin Van Buren, Aug. 18, 1840, quoted in Weisenburger, *Passing of the Frontier*, 395.

81. Weisenburger, *Passing of the Frontier*, 396; Smith, *Liberty and Free Soil Parties*, 59.

82. *Philanthropist*, Nov. 25, 1840; *Emancipator*, Nov. 5, 1840. Also attributed Liberty support in Ohio to ex-Democrats. See also Volpe, *Forlorn Hope*, 167n38.

83. *Philanthropist*, Oct. 28, 1840. The Liberty Party vote in Ohio was also depressed by a late Whig maneuver. Perhaps to take advantage of Morris's prominence within the new party, just days before the election, Whigs papers claimed that Democrats were distributing Birney tickets. In Bailey's view, this trick persuaded many Whigs that his candidacy "was but a Van Buren trick" (*Philanthropist*, Nov. 11, 1840).

84. Caleb Atwater, *A History of the State of Ohio: Natural and Civil* (Cincinnati: Glezen & Shepard, 1838), 432. Using the report of the Ohio Anti-Slavery Society of May 1837, Atwater reported 17,253 abolitionists in the state. Allowing for only modest growth during their continued efforts over the next three years, the society's membership by 1840 was certainly over twenty thousand. Thus, Birney did not receive 5 percent of the antislavery vote.

85. Morris to Bailey, *Philanthropist*, Oct. 28, 1840.

8. A TORRENT OF ELOQUENCE AND ARGUMENT

1. *Philanthropist*, July 14 and Aug. 8, 1841.

2. *Philanthropist*, Oct. 28, 1840.

3. *Philanthropist*, Oct. 28, 1840. See Stanley Harrold, *American Abolitionism* (Charlottesville: Univ. of Virginia Press, 2019), 74–92.

4. *Philanthropist*, Nov. 25 and Dec. 16, 1840; *Emancipator*, Nov. 12 and Dec. 17, 1840.

NOTES TO PAGES 110–114

5. Hugh Davis, *Joshua Leavitt: Evangelical Abolitionist* (Baton Rouge: Louisiana State Univ. Press, 1990), 176–77. For the operation and efficacy of this and earlier lobbying efforts, see Corey Brooks, "Stoking the 'Abolition Fire in the Capital': Liberty Party Lobbying and Antislavery in Congress," *Journal of the Early Republic* 33, no. 3 (Fall 2013): 523–47.

6. Theodore C. Smith, *The Liberty and Free Soil Parties in the Northwest* (New York: Longmans, Green, 1897), 50.

7. *Philanthropist*, Dec. 16, 1840.

8. *Philanthropist*, Jan. 13, 1841.

9. *Philanthropist*, Jan. 13, 1841.

10. *Philanthropist*, Jan. 13, 1841.

11. *Philanthropist*, Jan. 13, 1841.

12. *Philanthropist*, Jan. 13, 1841.

13. *Philanthropist*, Jan. 27, 1841.

14. *Philanthropist*, Jan. 27, 1841. A correspondent to Joshua Leavitt described Morris's speech to the convention as "noble and heart-stirring" (*Emancipator*, May 13, 1841).

15. *Philanthropist*, Jan. 27, 1841.

16. Montgomery County had provided only seven votes for Birney in the 1840 election. Vernon L. Volpe, "The Ohio Election of 1838: A Study in the Historical Method?" *Ohio History Journal* 95 (1986): 94. Montgomery County was also home to the delegate to the Ohio Democratic Convention, who a year earlier described Morris as a "rotten branch that should be lopped off," which preceded Morris's expulsion from the party (*Philanthropist*, Jan. 28, 1840).

17. Thomas Clegg and others to Morris, May 6, 1839, *Philanthropist*, Feb. 17, 1841.

18. Morris to Dear Sir, May 10, 1839, *Philanthropist*, Feb. 17, 1841.

19. *Dayton Transcript*, Jan. 27, 1841; *Philanthropist*, Feb. 3 and 17, 1841. In spite of this experience, abolitionists in Dayton urged him to return in the fall to speak (*Philanthropist*, July 14, 1841). Morris reported that some claimed that the mob had been roused by fears of "amalgamation." He described this fear as a "ridiculous and . . . exploded opinion" unworthy of serious thought.

20. Morris to William McKinney, mayor of Dayton, Feb. 10, 1841, *Philanthropist*, Feb. 17, 1841.

21. Morris to William, McKinney, mayor of Dayton, Feb. 10, 1841, *Philanthropist*, Feb. 17, 1841. For the history of the Ohio Constitution of 1802, see Kate Masur, *Until Justice Be Done: American's First Civil Rights Movement from the Revolution to Reconstruction* (New York: W. W. Norton, 2021), 15.

22. *Emancipator*, Feb. 4, 1841; *Philanthropist*, Jan. 13 and Mar. 24, 1841.

23. Smith, *Liberty and Free Soil Parties*, 50. Johnson described Tyler's succession as "perhaps the most important event aiding the Liberty Party in these early years." Reinhard D. Johnson, *Liberty Party: Antislavery Third-Party Politics in the United States* (Baton Rouge: Louisiana State Univ. Press, 2009), 26. For example, Salmon Chase had campaigned for Harrison and ran as a Whig candidate for city office in April, but Tyler's elevation to the presidency "triggered" Chase's decision to abandon the Whigs. By the end of 1841, he had aligned himself with the Liberty Party. Frederick J. Blue, *Salmon P. Chase: A Life in Politics* (Kent, OH: Kent State Univ. Press, 1987), 44–45.

NOTES TO PAGES 114–119   211

24. *Emancipator*, July 1, 1841.

25. *Emancipator*, May 20, 1841; Smith, *Liberty and Free Soil Parties*, 51.

26. *Address* in *Emancipator*, May 27, 1841.

27. *Philanthropist*, May 19, 1841.

28. *Philanthropist*, May 26, 1841.

29. *Philanthropist*, June 9, 1841, reprinted in *Emancipator*, June 17, 1841.

30. *Emancipator*, July 1, 1841.

31. Masur, *Until Justice Be Done*, 190.

32. Masur, *Until Justice Be Done*, 190, quoting *Cincinnati Enquirer*, Aug. 10, 1841.

33. *Philanthropist*, Aug. 11, 1841. Morris not only urged equal justice for all without regard to color but also defended Black voting by commenting favorably on the early practice of Blacks voting in Ohio under the Northwest Ordinance.

34. *Philanthropist*, Aug. 11, 1841. This theme of an aristocratic slave power denigrating all labor became a consistent one in Liberty Party campaigns. See Alan M. Kraut. "Partisanship and Principles: The Liberty Party in Antebellum Political Culture," in *Crusaders and Compromisers: Essays of the Relationship of the Antislavery Struggle to the Antebellum Party System* (Westport, CT: Greenwood Press, 1983), 86.

35. Hugh Davis, *Joshua Leavitt: Evangelical Abolitionist* (Baton Rouge: Louisiana State Univ. Press, 1990), 171–75, 184.

36. *Philanthropist*, Sept. 1, 1841.

37. *Philanthropist*, July 14 and 21, Aug. 4, and Sept. 22, 1841.

38. Morris to Dear Sir, Oct. 2, 1841, *Emancipator*, Dec. 16, 1841, declining to attend the Michigan State Liberty Party convention because he was "confined to [his] room and bed with sickness." By early November, however, he was promising to attend the Indiana State Anti-Slavery Society meeting (*Philanthropist*, Nov. 10, 1841).

39. Total vote in *Philanthropist*, Oct. 5, 1843. For Whig defections, see Edgar A. Holt, *Party Politics in Ohio, 1840–1850* (Columbus, OH: F. J. Heer Printing, 1930), 189–90.

40. *Philanthropist*, Dec. 8, 1841.

41. Morris to Gentlemen, Dec. 11, 1838, *Philanthropist*, Jan. 22, 1839.

42. *Philanthropist*, Dec. 8, 1841. Although Morris initially employed extremely broad language ("forever abolished throughout our country"), he subsequently limited his claim to "all places over which Congress has exclusive power of legislation." He had not yet renounced the federal consensus.

43. Chase to Lewis Tappan, Mar. 18, 1847, quoted in William M. Wieck, *The Sources of Antislavery Constitutionalism in America, 1760–1848* (New York: Cornell Univ. Press, 1977), 209; see also James Oakes, *The Crooked Path to Abolition: Abraham Lincoln and the Antislavery Constitution* (New York: W. W. Norton, 2021), 2–3.

44. Theodore Weld had hinted at this possibility in 1838 but focused on congressional power to abolish slavery in the District without transgressing the Fifth Amendment. Theodore Weld, "Power of Congress," in Jacobus tenBroek, *Equal under Law: The Antislavery Origins of the Fourteenth Amendment* (London: Collier Books, 1969), 271–76. For him, the common law was at least as much of an obstacle to slavery as the Constitution (Wiecek, *Antislavery Constitutionalism*, 189–90). In rejecting Calhoun's argument that the Constitution protected property in slaves, Weld followed Morris's *Incendiary Publications* speech closely, but also developed the idea that the slaves' property inter-

212   NOTES TO PAGE 119

est in themselves was protected by the Fifth Amendment. Theodore Weld, "Power of Congress," in Jacobus tenBroek, *Equal under Law: The Antislavery Origins of the Fourteenth Amendment* (London: Collier Books, 1969), 271–72. Weld's goal, however, was to prove Congress's power to abolish slavery, not its inability to establish it. The *Emancipator's* December 24, 1841, headline proclaiming slavery unconstitutional and front-page treatment of Morris's response indicates that the unconstitutionality of Congress establishing slavery was, if not new, an unfamiliar and almost revolutionary idea.

45. Act Concerning the District, 6th Congress, Session II, Chapter 15; Section I (Feb. 27, 1801).

46. *Emancipator*, Dec. 24, 1841. By this time the *Emancipator* had a weekly circulation of over two hundred thousand copies, providing Morris with immediate national exposure for his constitutional views. Avery O. Craven, *The Coming of the Civil War: A Stimulating and Profound Analysis of the Factors Which Brought a Nation into War with Itself* (Chicago: Univ. of Chicago Press, 1957), 145.

47. Stephen Middleton, *Ohio and the Antislavery Activities of Attorney Salmon Portland Chase, 1830–1849* (New York: Garland Publishing, 1990), 93–103, 114–21. In developing his arguments in the Matilda case, Birney and Chase had drawn heavily on Morris's ideas expressed in his speech on incendiary publications. Jonathan H. Earle, *Jacksonian Antislavery and the Politics of Free Soil, 1824–1854* (Chapel Hill: Univ. of North Carolina Press, 2004), 240n57. For the substance of the arguments, see Harold M. Hyman and William M. Wiecek, *Equal Justice under Law: Constitutional Development 1835–1875* (New York: Harper & Row, 1982), 106–7.

48. Chase to Charles D. Cleveland, Aug. 29, 1840, in John Niven, *The Salmon P. Chase Papers* (Kent, OH: Kent State Univ. Press, 1994), 2:69–71. Salmon Chase, July 16, 1840, diary entry, quoted in Robert Bruce Warden, *An Account of the Private Life and Public Service of Salmon Portland Chase* (Cincinnati: Wilstach, Baldwin, 1874), 288.

49. Chase to Charles D. Cleveland, Aug. 29, 1840 in John P. Niven, *Salmon P. Chase Papers*, 69–71. Harrison had lived in Cincinnati for several years. He and Chase were well acquainted. Chase's relationship with Harrison was strong enough that Harrison had sent Chase to meet with Bailey in the summer of 1840 to attempt to change Bailey's mind about supporting Birney. Chase failed to change Bailey's view, but Chase remained firmly in the Whig camp. Salmon Chase, July 1, 1840, diary entry, quoted in Warden, *Private life and Public Service*, 287; John P. Niven, *Salmon P. Chase: A Biography* (New York: Oxford Univ. Press, 1995) 57–58.

50. Albert Bushnell Hart, *Salmon P. Chase* (Philadelphia: Chelsea House, 1980), 88; Niven, *Salmon P. Chase*, 65; Smith, *Liberty and Free Soil Parties*, 40; Chase to Charles D. Cleveland, Oct. 22, 1841, in Niven, *Salmon P. Chase Papers*, 79–81. In many respects, Chase found himself in a similar position to Morris a year earlier: "he had nowhere else to go politically" (Niven, *Salmon P. Chase*, 62). For the September 1841 Cincinnati riot, see Leonard L. Richards, *Gentlemen of Property and Standing: Anti-Abolition Mobs in Jacksonian America* (New York: Oxford Univ. Press, 1970), 122–29.

51. *Philanthropist*, Dec. 22, 1841. Masur describes this meeting as the "first statewide Liberty Party convention" overlooking the January 1841 Columbus Convention (*Until Justice Be Done*, 192).

NOTES TO PAGES 119–122

52. Joel Goldfarb, "The Life of Gamaliel Bailey, Prior to the Founding of the National Era: The Orientation of a Practical Abolitionist" (PhD diss., Univ. of California, 1958)," 246.

53. Eric Foner, *Free Soil, Free Labor, Free Men: The Ideology of the Republican Party before the Civil War* (New York: Oxford Univ. Press, 1970), 80.

54. Niven, *Salmon P. Chase,* 61; Stanley Harrold, *Gamaliel Bailey and Antislavery Union* (Kent, OH: Kent State Univ. Press, 1986), 26.

55. Harold, *American Abolitionism,* 97.

56. Harrold, *Gamaliel Bailey,* 44; William Birney to Birney, June 9, 1842, in Dwight L. Dumond, *Letters of James Gillespie Birney, 1831–1857* (New York: D. Appleton Century, 1938), 697–98.

57. Chase to Joshua Giddings, Dec. 30, 1841, in Niven, *Salmon P. Chase Papers,* 81–83.

58. Reinhard D. Johnson, *Liberty Party: Antislavery Third-Party Politics in the United States* (Baton Rouge: Louisiana State Univ. Press, 2009), 181.

59. The *Emancipator* thought that the nomination of the former Whig King and the prominent role "of so uncompromising a democrat as Thomas Morris" demonstrated that the Liberty Party was not stalking horse for either of the two national parties (*Emancipator,* Jan. 13, 1842).

60. *Philanthropist,* Jan. 12, 1842.

61. Harrold, *Gamaliel Bailey,* 57–58.

62. Chase to Charles D. Cleveland, Oct. 22, 1841, in Niven, *Salmon P. Chase Papers,* 79–81.

63. *Philanthropist,* Jan. 12, 1842.

64. William M. Wiecek, *The Sources of Antislavery Constitutionalism in America, 1760–1848* (New York: Cornell Univ. Press, 1977), 212.

65. *Philanthropist,* Jan. 12, 1842.

66. *Philanthropist,* Jan. 12, 1842.

67. This insight was Chase's and was a lasting contribution to political antislavery ideology (Foner, *Free Soil, Free Labor, Free Men,* 79–80).

68. *Philanthropist,* Jan. 12, 1842.

69. The 1841 New York City Convention Address claimed that "the redress of the slave's wrongs . . . [were] the great paramount object of our political endeavors." The party's "test questions" were "emancipation, abolition, human freedom" (Johnson, *Liberty Party,* 25).

70. Richard H. Sewell, *Ballots for Freedom: Antislavery Politics in the United States, 1837–1860* (New York: Oxford Univ. Press, 1976), 90–91. As Bailey would later state the matter more starkly, "a political party is not a church or a philanthropic association." Quoted in James Brewer Stewart. *Abolitionist Politics and the Coming of the Civil War* (Amherst: Univ. of Massachusetts Press, 2008).

71. *Cincinnati Enquirer,* n.d., *Philanthropist,* Jan. 12, 1842. The comment about the quality of Morris's mind is even more remarkable considering the source—John Brough. Although now the editor of the *Enquirer* (Masur, *Until Justice Be Done,* 190), Brough was a member of the committee that questioned Morris in 1838; supported Tappen and the 1839 Ohio Fugitive Slave Law; and denied the rights of Blacks to petition the

214 NOTES TO PAGES 122–125

general assembly. He was one of the Ohio legislators Morris had described in 1839 as "a class of small politicians . . . [who] draw a precarious . . . existence from the putrid mass of prejudice." In acknowledging the quality of Morris's mind, however, Brough was not alone. References to Morris's intellect, despite his lack of formal education, were common in the Democratic press throughout Morris's career. See, for example, *Western Hemisphere,* June 11, 1834.

72. *Philanthropist,* Jan. 12, 1842.

73. *Daily Cincinnati Republican,* n.d., *Philanthropist,* Jan. 19, 1842.

74. *Ohio Free Press,* n.d., *Emancipator,* Nov. 18, 1841.

9. INDEPENDENT OPINIONS AND ULTRA DOCTRINES

1. Dwight L. Dumond, ed., *Letters of James Gillespie Birney, 1831–1857* (New York: D. Appleton, 1938), 490n2.

2. *Emancipator,* Jan. 13, 1842.

3. Frederick J. Blue, *Salmon P. Chase: A Life in Politics* (Kent, OH: Kent State Univ. Press, 1987), 44–45; David F. Hughes, "Salmon P. Chase: Chief Justice," *Vanderbilt Law Review* 18 (1965): 569, 572, 578–79. Rutherford B. Hayes and Ebeneezer R. Hoer, quoted in Charles Fairman, *History of the Supreme Court of the United States, Reconstruction and Reunion 1864–1888* (New York: Macmillan, 1971), 6:1474–75; Eric Foner, *The Fiery Trial: Abraham Lincoln and American Slavery* (New York: W. W. Norton, 2010), 43; see also Frederick J. Blue, "From Right to Left," *Northern Kentucky Law Review* 21, no. 3 (1993): 3–22, noting Chase's "elitism and pompous nature along with a degree of smugness."

4. William Birney to Birney, Feb. 26, 1844, in Dumond, *Letters of James Gillespie Birney,* 794–95.

5. *Philanthropist,* Jan. 12, 1842.

6. Betty Fladeland, *James Gillespie Birney: From Slaveholder to Abolitionist* (New York: Cornell Univ. Press, 1955), 215.

7. *Philanthropist,* Dec. 12, 1841. The *Emancipator,* December 16, 1841, also printed the Indiana resolution, but with an accompanying explanation that it related to the Liberty Party platform, not candidates.

8. *Philanthropist,* Jan. 12, 1842.

9. Chase to Birney, Jan. 21, 1842, in John Niven, *The Salmon P. Chase Papers* (Kent, OH: Kent State Univ. Press, 1994), 84–85; Fladeland, *James Gillespie Birney,* 216–18. William Birney's claim, five decades later, that Chase "cordially supported Mr. Birney as a candidate for the presidency" was simply wishful thinking. William Birney, *James G. Birney and His Times: The Genesis of the Republican Party* (New York: Bergman Publishers, 1890), 260–61.

10. Birney to Leavitt, Jan. 10, 1842, in Dumond, *Letters of James Gillespie Birney,* 645–56; Leavitt to Birney, Jan. 18, 1842, in Dumond, *Letters of James Gillespie Birney,* 659–60.

NOTES TO PAGES 125–128

11. Stewart to Birney, Apr. 14, 1842, in Dumond, *Letters of James Gillespie Birney*, 689–90. Stewart also communicated his displeasure to Bailey and Chase and reminded them that a second convention in 1843 was expected (*Philanthropist*, Mar. 1, 1843).

12. Leavitt to Birney, Feb. 14, 1842, *Philanthropist*, Mar. 1, 1843, 675–76. One month later, Leavitt wishfully editorialized that he anticipated that Ohio would "cast one-tenth of the electoral vote of the Union for Birney and Morris in 1844" (*Emancipator*, Mar. 10, 1842). Neither Birney nor those around him had any intention of yielding to Chase's request.

13. Birney to Chase, Feb. 2, 1842, in Dumond, *Letters of James Gillespie Birney*, 670–72; see Blue, *A Life in Politics*, 47–50. Birney's response merely confirmed Chase's concerns. His goal, and that of his friends, was not to nominate abolitionists and to distinguish the Liberty Party from abolitionism (*Philanthropist*, Feb. 9, 1842).

14. Morris et al. to Joshua Leavitt, Feb. 9, 1842, *Emancipator*, June 9, 1842.

15. Morris et al. to Joshua Leavitt, Feb. 9, 1842, *Emancipator*, June 9, 1842.

16. Reinhard D. Johnson, *The Liberty Party: Antislavery Third-Party Politics in the United States* (Baton Rouge: Louisiana State Univ. Press, 2009), 32.

17. The letter's language makes Chase or Bailey the probable author. See Chase to Charles D. Cleveland, Oct. 22, 1841, in Niven, *Salmon P. Chase Papers*, 79–81, and Bailey's editorial in *Philanthropist*, Feb. 9, 1842.

18. A few months later, Chase would again attempt to use Morris to improve abolitionists' view of his conduct. Chase's recognition of Morris's influence caused him to employ him as cocounsel in the VanZandt case in the spring of 1842 John P. Niven, *Salmon P. Chase: A Biography* (New York: Oxford Univ. Press, 1995) 78.

19. In Morris's October 2, 1841, letter (*Emancipator*, Dec. 16, 1841) to the Michigan Liberty Party, he told his readers that he had "full confidence" that slavery would be "entirely abolished."

20. *Philanthropist*, Feb. 9, 1842. Bailey was reacting to the "Address to the Slaves," which had been adopted by the New York State Anti-Slavery Society meeting at Peterboro on January 19, 1842 (*Emancipator*, Feb. 3 and 10, 1842).

21. Eli Nichols to Bailey, Apr. 13, 1842, *Philanthropist*, May 11, 1842.

22. Niven, *Salmon P. Chase*, 73–74. Fladeland, *James Gillespie Birney*, 218–19; Dumond, *Letters of James Gillespie Birney*, 690. Niven characterized Chase's behavior during the evening as at least "somewhat duplicitous." Morris does not appear to have attended this meeting.

23. Before Chase wrote his letter, Birney wrote Smith to report on his meeting with Chase. When Chase's letter arrived, Smith was ready. Stanley Harrold, *Gamaliel Bailey and Antislavery Union* (Kent, OH: Kent State Univ. Press, 1986), 61.

24. Stanley Harrold, *The Rise of Aggressive Abolitionism: Addresses to the Slaves* (Lexington: Univ. Press of Kentucky, 2004), 84.

25. Text of address in Harrold, *The Rise of Aggressive Abolitionism*, 153–61.

26. Harrold, *The Rise of Aggressive Abolitionism*, 77.

27. Harrold, *The Rise of Aggressive Abolitionism*, 83–86.

28. Chase to Gerrit Smith, May 14, 1842, in Niven, *Salmon P. Chase Papers*, 96–99.

29. Chase to Gerrit Smith, May 14, 1842, in Niven, *Salmon P. Chase Papers*, 96–99. Chase did not identify the individual whose opinion made support for the federal consensus only "almost unanimous." By the summer of 1842, however, Morris was changing his mind on his commitment to the federal consensus. William Birney to Birney, Feb. 26, 1844, in Dumond, *Letters of James Gillespie Birney*, 794–95. Chase's somewhat cryptic allusion to the lack of total unanimity, coupled with Morris's absence from the dinner with Birney, suggests Chase's concern with Morris's "ultra opinions" started as early as the spring of 1842.

30. Chase to Gerrit Smith, May 14, 1842, in Niven, *Salmon P. Chase Papers*, 96–99.

31. Chase to Gerrit Smith, May 14, 1842, in Niven, *Salmon P. Chase Papers*, 96–99.

32. *Philanthropist*, Jan. 13, 1841.

33. Gerrit Smith, *Cazenovia Abolitionist*, July 12, 1842, *Philanthropist*, Aug. 27, 1842. Smith's public letter was in response to Bailey's criticism of the Peterboro address (*Philanthropist*, Feb. 9, 1842).

34. *Philanthropist*, Feb. 9, 1842.

35. Niven, *Salmon P. Chase*, 82.

36. Bertram Wyatt-Brown, *Lewis Tappan and the Evangelical War against Slavery* (Cleveland: Press of Case Western Reserve, 1969), 276–77.

37. David Brion Davis, *The Slave Power Conspiracy and the Paranoid Style* (Baton Rouge: Louisiana State Univ. Press, 1970), 43–46.

38. Cong. Globe, 27th Cong., 2nd Sess., 173–74 (1841–42). The claim that abolition was part of a British plot to destroy America appears to have begun in the North and dogged the movement for years. See Leonard L. Richards, *Gentlemen of Property and Standing: Anti-Abolition Mobs in Jacksonian America* (New York: Oxford Univ. Press, 1970), 62–71. Wise's particular allegations were made in the midst of Southern uproar over the *Creole* affair. By this time, even Calhoun endorsed the view that Britain was plotting with abolitionists. Robert Elder, *Calhoun: American Heretic* (New York: Basic Books, 2021), 393–94.

39. *Philanthropist*, Feb. 22, 1842.

40. *Philanthropist*, May 25 and June 22, 1842; *Emancipator*, June 16, 1842.

41. *Emancipator*, Aug. 18 and Sept. 15, 1842. Participation in the fall campaign appears to have had a substantial impact on Lewis. Prior to the work, he had consistently denied any interest in supporting abolitionists and was firmly in Chase's camp. After working on the campaign, however, he became convinced that it was "a great mistake for any anti-slavery man or party to seek any distinction from what the world calls abolitionists" (Lewis to Bailey, *Philanthropist*, Oct. 22, 1842). This change of heart may have resulted from Chase's absence from the speaking tour and Lewis's continued exposure to Morris's ideas.

42. Francis P. Weisenburger, *The Passing of the Frontier 1825–1850: The History of the State of Ohio* (Columbus: Ohio State Archaeological and Historical Society, 1941), 402–9; Edgar A. Holt, *Party Politics in Ohio, 1840–1850* (Columbus, OH: F. J. Heer Printing, 1930), 70; see also James Roger Sharp, *The Jacksonians Versus the Banks: Politics in the States after the Panic of 1837* (New York: Columbia Univ. Press, 1970), 123–59.

43. "Address of the State Central Committee," *Philanthropist*, July 9, 1842.

44. Jonathan H. Earle, *Jacksonian Antislavery and the Politics of Free Soil, 1824–1854* (Chapel Hill: Univ. of North Carolina Press, 2004), 144–46; Harrold, *Gamaliel Bailey*, 45. The move from the Whig position of 1840 is dramatic. John Ashworth, *Slavery, Capitalism, and Politics in the Antebellum Republic*, vol. 1, *Commerce and Compromise, 1820–1850* (Cambridge: Cambridge Univ. Press, 1995), 396–97. Among the leadership, "only Morris was a bona fide radical Jacksonian in the 1830s" (Earle, *Jacksonian Antislavery*, 144). Although Bailey had been impressed with Leavitt's essentially Jacksonian economics in September 1840, the new leadership (Chase, Lewis, and King) were staunch Whigs. Hugh Davis, *Joshua Leavitt: Evangelical Abolitionist* (Baton Rouge: Louisiana State Univ. Press, 1990), 166–70.

45. This emphasis on economic issues troubled some. See Birney to Chase, Feb. 2, 1842, in Dumond, *Letters of James Gillespie Birney*, 670–72. The address reflects Chase's "political transition" from Pro-bank Whiggery to sympathy with Jacksonian financial policies." Sean Wilentz, *No Property in Man: Slavery and Antislavery at the Nation's Founding* (Cambridge, MA: Harvard Univ. Press, 2018), 224–25. A few years earlier, Bailey had concluded the "Democracy has done so many infamous things, that were it not for Thomas Morris, . . . the very name would nauseate an honest stomach" (*Philanthropist*, Sept. 24, 1839). Morris's influence on Bailey's changed political philosophy was evident to readers of the *Philanthropist*: "I do fully believe it is . . . your object to break the Whig party . . . and you have got a fit companion for your labors, Thomas Morris" (E. Connor to Bailey, Nov. 3, 1843, *Philanthropist*, Nov. 22, 1843).

46. "Interrogatories Propounded to Judge King at Cincinnati," Aug. 22, 1842, quoted in Kate Masur, *Until Justice Be Done: America's First Civil Rights Movement from Reconstruction* (New York: W. W. Norton, 2021), 194. Compare Morris, To the Democratic Portion of the People of Ohio: "Democracy ['s] . . . aim is equal and exact justice to men of all climes and colors" (*Philanthropist*, Aug. 11, 1841; *Emancipator*, Nov. 14, 1841).

47. Theodore C. Smith, *The Liberty and Free Soil Parties in the Northwest* (New York: Longmans, Green, 1897), 56.

48. *Philanthropist*, Jan. 12, 1842.

49. *Daily Ohio Statesman*, Dec. 8, 1842.

50. William Birney to Birney, Feb. 26, 1844, in Dumond, *Letters of James Gillespie Birney*, 794–95.

51. Leavitt to Birney, June 19, 1842, in Dumond, *Letters of James Gillespie Birney*, 699.

52. Chase to Lewis Tappan, Sept. 15, 1842, quoted in Joseph G. Rayback, "Liberty Party Leaders of Ohio: Exponents of Antislavery Coalition," *Ohio Archaeological and Historical Quarterly* 57, no. 2 (Apr. 1948): 171.

53. *Emancipator*, May 5, 1842.

54. William Birney to Birney, Feb. 28, 1843, in Dumond, *Letters of James Gillespie Birney*, 720–21. Goldfarb believes that Chase and Bailey convinced Morris to decline. Joel Goldfarb, "Life of Gamaliel Bailey, Prior to the Founding of the National Era: The Orientation of a Practical Abolitionist" (PhD diss., Univ. of California, 1958), 272. Harrold, however, accepts William Birney's explanation that Bailey's opposition forced Morris to decline (Harrold, *Gamaliel Bailey*, 64). Given Morris's personality, it is unlikely he would have acted solely to appease Bailey.

NOTES TO PAGES 133–136

55. *Philanthropist*, Jan. 11, 1843.

56. *Philanthropist*, Jan. 11, 1843. Morris may have intended this remark to be limited to slavery in the District of Columbia and the territories. But he was clearly considering federally mandated emancipation in the slave states, and would publicly explain his theory of congressional power to abolish slavery in the states later that summer before the Albany nominating convention met.

57. *Philanthropist*, Jan. 11, 1843. This position on fugitive slaves appears to have been made with VanZandt case in mind, but was also consistent with the one held at the time by Birney. Birney to Chase, Feb. 20, 1842, in Dumond, *Letters of James Gillespie Birney*, 650.

58. Fladeland, *James Gillespie Birney*, 216. Compare with Richard H. Sewell, *Ballots for Freedom: Antislavery Politics in the United States, 1837–1860* (New York: Oxford Univ. Press, 1976), 121; Rayback, "Liberty Party Leaders of Ohio," 170.

59. Wyatt-Brown, *Lewis Tappan*, 274.

60. William Birney to Birney, Feb. 28, 1843, in Dumond, *Letters of James Gillespie Birney*, 720–21.

61. Chase to Lewis Tappan, Feb. 15, 1843, in Niven, *Salmon P. Chase Papers*, 101–3. Johnson says Bailey and Chase "had pressured Morris to decline the nomination" (*Liberty Party*, 182). Goldfarb thought Morris's rejection of the nomination was Chase and Bailey's "trump card" in their effort to convene a second nominating convention ("Life of Gamaliel Bailey," 272).

62. Morris to Thomas Clegg, *Philanthropist*, Feb. 17, 1841.

63. *Philanthropist*, Jan. 11, 1843.

64. Bailey to Birney, Mar. 31, 1843, in Dumond, *Letters of James Gillespie Birney*, 726–27.

65. Morris to Bailey, Mar. 20, 1843, *Philanthropist*, Mar. 29, 1843.

66. Morris to Bailey, Mar. 20, 1843, *Philanthropist*, Mar. 29, 1843. Leavitt reprinted the letter in its entirety three weeks later in the *Emancipator*, April 20, 1843.

67. Goldfarb, "Life of Gamaliel Bailey," 316–17; see also Johnson, *Liberty Party*, 183.

68. Donald F. Melhorn Jr., *Lest We Be Marshalled: Judicial Powers and Politics in Ohio, 1806–1812* (Akron, OH: Univ. of Akron Press, 2003), 119–46; William T. Utter, *The Frontier State, 1803–1825* (Columbus: Ohio State Archaeological and Historical Society, 1942), 43–51.

69. Leavitt to Birney, Feb. 10, 1843, in Dumond, *Letters of James Gillespie Birney*, 713–16. Leavitt had long envisioned Morris presiding in the Senate as vice president. In March, 1839, in the aftermath of Morris's reply to Clay, Leavitt claimed Morris was "notching his name in the Senate Chamber . . . by which he will be remembered till he comes again—probably to preside over the body which forbade him to speak" (*Emancipator*, Feb. 28, 1839).

70. William Birney to Birney, Feb. 28, 1843, in Dumond, *Letters of James Gillespie Birney*, 720–22; Niven, *Salmon P. Chase Papers*, 67. William Birney's assessment, which downplayed the philosophical differences between Bailey and Morris, may have some merit. Even Bailey's biographer concedes that Bailey "coveted the prestige and personal political influence" (Harrold, *Gamaliel Bailey*, 56).

NOTES TO PAGES 136–138 219

71. *Philanthropist*, Mar. 1, 1843.

72. Niven, *Salmon P. Chase*, 67.

73. Goldfarb argued that Bailey had "reluctantly consented" to try to replace Birney, and that it was Birney's opposition to democracy that persuaded him to support Chase's effort. Bailey's more recent biographer believed that Bailey "grew increasingly disenchanted with the ticket" when "Birney identified with opponents of Bailey's conception of the Liberty Party and Morris became the leader of a similar radical faction in Ohio" (Goldfarb, "Life of Gamaliel Bailey," 250–56, 268; Harrold, *Gamaliel Bailey*, 63). Morris's refusal to follow Bailey's conversion away from abolition may also have contributed to the dispute. Bailey had initially expected that the Liberty Party would draw Chase to abolitionism. Instead, Chase converted Bailey to nonabolition (Harrold, *Aggressive Abolitionism*, 97). Whatever may have been his motivation to replace Birney, Bailey needed no encouragement to seek Morris's removal from the ticket. Johnson characterizes Bailey's motivation as "personal pique toward Morris" (*Liberty Party*, 41).

74. Bailey to Birney, Mar. 31, 1843, in Dumond, *Letters of James Gillespie Birney*, 726–27. The sincerity (as well as the accuracy) of Bailey's justification for opposing Morris is more than open to the question. Although claiming that Morris was his "friend," Bailey told William Birney "that he disliked Mr. Morris." William Birney to Birney, Feb. 28, 1843, in Dumond, *Letters of James Gillespie Birney*, 721. Opposition to Black suffrage was common among abolitionists. Harrold noted "Bailey's ambivalent attitude toward black rights in the 1840's" (Harrold, *Gamaliel Bailey*, 221n13). Moreover, William Jay, whom the editor supported as an alternative to Birney, also opposed Black voting. William M. Wiecek, *The Sources of Antislavery Constitutionalism in America, 1760–1848* (New York: Cornell Univ. Press, 1977), 156. While professing admiration for "the independence with which [Morris] forms his opinions and the boldness with which he utters them," Bailey found Morris's views on the power of Congress to abolish slavery in the states detrimental to the Liberty Party cause (Goldfarb, "Life of Gamaliel Bailey," 319).

75. Gerrit Smith to Bailey, Sept. 13, 1842, from the *Cazenovia Abolitionist*, *Philanthropist*, Oct. 15, 1842. Smith's recollection of a position taken by Morris during his Senate reelection efforts three years earlier and use of it to criticize the Ohio Liberty Party is extraordinary evidence of the extent that political abolitionists paid attention to (and remembered) Morris's views. For the background on the dispute between Bailey and Gerrit Smith, see Harrold, *Gamaliel Bailey*, 58–61.

76. Harrold, *Gamaliel Bailey*, 64–65; William Birney to Birney, Feb. 28, 1843, in Dumond, *Letters of James Gillespie Birney*, 720–22. Bailey may also have been aware, or at least suspected, that Birney had preferred Dr. Julius LeMoyne for the vice president spot (Leavitt to Birney, Feb. 10, 1843, and Birney to Charles Stewart and Joshua Leavitt, Aug. 17, 1843, in Dumond, *Letters of James Gillespie Birney*, 715, 754–58) and expected Birney to use his influence to remove Morris from the ticket.

77. Vernon L. Volpe, *Forlorn Hope of Freedom: The Liberty Party in the Old Northwest, 1838–1848* (Kent, OH: Kent State Univ. Press, 1990), 104.

78. Wiecek, *Antislavery Constitutionalism*, 156.

79. Gerald Sorin, *Abolitionism: A New Perspective* (Westport: Praeger Publishers, 1972), 86; see also Manisha Sinha, *The Slave's Cause: A History of Abolition* (London:

Yale Univ. Press, 2016), 465; Aileen S. Kraditor, *Means and Ends in American Abolitionism: Garrison and His Critics on Strategy and Tactics, 1834–1850* (New York: Pantheon Books, 1969), 38; Davis, *Joshua Leavitt*, 248; Margaret L. Plunkett, "A History of the Liberty Party, with Emphasis on Its Activities in the Northeastern States" (PhD diss., Cornell Univ., 1930), 13. Even Eric Foner, although viewing Morris generally favorably, agreed. Eric Foner, *Politics and Ideology* in the *Age of the Civil War* (New York: Oxford Univ. Press, 1980), 78. More recently some historians have concluded Morris had changed his position by the time of Bailey's letter. See, for example, Johnson, *Liberty Party*, 255; Sean Wilentz, *Rise of American Democracy: Jefferson to Lincoln* (New York: W. W. Norton, 2005), 908n16; Sewell, *Ballots for Freedom*, 100. Sewell says that Morris changed "his opposition to Negro suffrage in the face of great pressure from other party members." Not only is there no evidence of pressure, Morris rarely responded well to pressure. More likely, Morris had changed his mind before Bailey wrote—at least by the time of his favorable comments on Blacks voting in his August 1841 address to Ohio Democrats—just as Birney thought.

80. For prevailing racial notions, see George M. Fredrickson, *The Black Image in the White Mind: The Debate on Afro-American Character and Destiny, 1817–1914* (New York: Harper and Row, 1971).

81. In Morris's response to the inquiry from the Democratic Committee seeking information from the senatorial candidates, he had said that he thought Blacks "ought to be protected in and enjoy their natural rights, but [he did] not believe it would be good policy . . . to admit them to the enjoyment of equal political or social privileges" (Morris to Committee, Dec. 11, 1838, reprinted in *Philanthropist*, Jan. 22, 1838).

82. Birney to Bailey, Apr. 16, 1843, in Dumond, *Letters of James Gillespie Birney*, 730–34. Birney's language is interesting. Morris had long supported "civil" rights for Blacks. In 1838, however, he had opposed "political and social" rights. On the distinction between civil and political rights, see Eric Foner, *The Second Founding: How the Civil War and Reconstruction Remade the Constitution* (New York: W. W. Norton, 2019), 6–7; Harold M. Hyman and William M. Wiecek, *Equal Justice under Law: Constitutional Development 1835–1875* (New York: Harper and Row, 1982), 396. In general, abolitionists did not equate voting with civil rights (Wiecek, *Antislavery Constitutionalism*, 156).

83. Lewis Tappan asked Bailey, "Why has [Morris's] opinion not been announced" before? He claimed "it would astound Eastern Liberty men." Louis Filler, *The Crusade against Slavery, 1830–1860* (New York: Harper and Brothers, 1960), 145. As part of his "private" effort to alert Eastern supporters of Birney (of which Tappan was not one), Bailey also wrote to Joshua Leavitt. Bailey to Birney, Mar. 31, 1843, in Dumond, *Letters of James Gillespie Birney*, 726.

84. Goldfarb, "Life of Gamaliel Bailey," 317–19.

85. Morris to William J. McKinney, Feb. 10, 1841, *Philanthropist*, Feb. 17, 1841.

86. Foner, *Second Founding*, 5.

87. *Philanthropist*, Aug. 11, 1841. At the time of the Ohio Constitutional Convention, there were fewer than 350 Black residents in the state. The Ordinance of 1787 said nothing about their voting, but the constitution adopted as a preliminary to statehood prohibited it (Utter, *Frontier State*, 21–22, 396).

NOTES TO PAGES 139–140

88. *Philanthropist*, June 9, 1841.

89. Proceedings of the Ohio Liberty Convention, *Philanthropist*, Jan. 11, 1843.

90. Cong. Globe, 25th Cong., 3rd Sess., appendix, 167–74 (1838–39).

91. Morris to Smith, Mar. 30, 1837, in Benjamin Franklin Morris, ed., *The Life of Thomas Morris: Pioneer and Long a Legislator of Ohio, and U.S. Senator from 1833 to 1839* (Cincinnati: Moore, Wilstach, Keys & Overend, 1856), 247–66; also Morris, *Life of Thomas Morris*, 339–40; Morris to Bailey, Dec. 23, 1840, *Philanthropist*, Dec. 23, 1840.

92. Goldfarb, "Life of Gamaliel Bailey," 317–19.

93. *Philanthropist*, May 26, 1841. The early nominations were exactly what Bailey had sought in the aftermath of Birney's 1840 showing (*Philanthropist*, Nov. 11, 1840). Harrold argues that the convention's willingness to place candidates nominated by other parties on the antislavery ticket was evidence of "less than hearty support for the Birney-Morris ticket" (Harrold, *Gamaliel Bailey*, 40). More likely, because 1841 was an off-year election with no statewide races, the resolution was designed to deal with local races in Ohio in districts where the Liberty Party was unable to field candidates (*Philanthropist*, June 9, 1841).

94. *Philanthropist*, June 9, 1841.

95. Allusions to character failings could be particularly damaging. Many Liberty leaders, especially those supporting Birney, were committed to the doctrine of "entire sanctification" growing out of the revivals of Charles Finney. This concept "demanded constantly expanding levels of holy living" and measured the character of individuals "in degrees of moral worth." This imperative of perfectionism "formed the motivational base for Liberty Party voting." Douglas M. Strong, *Perfectionist Politics: Abolition and the Religious Tensions of American Democracy* (New York: Syracuse Univ. Press, 1999), 71–72, 83–84.

96. For example, Birney was apparently both aware and willing to share information about Morris's reputation. See Myron Holley to Birney, Jan. 1, 1849, in Dumond, *Letters of James Gillespie Birney*, 518.

97. Goldfarb acknowledged that many of these "other accounts . . . consisted of vague objections to [Morris's] personality, integrity and private habits" ("Life of Gamaliel Bailey," 317). Harrold argues that Morris's "repeated verbal clashes with Bailey . . . confirmed Bailey's belief that Morris' personality hurt the party's chances of attracting new adherents" (*Gamaliel Bailey*, 63). Whether it was the substance of the clashes (Morris's radicalism) or simply Morris's refusal to follow Bailey's lead, Bailey no longer approved of Morris.

98. Morris, *Life of Thomas Morris*, 402; *Signal of Liberty*, Aug. 5, 1844; W. H. Brisbane, *An Eulogium on the Life and Character of the Late Thomas Morris* (Cincinnati: L'Horriedieu, 1845), 10–11. James Swing, whose family knew Morris well, recalled that "though never a professedly pious man, [Morris] made the most effective use of his knowledge of the Scriptures in his public speeches." James B. Swing, "Thomas Morris," *Ohio Archeological and Historical Quarterly* 10 (1902): 352.

99. *Signal of Liberty*, Aug. 5, 1844.

100. Goldfarb, "Life of Gamaliel Bailey," 301–5; Sorin, *Abolitionism*, 44–52. By the time of Bailey's letter to Birney, however, Bailey was questioning his own attachment

to organized religion (*Philanthropist*, Apr. 15, 1843). Two years later, he resigned from church membership (*Philanthropist*, July 16, 1845).

101. Elk Lick Mill has been restored and relocated to Heritage Village Museum operated by Historic Southwest Ohio, Inc. Steve Preston, "Heritage Village Guest Post: Slavery, Politics, and Elk Lick House," *Harriet Beecher Stowe House* (Sept. 29, 2020), https://stowehousecincy.org/blog/heritage-village-guest-post-slavery-politics-and-elk-lick-house.

102. *Signal of Liberty*, Oct. 14, 1844. Although he may have been converted to temperance late in life, Morris's son's claim that Morris "believed the traffic in spirituous liquors . . . was a moral wrong" is difficult to reconcile with his early tavern ownership and investment in his son-in-law's distillery (Morris, *Life of Thomas Morris*, 32).

103. *Emancipator*, July 13, 1843. In general, Liberty Party members were much more amenable to Morris's radical constitutional views than the Cincinnati followers of Chase and Bailey (Johnson, *Liberty Party*, 183).

104. *Emancipator*, July 13, 1843.

105. Morris's tendency to state his case in language others found excessive and to refuse to change his position was a long-standing and widely recognized trait. For example, as he had told Alexander Campbell six years earlier, "I shall never humble myself . . . so as to admit the right, in the remotest possibility, of anyone to question me as to my particular expressions." Morris to Alexander Campbell, Nov. 13, 1837, *Philanthropist*, Dec. 26, 1837. Nor did Morris readily modify a position he had taken. During the Senate debate on the admission of Michigan as a state, Senator Buchanan observed that, although Morris had said he was open to changing his mind, "he had taken such a strong ground that it would take the eloquence of an angel to convince him, or shake his opinion." Cong. Globe, 24th Cong., 2nd Sess., 60 (1836–37).

106. Birney to Bailey, Apr. 16, 1843, in Dumond, *Letters of James Gillespie Birney*, 730–31. Bailey had also objected to Birney's views on democracy (Sewell, *Ballots for Freedom*, 121–24). He apparently continued his whispering campaign about Birney's antidemocratic views. William Birney to Birney, Apr. 29, 1843 ("made use . . . of words dropped by you"), in Sewell, *Ballots for Freedom*, 736–38; Samuel Lewis to Birney, May 28, 1843 ("rumors are circulating") and William Birney to Birney, Aug. 7, 1843 ("detraction of your political sentiments, representing you as a foe to our . . . country"), in Sewell, *Ballots for Freedom*, 750–53.

10. THE POWER TO ABOLISH SLAVERY IN EVERY STATE

1. *Philanthropist*, Aug. 9, 1843. Remarkably, at the same time Chase and Bailey were pressing for William Jay, Jay was threatening to become a "disunionist." Aileen S. Kraditor, *Means and Ends in American Abolitionism: Garrison and His Critics on Strategy and Tactics, 1834–1850* (New York: Pantheon Books, 1969), 31, 66.

2. *Philanthropist*, Aug. 9, 1843.

3. Chase to Lewis Tappan, Feb. 15, 1843, in John Niven, *The Salmon P. Chase Papers* (Kent, OH: Kent State Univ. Press, 1994), 101–3.

NOTES TO PAGES 144–146

4. Birney to Charles Stewart, Aug. 15 and Aug. 17, 1843, in Dwight L. Dumond, *Letters of James Gillespie Birney, 1831–1857* (New York: D. Appleton Century, 1938), 754–58.

5. *Emancipator*, Sept. 7, 1843. Alvan Stewart and William Goodale, both of whom thought slavery unconstitutional everywhere, were also members of the committee. Reinhard D. Johnson, *The Liberty Party: Antislavery Third-Party Politics in the United States* (Baton Rouge: Louisiana State Univ. Press, 2009), 36. Stewart and Goodell did not press their radical antislavery views on the platform committee.

6. Alan M. Kraut, "Partisanship and Principles: The Liberty Party in Antebellum Political Culture," in *Crusaders and Compromisers: Essays on the Relationship of the Antislavery Struggle to the Antebellum Party System*, ed. Alan M. Kraut (Westport, CT: Greenwood Press, 1983), 85–86.

7. William M. Wiecek, *The Sources of Antislavery Constitutionalism in America, 1760–1848* (New York: Cornell Univ. Press, 1977), 217; Johnson, *Liberty Party*, 38.

8. Wiecek, *Antislavery Constitutionalism*, 208.

9. *Emancipator*, Sept. 7, 1843.

10. Wiecek, *Antislavery Constitutionalism*, 218.

11. Gerald Sorin, *Abolitionism: A New Perspective* (Westport: Praeger Publishers, 1972), 85.

12. *Emancipator*, Sept. 7, 1843.

13. Chase to Lewis Tappan, Sept. 12, 1843, in Niven, *Salmon P. Chase Papers*, 103–4.

14. *Emancipator*, June 9, 1842.

15. See, for example, Cong. Globe, 24th Cong., 1st Sess., 77 (1836); Morris to People of Ohio, Nov. 23, 1838, *Emancipator*, Dec. 29, 1838.

16. James Oakes, *The Crooked Path to Abolition: Abraham Lincoln and the Antislavery Constitution* (New York: W. W. Norton, 2021), 86–93; Wiecek, *Antislavery Constitutionalism*, 212. Estimates of how long would be required for this approach to end slavery ranged from twenty-five to one hundred years. Oakes, *Crooked Path*, 91–93.

17. William Birney to Birney, Sept. 24, 1843, in Dumond, *Letters of James Gillespie Birney*, 761.

18. Cong. Globe, 24th Cong., 1st Sess., 283–84 (1836); see also Morris to Alexander Campbell, Nov. 13, 1837, *Philanthropist*, Dec. 26, 1837.

19. Cong. Globe, 25th Cong., 2nd Sess., 97–98 (1837–38). Lincoln apparently also subscribed to this view both at the time of Calhoun's Resolutions and twenty years later during his debates with Stephen Douglas. Noah Feldman, *The Broken Constitution: Lincoln, Slavery and the Refounding of America* (New York: Farrar, Strauss & Corex, 2021), 57–58, 118.

20. *Emancipator*, Dec. 29, 1838.

21. According to Stewart, there was "not a slave at this moment, in the United States upon the terms . . . of the Constitution." Because slavery was unconstitutional under the Fifth Amendment, Congress had the power to pass a "declaratory" act confirming the abolition of slavery. Alvan Stewart, "A Constitutional Argument on the Subject of Slavery," in Jacobus tenBroek, *Equal under Law: The Antislavery Origins of the Fourteenth Amendment* (London: Collier Books, 1969), 289, 295, appendix A. Stewart's views on the Constitution led him to conclude that an independent antislavery party

was "imperative." From his position as president of the New York State Anti-Slavery Society, he worked continuously from 1839 on to bring about a new party. By 1839, he "had emerged as the leading spokesman for an antislavery political party." Richard H. Sewell, *Ballots for Freedom: Antislavery Politics in the United States, 1837–1860* (New York: Oxford Univ. Press, 1976), 49–54.

22. Wiecek, *Antislavery Constitutionalism*, 254–55; Jacobus tenBroek, *Equal under Law: The Antislavery Origins of the Fourteenth Amendment* (London: Collier Books, 1969), 66–72.

23. *Emancipator*, May 17, 1838.

24. [Morris] to Dear Sir, Jan. 5, 1839, *Philanthropist*, Jan. 29, 1839.

25. Kraditor, *Means and Ends*, 187.

26. Hugh Davis, *Joshua Leavitt: Evangelical Abolitionist* (Baton Rouge: Louisiana State Univ. Press, 1990), 147; Wiecek, *Antislavery Constitutionalism*, 255. Betty Fladeland, *James Gillespie Birney: From Slaveholder to Abolitionist* (New York: Cornell Univ. Press, 1955), 178–79. The debate lasted three days. Margaret L. Plunkett, "A History of the Liberty Party, with Emphasis on Its Activities in the Northeastern States" (PhD diss., Cornell Univ., 1930), 145–49. Liberty leaders recognized that the *Barron* decision had made the argument untenable. See Chase to Lewis Tappan, Mar. 18, 1847, quoted in Plunkett, "A History of the Liberty Party," 153.

27. *Philanthropist*, May 22, 1838. For the obvious flaws in Stewart's argument, see Wiecek, *Antislavery Constitutionalism*, 256–57. Bailey recognized these flaws but went further. He argued both that the Constitution recognized slavery and that "persons" did not include slaves. Bailey did not change his mind until 1843 (*Philanthropist*, Feb. 22, 1843).

28. William Birney to Birney, Sept. 24, 1843, in Dumond, *Letters of James Gillespie Birney*, 761.

29. Cong. Globe, 24th Cong., 1st Sess., appendix, 283–84 (1836).

30. Cong. Globe, 25th Cong., 3rd Sess., appendix, 172 (1839).

31. *Philanthropist*, Dec. 8, 1841.

32. In May 1839, Morris suggested that if Congress could make counterfeiting or treason by a slave a crime or provide for a slave's enlistment, "the power of Congress in anyone of [those] cases, would lead," as necessary consequences, "to a power over the whole slave system." Morris to Bailey, n.d., in Morris, *Life of Thomas Morris*, 241. He does not appear to have ever followed up on this musing, nor promoted the view further.

33. *Philanthropist*, July 5, 1843.

34. *Philanthropist*, July 5, 1843.

35. *Philanthropist*, July 5, 1843. Although the basis for his change of mind is unclear, by the next summer in the midst of the 1844 presidential campaign, King had decided Congress did have the power to abolish slavery in the states and was sustaining that position in debates with Joshua Giddings. Richard H. Brackin to Birney, July 31, 1844, in Dumond, *Letters of James Gillespie Birney*, 827–29.

36. Wiecek, *Antislavery Constitutionalism*, 83.

37. Cong. Globe, 25th Cong., 2nd Sess., appendix, 160 (1837–38).

NOTES TO PAGES 149–151

38. Earlier antislavery writers had used the Preamble as part of their arguments. For example, Angeline Grimké argued that slavery violated the principles of the Preamble, "but she had not mounted a legal argument against slavery" (Feldman, *The Broken Constitution*, 65, 68). Grimké's husband, Theodore Weld, used the Preamble to support the notion that abolishing slavery in the District was a proper exercise of congressional power to legislate for the District of Columbia (Weld, "Power of Congress," in tenBrock, *Equal under Law*, 277). G. W. F. Mellen, in *An Argument on the Unconstitutionality of Slavery: Embracing an Abstract of the Proceedings of the National and State Conventions on this Subject* (Boston: Saxton and Peirce, 1841), 56–65, 427–28, discussed the Preamble as part of his claim that slavery was unconstitutional. Mellen was "flamboyantly eccentric, if not mad" and his work "was not particularly significant" (Wiecek, *Antislavery Constitutionalism*, 256). Neither author, however, treated the Preamble as a separate grant of power to Congress (cf. Oakes, *Crooked Path*, 35).

39. *Barron v. Mayor & City Council of Baltimore*, 32 U.S. 243 (1833).

40. *Emancipator*, Dec. 29, 1838. This was the position Henry Clay advocated in his amendment to Calhoun's Fifth Resolution. Cong. Globe, 25th Cong., 2nd Sess., appendix, 59 (1837–38); Resolution in Cong. Globe, 25th Cong., 2nd Sess., appendix, 96–98; Wiecek, *Antislavery Constitutionalism*, 188.

41. This argument appeared to be endorsed by two justices in *Groves v. Slaughter*, 40 U.S. 449 (1841): 506–8. Although in separate dicta, Justice McClean and Chief Justice Taney agreed that the "Constitution treats slaves as persons," McClean thought this meant that Congress could not enact slavery (Morris's position). Taney thought this meant Congress could not act on slavery (in particular the Commerce Clause did not apply) because slaves were not an article of commerce (property) under the Constitution. See Harold M. Hyman and William M. Wiecek, *Equal Justice under Law: Constitutional Development 1835–1875* (New York: Harper and Row, 1982), 101–2.

42. This was the position that troubled Chase and Bailey in their effort to attract nonabolitionists to the party. Yet, even among Free-Soilers, the view persisted. "We should let slaveholders understand that we make war upon the institution of slavery itself wherever it exists; and, when we have strength to legislate for its over throw in the States, . . . we shall find Constitutional powers through which to exert that strength." E. S. Hamlin to Chase, Apr. 25, 1850, in Sewell, *Ballots for Freedom*, 190.

43. Wiecek, *Antislavery Constitutionalism*, 249.

44. Akhil Reed Amar, *The Law of the Land: A Grand Tour of Our Constitutional Republic* (New York: Basic Books, 2015), 111–15. Amar adds the clauses that forbid the nation (article I, §9) and states (article I, §10) from granting titles of nobility and require the federal government to guarantee that each state has a republican form of government (article IV, §4) to his Preamble analysis.

45. *Philanthropist*, July 5, 1843. Bailey, while publicly dissenting from Morris's radical constitutional view, told Chase privately that the meeting was "the best yet held in the State; 1500 people; excellent speeches; King, Lewis, Morris, Hudson and others." Chase diary entry, June 23, 1843, in Robert Bruce Warden, *An Account of the Private Life and Public Service of Salmon Portland Chase* (Cincinnati: Wilstach, Baldwin, 1874), 299. Within two years, both William Goodell and Lysander Spooner published

books defending the notion that slavery was unconstitutional. By 1847, Birney came to a similar conclusion. Morris's position differed: slavery was not unconstitutional; rather, Congress had the constitutional power to abolish slavery not only in the territories but in the states as well.

46. For the background of the Ohio antislavery organizational split, see Stanley Harrold, *Gamaliel Bailey and Antislavery Union* (Kent, OH: Kent State Univ. Press, 1986), 44–45.

47. Stanley Harrold, *American Abolitionism* (Charlottesville: Univ. of Virginia Press, 2019), 95; Manisha Sinha, *The Slave's Cause: A History of Abolition* (London: Yale Univ. Press, 2016), 265, 464–65; Johnson, *Liberty Party*, 293–94.

48. *Philanthropist*, Sept. 13, 1843.

49. Henry Mayer, *All on Fire: William Lloyd Garrison and the Abolition of Slavery* (New York: St. Martin's Press, 1998), 362.

50. *Philanthropist*, Sept. 13, 1843. Goldfarb, overlooking Morris's resolutions at the June 1843 Ohio State Antislavery Society meeting, argued that it was not until this meeting of Garrisonians "that Morris definitely declared his advocacy of the doctrine that Congress could abolish slavery with the states." Joel Goldfarb, "The Life of Gamaliel Bailey, Prior to the Founding of the National Era: The Orientation of a Practical Abolitionist" (PhD diss., Univ. of California, 1958), 283.

51. William Birney to Birney, Sept. 24, 1843, in Dumond, *Letters of James Gillespie Birney*, 761. See also, Goldfarb, "Life of Gamaliel Bailey," 277: In 1843 there was "a great deal of animosity towards Bailey and Chase even by many Ohio Liberty men." By the end of the 1844 campaign, even William Birney had lost his enthusiasm for Chase. In a letter to his father written two weeks before Morris's death, William Birney described Chase and his supporters as "a temporizing, bargain and sale class of politicians who sought "to sacrifice our purity as a party." He was convinced that in Ohio "the old stock of abolitionists understand Mr. Chase and distrust him." William Birney to Birney, Nov. 25, 1844, in Dumond, *Letters of James Gillespie Birney*, 887.

52. Johnson, *Liberty Party*, 182–83.

53. *Philanthropist*, Feb. 14, 1844. Johnson implies that Morris was the primary promoter of these resolutions at the convention (*Liberty Party*, 183). Although the convention's actions reflect the acceptance of his constitutional views, Morris did not attend the meeting. See *Philanthropist*, February 14, 1844, for a list of convention attendees. Rather, "Bailey was the leading spirit of the Convention and pulled the wires with much skill" (*Ohio State Journal*, Feb. 14, 1844).

54. Harrold, *Gamaliel Bailey*, 67. Harrold argues that Bailey's acceptance of the resolution was part of his effort to reconcile with Morris (*Gamaliel Bailey*, 61–62). Bailey's concession, however, may well have been motivated by the change in position of other Ohio Liberty Party leaders. By early 1844, King, Lewis, and even Chase had concluded that Congress could reach slavery in the states (Wieck, *Antislavery Constitutionalism*, 216; Chase to Birney, Apr. 2, 1844, in Dumond, *Letters of James Gillespie Birney*, 805–6). Chase's position, however, was not for public consumption (Kraditor, *Means and Ends*, 227n21; cf. Oakes, *Freedom National*, 28): "Chase was convinced that it was . . . constitutionally incorrect . . . to deny that the Constitution protected slavery in the states." Chase would temper the Ohio resolution to eliminate the reference to

NOTES TO PAGES 152–155

the unconstitutionality of slavery in the states and incorporate the pairing of the Preamble with the Fifth Amendment into the Free-Soil Party's 1848 Platform to deny the constitutionality of slavery in the territories (Oakes, *Crooked Path*, 44).

55. *Philanthropist*, July 26, 1843.

56. *Philanthropist*, Aug. 9, 1843.

57. *Philanthropist*, Oct. 18, 1843.

58. Niven, *Salmon P. Chase*, 77–83. The effort to replace Birney had "led to a great deal of animosity towards Bailey and Chase even by many Ohio Liberty men" (Goldfarb, "Life of Gamaliel Bailey," 277).

59. Chase and Morris were likely encouraged that McClean would hear the case. He had already acknowledged that the Constitution treated slaves as persons and that slavery was "local in its character" so that "the power over slavery belongs to the states." *Groves v. Slaughter*, 40 U.S. 449 (1841) (McClean dissenting). The justice had also become part of Bailey's social circle in Cincinnati (Harrold, *Gamaliel Bailey*, 26).

60. *Jones v. VanZandt*, 13 F Cases 1040 (No. 7501)(CCD, Ohio, 1843) and *Jones v. VanZandt*, 13 F Case 1047 (No. 7502)(CCCD Ohio, 1843); Warden, *Private Life and Public Service*, 296–98. Birney's son believed that these arguments were derived from a "memorial" (in *Signal of Liberty*, Jan. 30, 1843) Birney had sent to the Michigan legislature. William Birney to Birney, July 13, 1843, in Dumond, *Letters of James Gillespie Birney*, 743. In at least this case, tenBroek's description of Birney as "a quartermaster of ideas in the movement rather than an original producer of them" is accurate (*Equal under Law*, 296). Birney's memorial was generally a repeat of arguments from the Ordinance of 1787 and Declaration of Independence, which both Chase and Morris had made for years. Morris had long believed that the absence of a right to jury trial in fugitive slave cases violated the Sixth Amendment and made the law unconstitutional. See *Emancipator*, Feb. 1, 1838.

61. *Philanthropist*, July 19, 1843.

62. *Jones v. VanZandt*, 13 F Cases 1040 (No. 7501)(CCD, Ohio, 1843) and *Jones v. VanZandt*, 13 F Case 1047 (No.7502)(CCCD Ohio, 1843). VanZandt lost and appealed to the United States Supreme Court. By the time of the appeal, Morris had died and William Seward joined Chase as VanZandt's counsel (Niven, *Salmon P. Chase*, 76–83).

63. *Emancipator*, Oct. 5, 1843.

64. *Emancipator*, Oct. 5, 1843.

65. *Emancipator*, Oct. 12, 1843.

66. *Emancipator*, Oct. 26, 1843.

67. William Birney to Birney, Jan. 12, 1844, in Dumond, *Letters of James Gillespie Birney*, 744; William Birney to Birney, Jan. 26, 1844, in Dumond, *Letters of James Gillespie Birney*, 776; William Birney to Birney, Feb. 28, 1843, in Dumond, *Letters of James Gillespie Birney*, 720–21.

68. William Birney to Birney, Jan. 12, 1844, in Dumond, *Letters of James Gillespie Birney*, 774.

69. William Birney to Birney, Jan. 12, 1844, in Dumond, *Letters of James Gillespie Birney*, 744. Morris "behaved like a perfect madman" when he failed to be elected to the Ohio Supreme Court" (Donald Ratcliffe, ed., "The Autobiography of Benjamin Tappan," *Ohio History Journal* 85 [Spring 1976]: 109, 146).

228   NOTES TO PAGES 155–158

70. Fladeland, *James Gillespie Birney*, 240, 32.

71. Harrold, *Gamaliel Bailey*, 67. Although Harrold says that Bailey "immediately sought reconciliation with Morris," Willian Birney believed that Chase's intercession had been necessary. William Birney to Birney, Jan. 12, 1844, in Dumond, *Letters of James Gillespie Birney*, 744.

72. Donald F. Melhorn, *Lest We Be Marshalled: Judicial Powers and Politics in Ohio, 1806–1812* (Akron, OH: Univ. of Akron Press, 2003), 124–25.

73. Myron Holley to Birney, Jan. 1, 1840, in Dumond, *Letters of James Gillespie Birney*, 518. If the Liberty leaders were aware of the accusation, by 1843 they had determined to overlook it and renominated Morris.

74. William Birney to Birney, Jan. 12 and Feb. 26, 1844, in Dumond, *Letters of James Gillespie Birney*, 774, 794–95.

75. William Birney to Birney, Jan. 12 and Feb. 26, 1844, in Dumond, *Letters of James Gillespie Birney*, 774, 794–95.

76. William Birney to Birney, Mar. 28, 1844, in Dumond, *Letters of James Gillespie Birney*, 802–4. Describing the conflict between Morris and the group led by Chase and Bailey as "the only feud that had serious repercussions in the Old Northwest, Johnson concludes that the "negative results were transitory and limited" (*Liberty Party*, 241). This outcome resulted more from Morris's death in 1844 than from any reconciliation.

77. Bertram Wyatt-Brown, *Lewis Tappan and the Evangelical War against Slavery* (Cleveland: Press of Case Western Reserve, 1969), 250–56. For Andrews's subsequent drift into anarchist thought and the notion of individual sovereignty, see Lewis Perry, *Radical Abolitionism: Anarchy and the Government of God in Antislavery Thought*, 2nd ed. (Knoxville: Univ. of Tennessee Press, 1995), 210–12.

78. Frederick Merk, *Slavery and the Annexation of Texas* (New York: Knopf, 1972), 45–54.

79. Merk, *Slavery and the Annexation of Texas*, 69, 81.

80. Walter R. Borneman, *Polk: The Man Who Transformed the Presidency and America* (New York: Random House, 2008), 87–88; William Birney to Birney, Mar. 28, 1844, in Dumond, *Letters of James Gillespie Birney*, 802–4. Similar letters were addressed to all candidates. Chase to Birney, Mar. 30, 1844, in Dumond, *Letters of James Gillespie Birney*, 804–6.

81. Elder, *Calhoun*, 419.

82. Adam Jewett to Chase, June 7, 1844, quoted in Stephen E. Maizlish, *The Triumph of Sectionalism: The Transformation of Ohio Politics, 1844–1856* (Kent, OH: Kent State Univ. Press, 1983), 33.

83. James Oakes, *The Scorpion's Sting: Antislavery and the Coming of the Civil War* (New York: W. W. Norton, 2014), 63–69; Johnson, *Liberty Party*, 316–17.

84. W. Birney to Birney, Feb. 26, 1844, in Dumond, *Letters of James Gillespie Birney*, 794–95. Reinhard Johnson concluded that Bailey's practice of excluding "items and opinions that he believed harmful to the overall goals presented a slanted view of Ohio Liberty affairs" (*Liberty Party*, 232). Ultimately, Birney would experience Bailey's editorial approach when Bailey refused to publish Birney's views. Birney to L. P. Noble, Sept. 13, 1847, in Dumond, *Letters of James Gillespie Birney*, 1082–83.

NOTES TO PAGES 158–159

85. W. Birney to Birney, Feb. 26, 1844, in Dumond, *Letters of James Gillespie Birney*, 794–95.

86. Henry B. Stanton to Salmon Chase, Feb. 6, 1844, in Niven, *Salmon P. Chase Papers*, 105; Morris to Dear Sir, Oct. 2, 1841, in *Signal of Liberty*, Nov. 17, 1841; Theodore C. Smith, *Liberty and Free Soil Parties in the Northwest* (New York: Longmans, Green, 1897), 86.

87. Smith, *Liberty and Free Soil Parties*, 73.

88. Edgar A. Holt, *Party Politics in Ohio, 1840–1850* (Columbus: F. J. Heer Printing, 1930), 202.

89. *Ohio Statesman*, May 29, 1844. The editor of the *Ohio Statesman* had attended the state Liberty Convention in Cincinnati in February. While there he told G. W. Ells (the former state representative who had been expelled from the Ohio Democrat Party at the same time as Morris) of his "contempt for Calhoun and his southern followers." Jonathan H. Earle, *Jacksonian Antislavery and the Politics of Free Soil, 1824–1854* (Chapel Hill: Univ. of North Carolina Press, 2004), 157.

90. Holt, *Party Politics in Ohio*, 205. When Polk failed to carry Ohio, Democrats blamed "the cursed abolitionists" claiming that Democratic abolitionists had voted for the Liberty Party while Whig antislavery men did not (Maizlish, *Triumph of Sectionalism*, 34).

91. Quoted in Holt, *Party Politics in Ohio*, 196–97; see also Smith, *Liberty and Free Soil Parties*, 71.

92. James Brewer Stewart, *Abolitionist Politics and the Coming of the Civil War* (Amherst: Univ. of Massachusetts Press, 2008).

93. Quoted in Holt, *Party Politics in Ohio*, 167.

94. James Brewer Stewart, "Abolitionists, Insurgents, and Third Parties: Sectionalism and Partisan Politics in Northern Whiggery, 1836–1844," in *Crusaders and Compromisers: Essays on the Relationship of the Antislavery Struggle to the Antebellum Party System*, ed. Alan M. Kraut (Westport, CT: Greenwood Press, 1983), 34; Stewart, *Abolitionist Politics*, 217–18.

95. In the letter Clay argued against the practicality of bringing Texas into the Union at the time. See Glyndon G. Van Deusen, *The Jacksonian Era 1828–1848* (New York: Harper & Row, 1963), 188–89; Smith, *Liberty and Free Soil Parties*, 76.

96. Holt, *Party Politics in Ohio*, 205; Fladeland, *James Gillespie Birney*, 234–35; Smith, *Liberty and Free Soil Parties*, 72.

97. Weisenburger, *Passing of the Frontier*, 439. Smith believed this report significantly undercounted King's total, which he places at "probably over 9,000" (*Liberty and Free Soil Parties*, 76).

98. *Philanthropist*, Oct. 22, 1844. Giddings "believed implicitly in the Garland forgery and . . . used it with deadly effect" (Smith, *Liberty and Free Soil Parties*, 113).

99. For example, see *Ohio State Journal*, Oct. 17, 1844. Alan Kraut thought the Whig deception "demonstrated its respect for the third party ("Partisanship and Principles," 82).

100. Fladeland, *James Gillespie Birney*, 244–51; Smith, *Liberty and Free Soil Parties*, 78–79.

101. William Birney to Birney, Nov. 25, 1844, in Dumond, *Letters of James Gillespie Birney*, 886–87. While not diminishing the impact of the Rohrbach forgery, Bailey

230 NOTES TO PAGES 159–162

consoled himself and his readers by looking forward to next year, saying, "while no party excitement disturbs the public reason, [we] must sow the seed, and at local election where no great interests are at stake to arouse selfishness, prejudice or passion, reap the fruit" (*Philanthropist*, Dec. 4, 1844).

102. Louis Filler, *Crusade against Slavery, 1830–1860* (New York: Harper and Brothers, 1960), 177; see also Van Deusen, *The Jacksonian Era*, 189.

103. Leonard L. Richards, *The Slave Power: The Free North and Southern Domination, 1780–1860* (Baton Rouge: Louisiana State Univ. Press, 2000), 145.

CONCLUSION

1. *Emancipator*, Feb. 21, 1839. Within weeks of his death, Morris had apparently already slipped into obscurity. His eulogist acknowledged, "A patriot and philanthropist has fallen. But the nation mourns not, the world knows it not." W. H. Bisbane, *An Eulogium on the Life and Character of the Late Thomas Morris* (Cincinnati: L'Horredieu, 1845), 10–11.

2. Kate Masur, *Until Justice Be Done: America's First Civil Rights Movement from Reconstruction* (New York: W. W. Norton, 2021), 113–14; Sean Wilentz, *Rise of American Democracy: Jefferson to Lincoln* (New York: W. W. Norton, 2005), 477; Jonathan H. Earle, *Jacksonian Antislavery and the Politics of Free Soil, 1824–1854* (Chapel Hill: Univ. of North Carolina Press, 2004), 38; Eric Foner, *Free Soil, Free Labor, Free Men: The Ideology of the Republican Party before the Civil War* (New York: Oxford Univ. Press, 1970), 91.

3. William Birney, *James G. Birney and His Times: The Genesis of the Republican Party* (New York: Bergman Publishers, 1890), 345. For earlier warnings by Morris of the Slave Power's threat, see, for example, Morris to Alexander Campbell, November 13, 1837, *Philanthropist*, December 6, 1837, and Morris to Joseph M. Trumon and others, May 11, 1838, *Philanthropist*, June 26, 1838.

4. David Brion Davis, *The Slave Power Conspiracy and the Paranoid Style* (Baton Rouge: Louisiana State Univ. Press, 1970), 18.

5. Marvin Meyers, *The Jacksonian Persuasion: Politics and Belief* (Stanford, CA: Stanford Univ. Press, 1960), 254; Foner, *Free Soil, Free Labor, Free Men*, 91; Manisha Sinha, *The Slave's Cause: A History of Abolition* (London: Yale Univ. Press, 2016), 352.

6. Davis, *Slave Power Conspiracy*, 85.

7. Eric Foner, *Politics and Ideology in the Age of the Civil War* (New York: Oxford Univ. Press, 1980), 48, 50.

8. James Oakes, *The Crooked Path to Abolition: Abraham Lincoln and the Antislavery Constitution* (New York: W. W. Norton, 2021), 35.

9. Morris to Eldest Son, Nov. 30, 1833, in Morris, *Life of Thomas Morris*, 345–56; see also Bailey to Birney, Mar. 31, 1842, in Dumond, *Letters of James Gillespie Birney*, 726–27: "I admire the independence with which he forms his opinions and the boldness with which he utters them."

10. James Oakes, *Freedom National: The Destruction of Slavery in the United States, 1861–1865* (New York: W. W. Norton, 2013), 6.

NOTES TO PAGES 162–164   231

11. Oakes, *Freedom National*, 6.

12. Oakes, *Freedom National*, 9.

13. Oakes, *Freedom National*, 18–19.

14. William M. Wiecek, *The Sources of Antislavery Constitutionalism in America, 1760–1848* (New York: Cornell Univ. Press, 1977), 20–39.

15. Oakes, *Freedom National*, 15–17.

16. Oakes, *Freedom National*, 26–27; National Liberty Party Platform, 1844, in Reinhard D. Johnson, *The Liberty Party: Antislavery Third-Party Politics in the United States* (Baton Rouge: Louisiana State Univ. Press, 2009), 315–22.

17. Cong. Globe, 25th Cong., 3rd Sess., 167–75 (1838–39).

18. *Philanthropist*, Oct. 2, 1838.

19. *Philanthropist*, May 19, 1841.

20. Sean Wilentz, *No Property in Man: Slavery and Antislavery at the Nation's Founding* (Cambridge, MA: Harvard Univ. Press, 2018), 225–26.

21. Wilentz, *No Property in Man*, 226. See also Sinha, *The Slave's Cause*, 477: Chase "elaborated" prior "abolitionist constitutionalism." Wilentz references Weld's 1838 pamphlet as a possible source for Chase's thought. Weld was certainly influential and Chase was undoubtedly familiar with his work, but most of Weld's analysis focused on an issue (the power of Congress to abolish slavery in the District), which was not particularly salient to Chase in the 1840s and 1850s. Chase's constitutional and political antislavery positions crystallized within a year of joining Morris in the Liberty Party. They changed little after 1843 (Foner, *Free Soil, Free Labor, Free Men*, 74–75, note 7). In 1837 Chase had drawn on Morris's constitutional theories in developing his Matilda argument, and over the ensuing years, Chase was repeatedly exposed to Morris's ideas in the local press and antislavery meetings. Whatever may have been Weld's impact, Morris's geographic proximity, prominence, and influence in southern Ohio antislavery circles argue for Morris as a primary source of much of Chase's theory. Indeed, Wilentz's summary of Chase's constitutional approach reads like a catalog of Morris's thought (Wilentz, *No Property in Man*, 224–26).

22. Oakes, *Crooked Path*, 2–5, 50–53.

23. Benjamin Franklin Morris, ed., *The Life of Thomas Morris: Pioneer and Long a Legislator of Ohio, and U.S. Senator from 1833 to 1839* (Cincinnati: Moore, Wilstach, Keys & Overend, 1856), xi. Chase's interest in Morris's ideas continued long after Morris's death. For example, in January 1857, while serving as governor of Ohio, Chase thought it important enough to record in his journal time spent reading *The Life of Thomas Morris*, which consisted of little more than a reprint of Morris's speeches and letters. John Niven, ed., *The Salmon P. Chase Papers* (Kent, OH: Kent State Univ. Press, 1994), 1:256, 259.

24. See, for example, Resolutions of Ohio Liberty Party 1844 Convention, *Philanthropist*, Feb. 14, 1844.

25. Staughton Lynd, *The Antislavery Vanguard: New Essays on the Abolitionists*, ed. Martin Duberman (New York: Princeton Univ. Press, 1965), 210.

26. Wieck, *Antislavery Constitutionalism*, 257.

27. William Goodell, *Views of American Constitutional Law in Its Bearing upon American Slavery*, 2nd ed. (Utica, NY: Jackson & Chaplin, 1845), 40–41, 84–86. Although

Goodell added the Necessary and Proper Clause to the Preamble argument, his analysis implicitly accepted Morris's view of the Preamble as an affirmative grant of power to Congress. The Necessary and Proper Clause only grants authority "to make laws . . . [in] execution of . . . all other powers vested by this Constitution in the Government of the United States" (article I, section 8, clause 17). The Preamble contained the grant of power.

28. Oakes, *Crooked Path*, 40.

29. Wieck, *Antislavery Constitutionalism*, 257. For the continued use of the Preamble in antislavery constitutionalism, see Oakes, *Crooked Path*, 96–97.

30. Wiecek, *Antislavery Constitutionalism*, 218.

31. William E. Nelson, *The Fourteenth Amendment: From Political Principle to Judicial Doctrine* (Cambridge, MA: Harvard Univ. Press, 1988), 91; see also Masur, *Until Justice Be Done*, 333–36.

32. John A. Neuenschwander, "Senator Thomas Morris: Antagonist of the South, 1836–1839," *Cincinnati Historical Society Bulletin* 32 (Fall 1974): 138.

33. Morris never recanted any of these positions. Garrison would have agreed with Morris's early denial of being an abolitionist. "One had to accept [Garrisonians] complete program in order to be included in their select group of abolitionists." Larry Gara, "Who Was an Abolitionist?," in *The Antislavery Vanguard: New Essays on the Abolitionists*, ed. Martin Duberman (New York: Princeton Univ. Press, 1965), 32–51.

34. Neuenschwander, "Senator Thomas Morris," 139.

35. Cong. Globe, 25th Cong., 3rd Sess., appendix, 173 (1839).

36. For many, immediatism "became a test of abolitionism" (Gara, "Who Was an Abolitionist?," 35). See also Stanley Harrold, *American Abolitionism* (Charlottesville: Univ. of Virginia Press, 2019), 2. Perhaps more importantly, unlike many Ohio antislavery politicians, after 1843 Morris did not deny being an abolitionist (Harrold, *American Abolitionism*), 47.

37. Morris, *Life of Thomas Morris*, xi.

38. Masur, *Until Justice Be Done*, 303–41.

Index

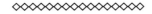

abductions, 54–56, 71–72
abolition and abolitionists, 162–63; actions of, 17–18, 64; and Black suffrage, 137–38; and Constitution, 150; in District of Columbia, 30, 48; during elections, 22–24, 72–74, 79–80; and expediency, 76; and free speech issues, 42–43; modern, 78–79; Morris's evolving views on, 2–4, 36–37, 47, 58–59, 65, 90–94, 97–99, 149, 157, 165–67; and political alliances, 100–107, 117, 132, 151, 152–53, 157–60, 161; in political maneuverings, 26–27, 56–57, 70, 85–87, 119–22, 125–30, 143–44, 156; publicity about, 34–35, 116; reactions to, 13–14, 17, 38, 52, 61–63, 66; and states' issues, 24–25, 145–48; support for, 20, 39–40, 45, 71, 90–94, 111–15
Adams, John Quincy, 13, 17, 23, 50, 130, 134
Advertiser (Cincinnati), 98
Alabama Beacon, 81
Allen, William, 62–63, 74
Amar, Akhil Reed, 150–51
American Anti-Slavery Society, 162; actions against, 13, 16–17, 72; actions by, 17–18, 91, 100–101, 102; disagreements within, 104, 147; political alliances of, 50, 95
American Colonization Society, 14, 16, 85–86
American Convention of Abolition Societies, 17
American Federalists and federalism, 56, 146

American & Foreign Anti-Slavery Society, 104
Amis, Junius, 22
Andrews, Stephen, 156
antiabolitionism, 17, 41, 99
antislavery movement: Constitution on, 4–7, 31, 53, 61, 89, 118–19, 146–47, 162–67; disagreements within, 102–4; growth of, 34–35, 43, 47; Morris's evolving views on, 2–3, 62–63, 65, 122, 157; as political issue, 12–13, 38, 66–69, 71–76, 79–81, 83, 86, 106–7, 116–17, 158–60; religion in, 44, 140, 166; resistance to, 13, 26–27, 100–101; and statehood issues, 23–24, 156; support for, 17–19, 40, 56, 71, 91–94, 109–10, 123, 140, 150
Arkansas, statehood for, 23–25, 32, 35

Bailey, Gamaliel: in antislavery movements, 106–7; colleagues at odds with, 123–25, 128, 129, 154–56; Liberty Party service by, 111–12, 119–20, 121, 126, 127, 143, 151, 152–53; moderate approach of, 132; Morris at odds with, 6–7, 133, 134–35, 136–39, 140–42, 147, 157–58; Morris cooperating with, 95–96, 110, 118; and third-party movement, 102–4, 105–7; work history of, 102
Bank of the United States, 2, 10–11, 35–37, 42, 63, 66, 115, 147

234   *INDEX*

Barron v. Baltimore, 150
Bayard, James A., 49
Beck, Isaac, 40
Benton, Thomas, 11, 45–46, 54, 59, 63
Biddle, Nicholas, 42
Birney, James, 39; actions against, 39–40, 41;
    Bailey's acquaintance with, 142; forgery
    used against, 159; as Liberty Party can-
    didate, 124–26, 127–28, 129–30, 132–34,
    136–37, 143–45, 156; in litigation, 51–52, 119;
    Morris's acquaintance with, 43–45, 50, 102,
    138, 140, 141; as publisher, 39, 42–43; and
    third-party movement, 103–7, 114, 115–16
Birney, William: on convention outcome,
    104; on forgery, 159; on Liberty Party dis-
    cord, 124, 132, 133, 134, 140, 145, 155; on
    Liberty Party leadership, 152–53; Liberty
    Party service by, 158; maneuverings by,
    157–58; on Morris's speech, 93
Black Laws, 81, 97, 99, 114
Blacks, free, 2, 14–15, 16, 43, 68–69, 70, 78,
    100, 116–17, 137–39
Britain, 130, 156
Brough, John, 77, 85, 116
Brown, Bedford, 27
Buchanan, James, 20, 21, 47, 63
Buchanan, Thomas, 74–75, 77, 85, 87
Burnett, Jacob, 41

Calhoun, John C.: alliances of, 10; as antiabo-
    litionist, 3–4, 8, 19–20, 87, 146; as cam-
    paign topic, 71–72; and Constitution, 1–2,
    30–35, 164; distrust of, 11; and mail cen-
    sorship, 35–36; Morris responding to, 74,
    75–76, 88, 148, 163; opinions on, 36–37;
    political maneuverings by, 13–14, 56–57;
    as pro-slavery, 26–29, 48–49, 57–63; on
    slaves as property, 30–31, 89; and state-
    hood issues, 157; targets of, 40, 43
Campbell, Alexander, 40–41, 55, 63
Charleston, South Carolina, 13
Chase, Salmon, 123–24; antislavery approach
    of, 147; conflict with, 124–29, 132–36,
    141; as defense lawyer, 51–52, 153–54; and
    Liberty Party leadership, 143–45, 152–53,
    155–56, 157–58; and Morris, 5, 7, 93, 118,
    120–22, 164, 167; political alliances of,
    107, 119–20, 129–30
Chase, Samuel, 9
Chevalier, Michael, 11
Cincinnati Anti-Slavery Society, 102
Cincinnati Daily Gazette, 52, 75
Cincinnati Enquirer, 116, 121–22
Cincinnati Republican, 122

civil rights, 36, 56, 68–69, 70, 131, 138, 139,
    141, 165, 166–67
Civil Rights Act (1866), 165, 167
Clay, Henry: Jackson's censure by, 10; and
    monetary policy, 2, 63; Morris's response
    to, 58, 83, 100, 101, 122, 161–62; as presi-
    dential candidate, 158–59; in Senate, 11;
    on slavery, 58, 85–90, 92–94, 164
Clermont County, Ohio, 8, 10, 40
Clermont County Anti-Slavery Society, 44
Cleveland Herald, 158–59
colonization movement, 2, 6, 14–16, 85–86,
    90, 165, 166
Commerce Clause, 89
Committee on the District of Columbia, 17,
    19, 47–48
Committee on Foreign Relations, 25
Confederation Congress, 43
Congress, and monetary policy, 10–11, 54, 63
Congress, and nullification, 10–11
Congress, on slavery issues: and Consti-
    tution, 144, 163, 167; in District of Co-
    lumbia, 23, 30–31, 32–34, 47–48, 76–78,
    84–85, 111, 118–19, 145–48, 165–66; and
    incendiary publications, 14, 25–29; in in-
    ternational trade, 64–65; and lobbyists,
    109–10; and mail censorship, 25–27, 29;
    and statehood, 24, 30, 46–47; and states'
    rights, 24–25, 30–34, 52, 57–60, 76–77,
    84–85, 96–97, 126–27, 145–51, 165–66
Congressional Globe, 28, 34, 87, 91
Constitution (US): ambiguity of, on slavery,
    3, 15, 52–53, 69–70, 129; as antislavery, 4,
    6, 61–62, 65, 76, 92, 115, 118–19, 148–52,
    163–67; attacks on, 11; and Fugitive Slave
    Act, 153–54; gag-rule contrary to, 111; in-
    terpretation of, 31–35, 57–59, 88–89,
    162–63; and monetary policy, 130–31; as
    pro-slavery, 29–32, 56, 57–59, 69–70, 88,
    99–100; slavery concept absent in, 1; and
    states' rights, 56, 59–60, 78, 85, 96–97,
    120–21, 128, 146–48
constitution, Ohio, 68, 114
Corwin, Tom, 16

Dayton, Ohio, riots in, 113, 138–39
Declaration of Independence, 76, 78, 89, 92,
    149, 163
Democrats, national-level, 24–25, 36–37, 39,
    45, 57, 74, 78–79, 95, 159
Democrats, Ohio: as antiabolitionist, 80,
    95–100, 106–7; as antislavery, 105–6, 131–
    32; beginnings of, 9–10; and elections,
    66–67, 71–74, 77–78; maneuverings by,

12; and monetary policy, 10, 11–12, 39, 131; and Morris, 67–68, 116–18; racism among, 70, 74–75, 116; and Slave Power, 83–84, 91; and Texas annexation, 158

Denison, Charles, 101

distillery, as strike against Morris, 141

Distribution Bill, 38–39, 53

District of Columbia, and Congress: antiabolition actions for, 36, 44, 86–87; antislavery actions for, 128; antislavery expectations for, 111; emancipation possible by, 6; power limitations of, 28, 31, 32–34, 47–48, 76–77, 78, 118–19, 145–48, 165–66; pro-abolition actions for, 2–4, 8, 17–20; pro-slavery actions for, 19, 56, 57–58

District of Columbia, and Constitution: abolition not prohibited for, 3–4, 32–34; ambiguity of, on slavery, 78, 145–46, 147–48; antiabolitionist interpretations, 30, 99; antislavery interpretations, 6, 76, 118–19, 128, 152, 167; and petitions to Congress, 19–20; pro-slavery interpretations, 57–58

District of Columbia, and President Van Buren, 74

doctrines, ultra, 124, 127

Dred Scott v. Sanford, 4, 30, 162

Duane, William, 10

Dumond, Dwight, 123

Earle, Thomas, 114

Early, Peter, 49

Elk Lick Mill, 140–41

emancipation, 6, 7, 14–15, 86, 90–91, 126, 129–30, 150, 166

Emancipator: on abolitionist organizations, 114; antislavery views published by, 75, 101, 128; influence of, 104–5; on legislative resolutions, 85, 87; on Morris, 63, 65, 77, 92, 97, 110, 117, 119, 154; on political conventions, 114–15, 123, 126, 133, 144

Evening Post (New York), 156

Ewing, Thomas, 8, 18, 45, 158

expediency, 36, 44, 48, 76, 101, 146

federal consensus: and Liberty Party, 120; and slavery, 15, 19, 31, 93, 126, 147, 161, 165–66, 167; and statehood, 24

Federalists and federalism, 35, 56, 60, 146

Fehrenbacher, Don, 30

Fifth Amendment, 19, 30, 32, 33, 69, 119, 144, 146–48, 149–50, 152

First Amendment, 18, 19

Flood, George, 98–99

Fourteenth Amendment, 167

Free-Soilers, 4, 164, 165

Fugitive Slave Clause, 29, 30–31, 32, 52, 53, 96–97, 153–54, 163

Fugitive Slave Laws, 4, 51–53, 81, 89, 96, 97, 131, 152, 153–54

gag rule, for antislavery petitions, 2, 18, 20, 42, 47, 110–11

Garland, J. B., 159

Garrison, William Lloyd, 91, 101–2, 151, 165

Garrisonians, 79, 104, 120, 151–52, 165–66

Giddings, Joshua, 158–59

Goodell, William, 5; *Views of American Constitutional Law,* 164–65

Goodenow, John Milton, 9

Great Britain, 130, 156

Hamer, Thomas, 41–42, 43, 77, 99

Hamilton Convention (1840), 105–7, 109, 110

Hammond, Charles, 52

Hammond, James, 18

handwriting, as evidence, 42

Harrison, William Henry, 102, 103–4, 106–7, 111

Hayne, Robert, 13

Holley, Myron, 102, 103

House of Representatives (Ohio), 8–9, 15, 42

House of Representatives (US), 3, 10, 17–18, 23, 110

Hubbard, Mr. (Michigan senator), 85, 87

impeachment proceedings, 9, 41, 77, 135, 154

incendiary publications, 13–14, 16–17, 19, 25–27, 28–29, 36, 38

Independent Treasury plan, 54, 57, 63–64, 66, 67

Indiana, and Liberty Party, 124–25

Jackson, Andrew: and antislavery mailings, 13–14, 25–26; censure of, 10, 12, 45–46; issues facing, 17; and monetary policy, 10–11, 39, 53–54, 147; Morris's support for, 2, 74; opposition to, 134; and statehood issues, 64

Jacksonians: and abolitionism, 36–37, 79–80; and civil rights issues, 70; and monetary policy, 39; Morris as, 1–2; in Ohio legislature, 9; and right of petition, 18, 62–63; Slave Power concept descended from, 4, 68–69, 93–94, 121, 161; and statehood issues, 47; and states' rights on slavery, 22–23, 24–25; and third-party movement, 117

Jay, John, 130

Jay, William, 134, 138, 143

Jefferson, Thomas, and Jeffersonian influence, 9, 10, 35, 36, 38, 65, 68, 154, 165
Johnson, Eliza, 54–56
Jollife, John, 40

Kelly, Abby, 104
Kendall, Amos, 13, 14
Kentucky, Ohio's relationship with, 54–56, 81, 83, 96, 131
King, Leicester, 70, 107, 120, 123, 130–31, 143–44, 149, 151, 156, 158
Kraditor, Aileen, 101, 147

Lane Seminary, 102
Lawrence, Matilda, 51–52, 119
Leavitt, Joshua, 104–5, 106, 110, 125–26, 127, 136, 145, 154, 161
LeMoyne, Julius, 103
Lewis, Samuel, 130, 143–44, 151, 152–53, 157, 158
Liberator, 91
Liberty Party: alliances of, 151–52; conflict within, 123–30, 132, 136–38, 145, 155–56; conventions and campaigns of, 120, 121–22, 124–28, 132–36, 140–41, 143–44, 152–53, 154–60; goals of, 120–21; leadership of, 119–20; Morris's participation in, 4, 6–7; values of changing, 165. *See also* Morris, Thomas, post-Senate life of; third-party movement
Lincoln, Abraham, 1
literature, antislavery. *See* incendiary publications
Lloyd, William, 46
lobbying, antislavery, 109–10
Locofocos, 39, 42, 106
Lucas, Robert, 16, 26

Mahan, John B., 71–72, 74, 97
Maine, influence of, 27
Mangum, Willie P., 11
Mansfield, Lord, 163
Marshall, John, 31
Massachusetts Liberty Party, 126
McClean, John, 10–11, 153
McDuffie, George, 11
Medary, Samuel, 69, 70, 107
Methodist Protestant, 102
Missouri Compromise, 23, 24
Missouri Crisis, 14, 30–31, 35
mob attacks, 13, 39–40, 42
Money Power, 34, 35, 69–70, 84, 89, 93–94, 98, 147, 162
Morris, S. J., 40

Morris, Thomas, 1–8, 140, 160–67
Morris, Thomas, as Ohio legislator, 8–9, 15–16, 155
Morris, Thomas, as Ohio Supreme Court Justice, 12, 135–36
Morris, Thomas, post-Senate life of: in conflicts, 123–24, 132–35, 136–37, 140–42, 155–56, 159; on Congressional power, 148–52; on constitutional issues, 146–47; and Democratic party, 96–102; influence of, 109–15, 118–22, 126–27, 131–32, 152–54, 157–58; as Liberty Party candidate, 110, 115–18, 130, 143–45, 156; and racial issues, 137–40; and third-party movement, 103–8
Morris, Thomas, as US Senator: and antislavery petitions, 8, 18, 19–21, 27–28, 46–50; antislavery work of, 83–85, 87–93, 95–96; in conflicts, 62–63; on Congressional power, 145–46, 146–47, 148; on constitutional issues, 30, 31–37, 51–53, 56, 58–62; and Democratic party, 74–75; election loss of, 79–82; and incendiary publications, 28–29; influence of, 93–94; issues facing, 9–12, 38–39, 45–46; on monetary policy, 54, 63–64, 66–67; in political maneuverings, 85–87; and racial issues, 55–56, 68–69, 75–79; reelection efforts of, 72–73; relationships of, 39–44; and statehood issues, 22–25, 64–65

National Bank, 63. *See also* Bank of the United States
Neuenschwander, John, 165
New England Federalists and federalism, 35
New York State Anti-Slavery Society, 86, 146–47
Northwest Ordinance. *See* Ordinance (1787)
nullification, 2, 10–11, 27, 34, 36–37, 60

Oakes, James, 4, 34, 162
Ohio American Antislavery Society, 151
Ohio Anti-Slavery Society, 16; actions by, 18, 45, 72; constitution of, 138; disagreements within, 120, 148; leadership of, 102, 103–4; membership of, 114; noncooperation with, 71; political alliances of, 41, 50, 115–16; views of, 23
Ohio General Assembly: and monetary policy, 63; Morris's service on, 2, 9–10; and Ohio Supreme Court, 12, 135–36; and Senate elections, 66–67, 72–75, 77–78; Slave Power's influence on, 81; on slavery

issues, 14–15, 52, 83–84, 131–32; on states' rights, 98–99; and Texas's status, 70–71

Ohio State Journal, 55, 67, 73

Ohio Statesman, 67, 69, 72, 74, 77, 80, 99, 100, 107, 158

Ordinance (1787), 24, 43, 52, 69, 139, 153, 154

Pakenham letter, 157

Pennsylvania Abolition Society, 17

Philanthropist: actions against, 39–40, 41, 42; antislavery actions of, 56, 65; on debate, 147; on discord within Liberty Party, 128, 129; on elections, 100, 107, 154; on fugitive slave issue, 51–52, 96; Morris excluded from, 6, 132, 142, 157–58; Morris included in, 34–35, 71, 83–84, 118, 149; Morris misunderstood by, 110; Morris supported by, 70, 72–73, 75, 91–93, 104, 115, 117, 122; ownership of, 120; on political campaigns, 130; on political conventions, 111, 124, 127; on political parties, 156–57

Pinkney, Henry, 47

Polk, James, 156–57, 158, 159–60

Preamble (US Constitution), 148–51, 152, 164

Preston, William, 64, 86

Prigg v. Pennsylvania, 96, 154

Quakers, 17, 20, 104

Rankin, John, 40, 44–45, 62

Republicans, 4, 7, 162, 164, 165

riots, 113, 138–39

Rives, William C., 48–49, 54, 61–62, 63

Ruggles, John, 27

senate (Ohio), 9

Senate (US): issues facing, 44; and monetary policy, 11; Morris addressing, 1, 87–88; and petition controversy, 19–21, 27–29, 47–50; political maneuverings in, 12, 79, 156; resolutions against slavery in, 56, 59, 64–65, 85; resolutions for slavery in, 56–58, 59–63, 85, 99; and statehood issues, 25; turmoil in, 10, 45–46. *See also* Morris, Thomas, as US Senator; slavery, congressional power over

Seward, William, 134

Shannon, William, 98, 99

slave catchers, 51, 54–55

Slave Power: danger of, 62, 147; and monetary policy, 117; Money Power connected with, 69–70, 98; Morris's realization of, 4–5, 34–35, 83, 161–62; Morris's response

to, 6, 7, 36, 56, 88–94, 96, 101, 138–39; as political issue, 112–13, 115, 120–22, 126–27, 128–29, 130, 137, 156–57, 163–67; strength of, 81–82, 107–8, 144; temptation of, 87; underestimated, 111

slavery: discussions about, 43–45; as election issue, 72; as freedom-of-speech issue, 25–26; and monetary policy, 130–31; Morris's changing attitudes toward, 35–37, 118; Morris speaking against, 75–76, 80–81, 90, 91–93, 95–96, 114, 116–17; petitions about, 17–21, 27–28, 46–50, 70, 74–75, 84, 86, 87–88; as political issue, 22–23, 38, 100–101, 129–30, 137, 139–40; as statehood issue, 23–25, 46–47, 64–65, 156; support for, 26–29

slavery, congressional power over: absent, 17, 19, 31, 35–36, 57–58, 96–97, 144, 145–46, 165–66; ambiguous, 18–19, 19–20, 28, 34, 76–77, 78, 118–19, 126–27, 148; present, 30, 32–34, 58–59, 109–11, 146–52, 157, 164, 167

slavery, constitutional power over: absent, 57–59, 99, 128; ambiguous, 1, 3, 28–30, 31–35, 56, 59–60, 76, 88, 100; present, accommodating, 3–7, 30; present, unaccommodating, 51–53, 60–61, 88–89, 92, 118–19, 120–21, 146–52, 153–54, 162–67

slaves: fugitive, 40, 51–52, 68, 96, 119, 153; insurrection encouraged in, 14, 128, 134; in persons or property debate, 1, 4, 19, 29–30, 32–34, 89, 150, 162–64; regard for, 84, 115. *See also* Fugitive Slave Clause; Fugitive Slave Laws

Smith, Gerrit, 127–28, 129, 137

Smith, Theodore C., 6, 44

Somerset v. Stewart, 163

South: antislavery actions against, 13–14, 17–18; appeasement of, 22, 25–26, 74–75, 95, 99–100; apprehension over, 25; attitudes toward, 82, 122, 138–39; challenges to, 28–29; on Constitution, 56; financial interests of, 11, 42; and North, 88; as political liability, 160; in political maneuverings, 19, 26–27, 56–57, 58, 61; power of, 35–37, 44, 62, 80–81, 90–92, 93–94; self-image of, 60

South Carolina, and nullification, 10–11

Specie Circular, 39, 45, 53–54

Stanton, Henry B., 50

State v. Hess, 42

Stewart, Alvan, 78, 125, 146–47, 149–50

Sturge, Joseph, 130

238 *INDEX*

Sub-Treasury Bill, 67
suffrage, Black, 43, 100–101, 137, 138, 139, 155
Supreme Court, Ohio, 9, 12, 41, 42, 135
Supreme Court, US, 35, 118, 150
Swift, Benjamin, 22, 56

Taney, Roger, 10, 30, 35
Tappan, Arthur, 77
Tappan, Benjamin, 9, 12, 77, 79, 156
Tappan, Lewis, 77, 79, 104, 129–30, 138, 144, 156
Tenth Amendment, 53, 96, 150, 154
territories, slavery in: abolition stopping, theory of, 145; Congressional power over, 6, 30, 43, 57–58, 76–77, 78, 85, 146, 147–48, 150; Constitutional power over, 6, 30, 57, 78, 147–48, 152, 166–67; federal consensus affecting, 24, 147, 167
Texas: annexation for, 45, 60, 64, 70–71, 156–57, 158–59; independence for, 25, 46–47, 64–65; and slave trade, 68
third-party movement, 83, 86, 93, 102–5, 109, 117, 123, 131, 158. *See also* Liberty Party
three-fifths clause, 29, 32, 35
Tipton, John, 47, 49
Tod, David, 77
Turner, Nat, legacy of, 2, 14–16, 18, 49
Tyler, John, 48, 114, 119, 123, 156

ultra doctrines, 124, 127

Van Buren, Martin: as antiabolitionist, 49, 65, 66, 74–75; Calhoun's support for, 56–57; enemies of, 134; issues facing, 53–54; Morris's support for, 64, 67; as presidential candidate, 13–14, 22–23, 36–37, 39, 157, 159; schemes against, 18–19; and Texas annexation, 156, 158
Vance, Joseph, 72
VanZandt, John, 153–54
Views of American Constitutional Law (Goodell), 164–65
voting rights, for Blacks. *See* suffrage, Black

Wade, Edward, 107
Walker, Robert J., 25, 64
Washington Globe, 18–19, 22, 80
Webster, Daniel, 11, 48, 62, 63
Weld, Theodore, 5, 39, 91, 110
Western Hemisphere, 11
Western Reserve (Ohio), 102, 105–6, 110, 159
Whigs: Democratic Party competing with, 13–14, 66–68, 71–74, 98; Liberty Party competing with, 106–7, 117, 154, 158–59; and monetary policy, 63; in presidential elections, 85–86; and Texas annexation, 70–71, 157, 158–59
Wiecek, William, 149, 150
Wise, Henry, 130
Worthington, Thomas, 9, 135
Wright, Elizer, 43
Wright, Silas, 11, 45, 54, 63, 64, 159–60
Wyatt-Brown, Bertram, 104